Form and Style

Form and Style

Research Papers, Reports, Theses

TWELFTH EDITION

Carole Slade *Columbia University*

Houghton Mifflin Company Boston New York

Senior Sponsoring Editor: Suzanne Phelps Weir
Development Editor: Janet Young
Project Editor: Jane Lee
Editorial Assistant: Talia Kingsbury
Senior Production Design Coordinator: Jodi O'Rourke
Senior Manufacturing Coordinator: Priscilla Bailey
Marketing Manager: Cindy Graff Cohen

Cover Image: Famous rock garden of Ryoanji Temple in Kyoto, by Kaz Mori. From The Image Bank.

Text Permissions

The authors and editors thank the following persons and publishers for permission to use copyrighted material.

Page 7: Reprinted with permission of Epixtech, Inc., Provo, UT. **Page 8:** Reprinted with permission of Epixtech, Inc., Provo, UT. **Page 16:** This homepage is reprinted with permission from The Northeast Document Conservation Center (NEDCC), 100 Brickstone Square, Andover, MA 01810 <www.nedcc.org>. **Page 68:** Copyright © 1998 by G. Beato. Reprinted with the permission of the author and *21stC: The World of Research at Columbia University.* **Page 77:** From *A Forest of Kings* by Linda Schele and David Freidel. Copyright © 1990 by Linda Schele and David Freidel. By permission of William Morrow and Company, Inc. **Pages 271–276:** Neal J. Roese, "Counterfactual Thinking," *Psychological Bulletin,* 1997, *121,* 133–148. Copyright 1997 by the American Psychological Association. Excerpted with permission.

Photo Permissions

Page 117: © J. Denham, *The Boston Globe,* November 18, 2000.

Printed in the U.S.A.

Library of Congress Control Number: 2001133347

ISBN: 0-618-41131-3

3456789-QUD-09 08 07 06

Contents

Preface

PART I: THE PROCESSES OF RESEARCH AND WRITING 1

Chapter 1: Writing Research Papers 2

Choosing a Topic 2
General Subject Area 3
Definition of the Topic 3
Formulating a Working Statement of the Topic 4

Collecting Information 5
Sources of Information 6
Evaluating Information 14
Recording Information 17
Understanding Information 17

Outlining the Paper 20
The Thesis Statement 20
Principles of Organization 20
Types of Outlines 22
Outline Formats 22
Parallelism in Outlines 23
Logical Consistency in Outlines 24

Writing the Paper 25
The First Draft 25
Revision 26
Editing 27
Format 27
Proofreading 28

Elements of Research Papers: Sample Pages 29

Chapter 2: Theses and Dissertations 39

The Preliminaries (Front Matter) 39
Abstract 40
Approval Sheet 40
Title Page 40
Copyright Page 42
Table of Contents 43

Lists of Tables and Figures 43
Clearance Forms 44
Acknowledgments 44
Preface 44

The Text (Body) of the Paper 44
Organization of Chapters 44
Chapter Titles and Headings 47

Reference Materials (Back Matter, or End Matter) 48
Appendix 48
Glossary 49
Notes 49
Bibliography, List of Works Cited, or References 49
Index 49

Elements of Theses and Dissertations: Sample Pages 51

Chapter 3: Quotations 58

Indirect Quotation (Summary and Paraphrase) 59

Direct Quotation 61
Short Quotations 62
Extended Quotations 63
Introducing Direct Quotations 68
Punctuating Direct Quotations 71

Chapter 4: Style and Mechanics 80

Style 80
Diction 81
Tone 81
Voice 81
Economy 82
Verb Tense 82
Sentence Structure 83
Parallelism 84
Coherence 85
Unbiased Language 85

Mechanics 87
Spelling 87
Abbreviations 87
Hyphenation 88
Italics 89
Titles of Works 90
Capitalization 93
Numbers 94
Enumeration 97

Editing and Proofreading 98

Chapter 5: Tables and Figures 99

Tables 99
Relationship Between Tables and Text 100
Captions 101
Numbering 102
Columns and Rows 102
Footnotes for Tables 103
Large Tables 104

Figures 104
Graphs 105
Relationship between Figures and Text 109
Notes for Figures 110

Tables and Figures: Sample Pages 111

Chapter 6: The Finished Copy 120

The Final Draft 120

Equipment and Supplies 120

Printing Your Paper 121
Numbering of Pages 122
Spacing 122
Quotations 125
Endnotes and Footnotes 126
Headings within Chapters 127
Tables and Figures 128
Chapter Numbers and Titles 129
Part-Title Pages 129
Bibliographies and Lists of Works Cited 130
Front Matter for a Thesis or Dissertation 130
Back Matter for a Thesis or Dissertation 133

PART II: SYSTEMS OF DOCUMENTATION 135

General Information on Documentation 136

Purposes of Notes and Parenthetical References 136
Identifying Sources of Information 137
Establishing the Validity of Evidence 137
Providing Cross-References within the Paper 137
Amplifying Ideas 137
Providing Additional Bibliography 138

The List of Sources 138
Alphabetization of Entries 139
Types of Bibliographies 140

Chapter 7: *Chicago Manual* Style 141

Endnotes and Footnotes 142
- Designation of Notes in the Text 142
- First Reference and Subsequent Reference 143

Bibliographies 150
- Books 151
- Multivolume Works and Series 157
- Periodicals 158
- Works of Literature 162
- Reference Works 163
- Public Documents 164
- Unpublished Sources 167
- Dissertations 169
- Nonprint Sources 169
- Electronic Sources 173

Examples of Footnote and Endnote Forms and Bibliography Forms 177

Chapter 8: Modern Language Association Style 214

Content of Parenthetical Citations 214

Placement and Punctuation of Parenthetical Documentation 219

The List of Works Cited 220

Works Cited Forms 223
- Books 223
- Articles in Periodicals 229
- Electronic Sources 232
- Other Sources 235

MLA-Style Shortened Forms of Publishers' Names and Imprints 239

Sample Pages 243

Chapter 9: American Psychological Association Style 245

Parenthetical Reference Citations in Text 246

Reference Forms 251
- Periodicals 252
- Books and Chapters of Books 255
- Technical and Research Reports 259
- Proceedings of Meetings 260
- Dissertations and Theses 261
- Unpublished Materials and Works of Limited Circulation 261
- Reviews and Published Interviews 262

Audiovisual Media 263
Electronic Sources 264

The List of References 269

Sample Pages 271

Chapter 10: *Columbia Guide to Online Style* 278
Humanities Style 279
Scientific Style 279

Appendix A: Legal Citation 281

Appendix B: Abbreviation of State Names 285

Glossary 287

Index 291

Preface

Although this book has long been entitled *Form and Style,* it covers not just matters of format and style but also the essential processes for writing any kind of paper based on research. Research papers draw on information gathered systematically from the Internet, the library, the laboratory, or through personal observation. Writers of research papers often work with materials compiled by others, but they make an original contribution by organizing the information in a new way or by drawing a new conclusion from existing knowledge. The writer's creativity reveals itself in the choices made at every stage: selecting the topic, locating appropriate sources, organizing information, and presenting a clearly written and accurately documented paper.

Research papers go by many names and take several forms, depending on the context and audience, as well as the level, scope, and nature of the paper. In general, the term *research paper* distinguishes a paper based on research from an essay, which usually draws exclusively on common knowledge, a personal interpretation of a text or condition, or the writer's experience. The word *report* usually refers to a thorough record or description of the results of firsthand experiences, empirical studies, or reading of primary sources. Although the writer of a report may evaluate or interpret the results, most often a report presents information as objectively as possible. The term *review article* designates a presentation of secondary sources organized, evaluated, and analyzed to present the current state of research on a topic. The word *thesis* commonly refers to a substantial research project. As the word, which also means a proposition or point of view defended through argument, implies, a thesis should draw an original conclusion based on information derived from research. A *dissertation* is a research paper submitted by a candidate for the doctoral degree. This paper requires more research and more extensive development of ideas than a master's thesis. The word *thesis* is sometimes used interchangeably with *dissertation.* For convenience and brevity, *Form and Style* refers to any paper based on research as a research paper.

Writers of research papers for college, graduate school, business, government, and professions will find the basic principles of research writing thoroughly yet succinctly described here. The review of the fundamental processes of research makes *Form and Style* suitable as a text in courses of many kinds: composition courses, writing courses in specific disciplines, and courses in research and methods at both the undergraduate and graduate levels. The book continues to serve experienced writers with its discussion of procedures for writing various types of theses, its thorough presentation of principles of documentation and bibliographic forms, and its comprehensive treatment of the conventions for presenting information.

Form and Style works well as either a reference work or an instructional text. The index allows the reader to locate particular subjects quickly and easily; the glossary provides explanations of terms and abbreviations. At the same time, because the book provides an approximately sequential guide to the processes of research and writing, some writers may wish to begin by reading straight through it.

Documentation Systems Covered

As before, *Form and Style* presents three frequently used documentation systems in separate chapters. The instructions for using these systems draw on the most recent editions of the three style sheets: *The Chicago Manual of Style,* 14th ed. (1993), *Publication Manual of the American Psychological Association,* 5th ed. (2001), and the Modern Language Association's *Handbook for writers of Research papers,* 5th ed. (1999) and *Style Manual and Guide to Scholarly Publishing,* 2nd ed. (1998), both by Joseph Gibaldi. These systems are abbreviated in *Form and Style* as *Chicago Manual,* MLA, and APA. For the first time, *Form and Style* also provides brief coverage of *Columbia Guide to Online Style*, by Janice Walker and Todd Taylor, abbreviated here as *CGOS*.

Remember that style sheets do not proclaim universal principles, but rather present a set of agreements that facilitate communication among persons who use them. For this reason, style sheets regularly change to accommodate new ideas and to reflect trends in style and language. To find out whether MLA, APA, or *CGOS* has recently made changes in policy, see the Web sites maintained by each organization, <www.mla.org>, <www.apastyle.org>, or <www.columbia.edu.cu.cup.cgos>. At present *Chicago Manual* does not have such a Web site.

Style sheets cannot possibly cover every situation you might encounter in conducting research and assembling a paper. When you encounter a problem not specifically treated by *Form and Style*, you should follow the general principles that govern the style sheet you are using, and most important of all, make consistent use of whatever format or rule you select.

Most writers choose a documentation system on the suggestions of an adviser, the requirements of a department or university, or the conventions of a field of study. In the absence of a recommendation, writers should use the widely accepted *Chicago Manual* system, whereas writers within particular disciplines can select either the MLA or the APA system. *Form and Style* also provides information on legal citation in Appendix A.

Organization and Coverage

Form and Style is divided into two sections: Part I, The Processes of Research and Writing, covers the essential procedures that most writers employ as they create a paper; Part II, Systems of Documentation, provides a general introduction to citation, followed by separate chapters on using *Chicago Manual,* MLA, APA, and *CGOS* documentation.

Part I: The Processes of Research and Writing

Chapters 1 through 6 focus on the processess required for producing a research paper. Over the past several editions *Form and Style* has gradually incorporated more information about accomplishing these goals on a computer, and this new edition assumes that all readers will be doing at least some of their research and writing on a computer.

For the sake of brevity and clarity, instructions and examples in these chapters draw on *Chicago Manual* style. Most of the principles also apply to MLA and APA styles, but where differences exist, the alternatives are provided. As an authority for usage and spelling, I continue to rely on *The American Heritage Dictionary*, 3rd ed. (Houghton Mifflin, 1993).

Chapter 1 explains the process of writing a research paper from the initial steps of choosing a topic and collecting information through outlining, drafting, and revising the paper. These explanations of fundamental principles make the book accessible and useful to undergraduates at all levels. Others may want to use this chapter to review the essential stages in writing a research paper. New features of this edition include sections on selecting a search engine or browser, evaluating Web sites, and collecting information from electronic sources. The chapter still includes discussion of the more valuable tools for traditional library research, such as *Subject Hearings of the Library of Congress,* which permits a researcher to identify related subjects in this fully articulated classification system.

Chapter 2 describes the standard elements of a thesis or dissertation and explains the usual requirements for the research and writing of such projects. The chapter offers guidelines for preparing three types of graduate papers: theses based on the collection of empirical data, theses based on critical analysis or philosophical speculation, and theses based on historical research.

Chapter 3 explains the basic principles of attributing ideas and quotations to their sources. Because most plagiarism results from careless application of the rules for documentation, the chapter reviews the methods for accurately documenting direct and indirect quotations. The current guidelines for introducing quotations are also explained.

Chapter 4 discusses the principles of grammar and mechanics most often needed in writing and revising research papers, as well as advice about the style, tone, and voice appropriate for research papers. Chapter 5, completely revised for this edition, offers instructions for preparing tables and figures, as well as for presenting figures, graphs, and computer-generated materials. The chapter now assumes that researchers will be presenting much of their data with computer-generated materials. Chapter 6 presents the process of preparing the finished copy and gives instructions for typing and printing. In all chapters, this edition addresses techniques for writing, revising, and proofreading on word processors and computers.

Part II: Systems of Documentation

Part II gives detailed coverage of the *Chicago Manual*, MLA, and APA documentation systems as well as brief coverage of *CGOS*. The introduction to this section reviews the principles of documentation applicable to all three systems, such as the purposes of citation and the organization of entries in bibliographies and lists of works cited.

Chapter 7 explains the *Chicago Manual* system for notes accompanied by a bibliography. A section of note and bibliography entries placed on facing pages helps the writer translate information about a work from bibliography form into note form, and vice versa. This edition adds note and bibliography forms for many new types of sources, with an emphasis on computer materials. Chapter 8 provides instructions for MLA documentation, Chapter 9 provides instructions for APA documentation, and Chapter 10 covers *CGOS*. The sample pages in APA format appear at the end of these chapters and are designed to clarify the distinction between formatting of references for a manuscript and a printed document. For ease of identification, a colored tab marks each chapter.

▪ Sample Pages

Sample pages in Chapters 1, 2, 5, 8, and 9 illustrate the formats for research papers and systems of documentation described in *Form and Style*. These pages are designed to resemble pages printed by a computer and will serve as models for research papers, theses, and dissertation. The appearance of any printed book necessarily differs from that of a typescript, particularly in its spacing, margins, and typefaces; therefore, the printed text of *Form and Style* may vary slightly from the format recommended here for typescripts.

Acknowledgments

As in previous editions, I heartily thank the colleagues and friends who have helped in various ways with the book. I am especially grateful to reviewers whose comments and suggestions informed this revision of *Form and Style:*

Edmund August, McKendree College
Suzanne S. Bourdess, Towson University
Prudence J. Gushwa, Minnesota State University—Mankato
Karen A. Holleran, Kaplan College
Sylvia Stacey, Oakton Community College
Marjorie Swann, University of Kansas
Dennielle True, Florida Gulf Coast University

Kittrell Rushing of the University of Tennessee at Chattanooga provided a particularly helpful review of the manuscript with respect to technological information.

Each time I work on an edition of *Form and Style* I think that I have had the best of all possible editors and that I could not possibly be so fortunate again. But Houghton Mifflin always comes through with more of the best possible editors. I want to thank Suzanne Phelps Weir, senior sponsoring editor, for including *Form and Style* in the excellent company of Houghton Mifflin's new titles and editions; Janet R. Young, development editor, for bringing this edition home on a schedule that seemed improbable and would have been impossible without her last-minute rescues; and Jane Lee, project editor, for the kind, good-humored messages she took the time to send even as she expertly juggled enormous batches of manuscript and page proofs. I am exceedingly grateful to all of them for their first-rate work.

As always, I am indebted to my students, who have helped me learn how to teach them to write research papers.

C. S.

I The Processes of Research and Writing

1 Writing Research Papers 2
2 Theses and Dissertations 39
3 Quotations 58
4 Style and Mechanics 80
5 Tables, Figures, and Computer Materials 99
6 The Finished Copy 120

1 Writing Research Papers

All you really need to get yourself started on a research paper is curiosity. If you have a desire to know more about a topic, you have the most important impetus for research. Curiosity will not let you settle for the easiest answers to your questions or allow you to leave important clues unexplored. Of course, research writing will not always be self-initiated. The reality is that teachers assign research papers and supervisors require research reports on subjects that may hold little interest for you. The processes of learning about a new topic and organizing the fruits of your research can be rewarding in themselves, however, if you proceed with the aim of learning as much as you can. All of the instructions and guidelines below, rather than ends in themselves, are the means to help you communicate your knowledge and ideas to others.

Whatever the subject or scope of your project, the procedures for writing a paper based on research are quite similar. The essential processes include (1) choosing a topic, (2) preparing a working bibliography, (3) collecting information, (4) outlining the paper, (5) drafting the paper, and (6) preparing the final copy. Although you will probably move through these steps more or less sequentially, you should not consider any of them fully completed until you hand in the final copy of the paper. For example, while you collect information, it is likely that you will also reframe your topic and take down information for your bibliography or list of works cited. And when you outline the paper, you may find that you need more information in certain areas. In drafting the paper you probably will find that you need to reorganize your outline. Your final paper will display the quality and scope of the work you put into each of these steps.

Choosing a Topic

Choosing a topic involves identifying a general subject area, defining the topic and narrowing it, and stating the topic as a question or hypothesis. As you gather information through research, you will want to reconsider all of these decisions and eventually to formulate a thesis statement. When you think you have enough evidence, write out a tentative thesis statement, but avoid considering it final until you have written through the entire paper. A misstated or inaccurate thesis statement left in place can thwart your efforts to write.

▪ General Subject Area

An instructor or adviser sometimes specifies a broad area of study. The instructor may assign a particular topic, provide a list of possible topics, or give the writer a free choice of topics. You can begin to consider possible topics for a research paper at the moment you decide to take the course. When taking notes on the lectures and readings, you can jot down subjects of interest. Graduate students can begin to compile a list of possible thesis or dissertation topics early in their academic careers, perhaps selecting graduate classes that will contribute to their knowledge of these subjects and trying out ideas in seminar presentations or papers.

Even in the fields that seem to have been well covered by other scholars, possibilities for further research can often be found. Scholars sometimes suggest undiscussed areas of inquiry or unresolved controversies in their own work; this kind of information often appears in the notes and the conclusions. Also, commonly held but unsubstantiated conclusions or new ways of testing the basic assumptions in a field can provide subjects for research. In considering the terminology in your discipline, you can often find innovative ways to illustrate it or even new definitions. Recently published books or developments in current events can afford new insight into existing theories and thus lead to opportunities for research; contradictions or disjunctions among the various books also suggest possible topics.

▪ Definition of the Topic

As you make decisions leading to a topic, you should also consider such factors as the importance of the subject, your ability to be objective (especially if the topic is controversial), and the time available for completing the assignment. Evaluate the possibilities according to the following criteria: importance and interest, opportunity for discovery and originality, manageability, and availability of resources. You do not want to begin working on a topic that is not significant, that has already been so thoroughly investigated that room for discovery does not exist, that is not practical under the circumstances, or that cannot be completed within the time allotted for the assignment.

IMPORTANCE AND INTEREST Naturally, you will want to devote your time to a topic of considerable importance and interest to your readers. To a certain extent, importance and interest are subjective judgments that depend on the nature of the assignment and the requirements of the instructor. A topic that seems trivial to persons in one field of study might hold great significance for specialists in another. Your instructor or adviser should confirm the importance of your topic, and your paper should convince readers of its significance.

In some cases, a clearly important subject, such as gun control, may not make a good topic if the extensive public debate hampers your ability to make an original contribution or if your strong feelings or personal experience prevent you from at least examining opposing viewpoints.

OPPORTUNITIES FOR DISCOVERY OR ORIGINALITY You may want to consider whether your topic permits you to contribute anything to the existing discussion. Most research papers for undergraduate courses do not require that you arrive at a completely new analysis or conclusion. Even so, you should try to avoid duplicating work that others have done. It is nearly always possible to take an original perspective.

For a thesis or dissertation, you need to make certain that you can make a new and significant contribution. Judgments about how much room the topic should allow for discovery or originality vary widely. It's a good idea to come to an understanding with your adviser about expectations for originality.

MANAGEABILITY Careful limiting of a topic will help you conduct research successfully. If a topic is too vague or broad, too narrow, or too specialized, you may not be able to find enough suitable material. A topic that is too broad will not give sufficient direction to research and probably will necessitate superficial treatment of the subject. A topic that is too narrow will yield inadequate information, limiting your ability to reach a valid conclusion. If a topic is too specialized or too technical, it may demand knowledge you cannot acquire in the time allotted for your project. For example, you probably would not want to choose a topic that requires extensive statistics unless you have some background in mathematics or can consult with a statistician. Ultimately, of course, readers will judge the manageability of your topic by the treatment you give it, because a good paper defends not only its content but also its scope.

AVAILABILITY OF RESOURCES Even if a topic is worthwhile and manageable, it may not be suitable if the necessary research materials are not available. Access to print and to electronic materials should help guide your choice of topic. If your research paper entails a survey or an experiment, you need to determine whether you can collect the required data within the time limits of the assignment.

▪ Formulating a Working Statement of the Topic

You might wish to state your topic as a question or as a hypothesis, depending on the nature of the subject and the assignment. Formulating the topic as a question prevents you from settling on a thesis without having tested it sufficiently with exploratory research.

Topics stated as questions

```
--Does the extensive use of e-mail communication affect the
organizational hierarchy in a business?
--Should any nation that explodes a nuclear device be
admitted to the so-called nuclear club?
```

Your question should be one to which you really would like to know the answer, and the answer should not be simple or obvious.

As you gather information, you may discover that you have asked the wrong question or that you are more interested in answering a related question. If so, you can revise your question. You will also be able to narrow your question as you work. A question about the psychological effects of computer-assisted instruction might be narrowed to focus on instruction in foreign languages, perhaps even on one specific language, possibly on one particular program for learning that language. Even in early stages of work, you can begin to formulate possible answers to your question in the form of preliminary thesis statements, which may have to be abandoned or refined as you continue exploring your topic.

For some fields of research, particularly those involving empirical or descriptive research, you may want to state your topic as a *hypothesis*, that is, a tentative explanation or argument that you will test, either with your own empirical research or a survey of data collected by others.

Topics stated as hypotheses

--The preponderance of evidence suggests that the planet is experiencing the phenomenon known as global warming.
--Television programs aired in prime time should (should not) be censored for sex and violence.

Drawing on the facts and ideas you find by doing research, you will test the hypothesis, and you will revise it as many times as your information warrants. For example, the writer of the sample paper "Are Books Obsolete?" (see the outline for this paper on page 31) began with the hypothesis that given rapid developments in computer technology, electronic materials will quickly replace printed books. After doing some research, she concluded that her initial hypothesis was wrong. (See page 45 for a more scientific definition of the word *hypothesis*.)

Your answer to the question or your revised hypothesis will become the *thesis statement*, or what some instructors call the *controlling idea*, of your paper.

Collecting Information

Once you have selected the broad subject of your paper, you can begin research to determine how to narrow and shape the topic. This effort should result in a *working bibliography*, a list of sources that appear to be relevant at the initial stage of your research. Developing the working bibliography requires knowledge of resources, both print and electronic, and of various ways to locate sources.

Information has never been more abundant or more readily available, especially to those with access to the Internet, or World Wide Web, an international electronic network of databases. This ease of acquiring some kinds of information does not necessarily make writing a research paper easier, however. Even if you have found all your sources in electronic form, you still have to read the material critically and take notes on it; develop your own perspective into a thesis statement; organize and outline your argument; and document your sources according to the requirements of the style sheet you are following.

Whether you plan to use print sources or electronic sources, or a combination of the two, you will do research with an *index*, a list of names or topics that is usually, but not necessarily, arranged in alphabetical order. Indexes can be valuable for locating journal and newspaper articles. Also, you may search the Internet by scanning different types of indexes of electronic materials.

■ Sources of Information

If you have access to a good library, you probably will want to begin by using its electronic and print resources.

LIBRARY CATALOGS Most libraries now permit you to search their more recent holdings in an electronic database, or online catalog. For materials acquired before a certain specified date, which varies by library, you will have to use the catalog in the form of paper cards arranged in drawers by author, title, and subject.

Subject listings

Subject listings are important tools for locating sources relevant to your topic; they indicate all the works in the library dealing with one subject. It is useful to note the subject areas under which the books for your topic are cataloged; those subject headings can lead you to related headings and additional sources of information. You can also find subject headings by looking up a general subject area, such as art, history, literature, linguistics, or physics, and noting the category headings, subheadings, and cross-references.

Cataloging system

The two cataloging systems you may encounter are the Library of Congress and the Dewey Decimal systems. The Dewey Decimal system is older, and most libraries no longer use it to catalog new materials. However, many libraries have books shelved under both systems, so you need to know the headings from both systems.

When you cannot find your topic in the catalog, consult the appropriate list of subject headings. For example, the term *Equal Rights Amendment* does not appear in the card catalog. By consulting a work on subject headings, you will discover that material on the ERA is filed under *Women's Rights—United States.* For a card catalog with headings based on the Dewey Decimal system, see *Sears List of Subject Headings* by Minnie Earl Sears (14th ed., edited by Martha T. Mooney [New York: Wilson, 1991]). For a card catalog with headings based on the Library of Congress system, see *Library of Congress Subject Headings* (24th ed., 5 vols. [Washington, D.C.: Library of Congress, Cataloging Distribution Service, 2001]).

Online library catalogs

Online library catalogs generally permit you to search by the categories traditionally used in the card catalog—author, title, and subject—as well as to conduct additional types of searches, such as for keywords, call numbers, or multiple subjects. The home page of the online library catalog normally provides information about the best approaches to searching (see Figure 1.1).

If the computer finds nothing in response to your request, first check the spelling of the words you entered. If you have spelled everything correctly, try a different kind of search, such as for the title rather than the author, or use some alternative keywords to designate the subject.

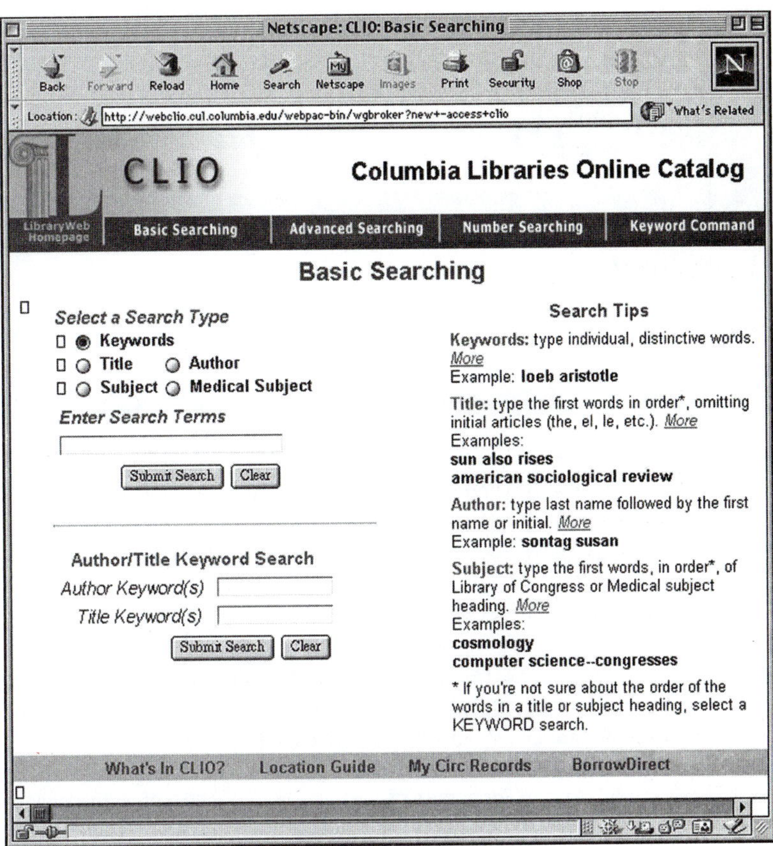

Figure 1.1. Home page of online catalog.

Many libraries now include current information in the online catalog about the availability of print materials: whether or not a book is checked out and the due date; the actual holdings of any particular periodical, indicating the span of years the library has subscribed and which volumes are missing or checked out; and materials that have been ordered or are being bound (see Figure 1.2).

In addition to retrieving information about the holdings of your own library, you may also be able to access the online card catalogs of some of the nation's major research libraries, such as the Library of Congress, the New York Public Library, and the University of California, to name only a few online services available nationwide. RLIN-BIB (Research Libraries Information Network—Bibliographic File), OCLC (Online Computer Library Center), and CURL Catalog (Consortium of Research Libraries) are national bibliographic databases that provide information about the location of books in libraries throughout the United States and in many other countries. WorldCat provides a merged catalog of more than 36 million entries from libraries around the globe. If you have a modem, a device that enables computers to communicate with each other over telephone lines, you may be able to access all this online library information from your personal computer.

Long View

Search: Author Browse = DASTON LORRAINE 1951
Record: 6 of 6

New Search | Brief View | Previous Record | Next Record | Back

Author: Daston, Lorraine, 1951- ①
Title: Wonders and the order of nature, 1150-1750 / ③
Description: ⑦ 511 p. : ⑧ ill. ; ⑨ 29 cm. ⑤
Published: ④ New York : Zone Books ; Cambridge, ④ Mass. : Distributed by the MIT Press, 1998. ⑥
LC Subjects: Science, Medieval. Science--History--18th century. Science--Philosophy--History. ⑩
Other Authors: Park, Katharine, 1950- ②
Notes: Includes bibliographical references (p. 451-497) and index.
Contents: Introduction: At the Limit -- I. The Topography of Wonder -- II. The Properties of Things -- III. Wonder Among the Philosophers -- IV. Marvelous Particulars -- V. Monsters: A Case Study -- VI. Strange Facts -- VII. Wonders of Art, Wonders of Nature -- VIII. The Passions of Inquiry -- IX. The Enlightenment and the Anti-Marvelous.
LCCN: 96049411
ISN: 0942299906

Location	Call Number	
SCIENCE ⑪	Q124.97 .D38 1998	
	Circulation Data	
⑫	Not checked-out	Item:

Location	Call Number	
BARNARD ⑬	Q124.97 .D38 1998	
	Circulation Data	
⑭	Not checked-out	Item:

New Search | Brief View | Previous Record | Next Record | Back

① Author of book
② Co-author of book
③ Title
④ Places of publication
⑤ Publisher
⑥ Date of publication
⑦ Number of pages in book
⑧ Indication of Illustrations
⑨ Height of book
⑩ Subject entries for book
⑪ ⑬ Call number
⑫ ⑭ Availability

Figure 1.2. Detailed report in online catalog.

PRINT INDEXES Indexes also comprise print reference works that can be valuable in formulating a working bibliography. Indexes are particularly useful for locating journal and newspaper articles, which are not entered in library catalogs. Some indexes contain abstracts, or brief summaries, of articles and book reviews; other indexes simply list books.

Indexes may be either general or specialized. General indexes cover a wide range of subjects because they list every article, editorial, or review in each issue of the periodicals they survey. Specialized indexes focus on specific fields and subject areas, often collecting material from a wide range of periodicals and books. As you work in a particular field, you will accumulate a list of relevant indexes. To find out whether your library owns an index on a particular subject, consult the catalog under the heading *Indexes,* or look up *Indexes* as a subdivision of a specific subject (as in *Spanish-American History—Indexes*).

A printed index will include a key to its organizational format and the abbreviations it uses. A brief study of this material before you turn to the index will help you to find the entries you want and to decipher the numbers and abbreviations used in a particular index.

A list of widely used general and specialized indexes appears below. The first date indicates the beginning of the series; the second date indicates the end of coverage.

INDEXES IN THE HUMANITIES

America: History and Life, 1974–
Art Index, 1929–
British Humanities Index, 1962–
Guide to the Performing Arts, 1957–
Humanities Index, 1974–; With *Social Sciences Index,* 1974–; Preceded by *Social Sciences and Humanities Index,* 1967–73; and by *International Index,* 1907–66
Index to Religious Periodical Literature, 1949–
International Bibliography of Historical Sciences, 1926–
Library Literature, 1933–
MLA International Bibliography of Books and Articles on the Modern Languages and Literatures, 1921–
Music Index, 1949–
Philosopher's Index, 1967–
World Literature Today, 1960–
Year's Work in Modern Language Studies, 1929–

INDEXES IN THE SCIENCES

Applied Science and Technology Index, 1958–
Biological and Agricultural Index, 1964–
Energy Index, 1973–
General Science Index, 1978–
Science Citation Index, 1964–

INDEXES IN THE SOCIAL SCIENCES

America: History and Life, 1964–
Education Index, 1929–61; 1969–
Educational Studies, 1973–
Historical Abstracts, 1955–

Index of Economic Articles, 1961–
International Bibliography of Economics, 1952–
International Bibliography of Political Science, 1952–
International Bibliography of Social and Cultural Anthropology, 1955–
International Bibliography of Sociology, 1952–
LLBA: Language and Language Behavior Abstracts, 1967–
Resources in Education, 1966–
Social Sciences Index, 1974–; See the listing above for accompanying *Humanities Index*

JOURNAL INDEXES

Business Periodicals Index, 1958–
Current Index to Journals in Education (CIJE), 1969–
New Periodicals Index, 1977–
Nineteenth-Century Readers' Guide, 1890–1922
Poole's Index to Periodicals, 1802–1907
Popular Periodicals Index, 1973–
Public Affairs Information Service (PAIS), 1915–
Readers' Guide to Periodical Literature, 1901–
State Education Journal Index, 1963–

NEWSPAPER INDEXES

Chicago Tribune Index, 1972–
Christian Science Monitor Index, 1960–
Los Angeles Times Index, 1972–
New York Times Index, 1851–
The Times Index (London), 1906–
Wall Street Journal Index, 1958–
Washington Post Index, 1972–

INDEXES TO GOVERNMENT PUBLICATIONS

American Statistics Index, 1973–
Congressional Information Service Index to Publications of the United States Congress, 1970–
The Monthly Catalog of the United States Government, 1898–

INDEXES TO PARTS OF BOOKS

Biography Index, 1946–
Essay and General Literature Index, 1900–

INDEXES TO BOOK REVIEWS

Book Review Digest, 1906–
Book Review Index, 1965–
International Bibliography of Book Reviews, 1971–
New York Times Book Review, 1896–

For an exhaustive listing of print reference works, see *Guide to Reference Books,* 10th ed., edited by Eugene P. Sheehy et al. (Chicago: American Library Association, 1986), and the supplement, *Guide to Reference Books Covering Materials from 1985–1990,* edited by Robert Balay and Eugene P. Sheehy (Chicago: American Library Association, 1992).

Online databases
CD-ROM databases

DATABASES, OR ELECTRONIC INDEXES Electronic databases take two forms: (1) online databases, which are retrieved by modem from a central databank or vendor, and (2) CD-ROM (Compact Disk—Read Only Memory) databases, which are on the same type of disk used for most musical recordings.

Many indexes and bibliographies are now available in both print and electronic form, either CD or online or both. These reference works include, to name only a few, *Arts and Humanities Citation Index, Biological Abstracts, Chemical Abstracts, Dissertation Abstracts International, Educational Resources Information Clearinghouse (ERIC), G. P. O. Monthly Catalog, Historical Abstracts, Humanities Index, Legal Resource Index, Linguistic and Language Behavior Abstracts, Modern Language Association Bibliography, Physics Abstracts, Public Affairs Information Services (PAIS), Philosopher's Index, Psychology Abstracts,* and *Sociological Abstracts.* These databases may be updated weekly, quarterly, or yearly; often the electronic version, in particular the online edition, is more current than the print one.

Other electronic databases have no equivalent in print form. Some of the most useful of these are Infotrac, which provides an index, along with abstracts or the full texts of articles in newspapers and journals, and *ProQuest Image,* which provides abstracts and articles from general-interest magazines from 1986 to the present.

Home use of electronic databases

Some encyclopedias, dictionaries, and other reference works may be purchased in CD-ROM form by individuals. To read these disks with a personal computer, you need a special drive unit. For information on materials available in CD-ROM form, see *CD-ROMs in Print: An International Guide to CD-ROM, CD-I, CDTV, and Electronic Book Products* (Westport, Conn.: Meckler, updated annually).

For information about online databases you can arrange to receive through a modem in your home, see the *Directory of Online Databases,* published quarterly, with two additional updates a year, by Cuadra/Elsevier.

Searching electronic databases

When you approach a new database, you will have to spend some time learning how it is organized, in the same way that you would have to peruse the table of contents and the index in a book. Most electronic databases have a "Help" program—an online instructional program—as well as brochures in print form. Because electronic sources have not been systematized by any one organization, they use a variety of different commands, symbols, and descriptors, which are the equivalent of subject headings in print sources. Often it is useful to call up one or more titles you have already identified as relevant to see how they are defined by a particular database. Some databases allow you to browse alphabetically through their list of subject descriptors. Other systems allow you to search for any word that appears in a title, abstract, or article, including publisher, date of publication, and language.

Boolean logic

Most database search mechanisms operate on the principle of a combinatory system known as Boolean logic (named for its inventor, George Boole), which locates keywords or subjects with the operators `AND`, `OR`, and `NOT`.

AND narrows a search by specifying two terms that must be in the same document.

(keyword=tennis and racquetball—for documents containing mentions of both of the sports, rather than either tennis or racquetball alone)

OR extends a search.

(keyword=(george or martha) washington—for documents that mention either George Washington or Martha Washington alone or both of them together)

NOT narrows a search by eliminating some documents likely to contain the term.

(keyword=earthquake not California—for documents dealing with earthquakes but not earthquakes in California)

You may use one Boolean operator, as in the examples just given, or several of them.

(keyword=movies and india not satyajit ray—for documents about films made in India but not those of the most well-known director in the West, Satyajit Ray)

Other positional operators

Many search mechanisms also use other positional operators, such as the following:

ADJ designates which of the terms should modify the other.

(keyword=cuban adj american—for documents about Cuban Americans)

NEAR searches for documents with two terms occurring near each other in any order.

(keyword=Madrid near Paris—for documents comparing the two cities rather than merely mentioning both of them)

WITH searches for terms close to each other in the same document in any order and not necessarily adjacent.

(subject=fish with pollution—for a document discussing the connection between pollution and populations of fish)

Wildcards

Databases often use wildcards, symbols that truncate a word, to enable the computer to call up the word with various endings. The most common ones are ? and *.

(keyword=histor? creates a search that will retrieve history, historical, historicism, historic)

Avoid using wildcards to shorten words because you will retrieve too many matches. For example, don't enter keyword=garb* if you are looking for the subject garbage, because you will pull entries including garb, garbanzo, and garble.

INTERNET Computer networks, known collectively as the Internet, permit computers all over the world to share computer files. For access to the Internet you need an account from an organization (most colleges and universities provide this service) or a subscription to a commercial online service, such as America Online, CompuServe, and many others.

URL codes

Your computer accesses the Web through a *browser,* a type of software. Netscape Navigator and Microsoft Internet Explorer are two commonly used browsers. To locate a Web site with your browser, enter the electronic address written in URL (Uniform Resource Locator) code, which is more or less the equivalent of a call number for a book. Typed into your browser, a URL address, such as <http://node.on.ca/tfl/multimedia/primer>, will bring this site to your screen.

Search engines

Your browser can also give you access to *search engines,* which are analogous in some ways to indexes, but lead to Web sites rather than to books.

Search engines operate on some variation of the keyword search described above, but they may conduct the search in quite different ways, which will produce different results. You probably will want to experiment with several search engines, first, to learn to exploit all their capabilities, and second, to learn which ones lead you to the best sites for your purposes. The most popular search engines are these:

Yahoo! <http://www.yahoo.com> deploys a hierarchical index, which means that it ranks entries in the order of their apparent relevance to your topic. Whereas most search engines gather information electronically, Yahoo! employs people to categorize information. As a result, you may receive fewer matches (organized by category, site, and Web page), but those you do find should be the ones most relevant to your work. Other search engines that work hierarchically are AlphaSearch <http://www.calvin.edu/library/as> and Infomine <http://infomine.ucr.edu>.

Google <www.google.com> works by locating your keywords within the documents in its index. Google arranges Web sites by the number of links to them from other Web sites, thus in effect using popularity as an index to value.

Most search engines operate by using a "robot" or "spider" to locate and index information in Web sites. Among the best of these search engines are AltaVista <http://www.altavista.com> and Go Network <http://infoseek.go.com>.

Some search engines, such as Inference Find <http://www.inferencefind.com> and MetaCrawler <http://www.metacrawler.com>, function by searching other search engines.

For detailed information about finding the right engine for your particular search, see Robert Berkman, *Find It Fast: How to Uncover Expert Information on Any Subject*, 5th ed. (New York: Harper Collins, 2000).

Electronic bookmarks

Keeping track of material on the Web requires constant attention to your potential use of the source. You may encounter information through a series of links from one source to another that may be difficult to retrace. For this reason most browsers have a *Bookmark* feature that allows you to create a personal list of sites you want to revisit. Some browsers have a *History* function that records your itinerary through the Web.

Web sites exist only in cyberspace, a virtual or nonexistent space. As a result, they can vanish from one day to the next. Providers may alter their sites at any time, so the site may exist in a form different from the one you encountered, thus foiling the reader who wishes to check your information. For this reason you need to remember to take down not only the address of the site but to record the date and time you accessed it. It is a good idea to download or print out any information you think might be useful; the copy will have the date and electronic address on it.

Evaluating Information

Before deciding to use a particular source, you should evaluate its relevance and suitability for your purposes.

PRINT SOURCES The principal qualities to notice in a print source are the qualifications and perspective of the author, the objectivity of the sources used, the date and form of publication, the level, and the source's primary or secondary nature for your purpose. For help in evaluating print sources, you may want to consult a compendium of book reviews, such as the *Book Review Index* or the *Book Review Digest,* both available in print and online.

The author's qualifications

An author's qualifications for writing a work, such as academic degrees, professional credentials, and experience and status in the field, may influence your choice of a source. Information about an author's qualifications may be found in the preliminary or appendix materials of the source itself, in a biographical dictionary or directory such as *Who's Who,* or in an encyclopedia.

The author's perspective

Every writer brings his or her own perspective to any piece of work. This authorial perspective may range from a personal inclination to a fully developed philosophy or theory about the subject. In more specialized works the author will usually have chosen a particular method for working on the subject from among various possible methods. The most reliable authors will state the theories and methods on which they operate. If the author does not identify the critical or analytical approach, you should do so yourself before deciding whether to invest time in studying the source.

Objectivity

The objectivity of a source is its lack of bias or prejudice. Total objectivity is not humanly possible, but the most valuable sources identify any biases that might be caused by the author's affiliations or allegiances—whether economic, political, philosophical, or religious. The writer of a study of the automotive industry based solely on information obtained from executives at Chrysler or Ford should make readers aware that the nature of the sources may have influenced the conclusions. Even if a writer does not reveal possible reasons for bias, you should try to discern them and evaluate the work accordingly.

Date and form of publication

The facts of publication can reveal a great deal about the potential usefulness of a source. The date of a work generally gives an indication of its perspective. A 1939 book on the Great Depression would differ greatly from a 1999 book on the same subject. Similarly, two books published in 2002, one in Europe and the other in the United States, would very likely differ in perspective on the United Nations, for example. The identity of the publisher can also suggest the nature of the source. A university publisher usually indicates that the book makes a substantial contribution to its field and that it may be intended for specialists. Commercial publishers release books for a wide range of readers, and their lists vary widely in level and quality. The history and reputation of the publishing house can help you estimate the usefulness of a book. Likewise, some journals submit articles to more rigorous editorial scrutiny than do others.

Level

The intended audience determines the level of a work with respect to diction, sentence structure, complexity, and assumed background knowledge.

You may find sources that are too technical and advanced; with these, you will need either to seek guidance in understanding them or omit them from your study. Similarly, avoid using works that are too general or simplistic for your purposes.

Primary and secondary sources

You need to consider whether your project requires primary or secondary sources and, if you will use both, whether a particular work is a primary or a secondary source in the context of your work. Primary sources are basic materials with little or no annotation or editorial alteration, such as manuscripts, diaries, letters, interviews, and laboratory reports. Secondary sources derive from primary materials and include analysis, interpretation, and commentary on primary materials.

Depending on the point of view of your research paper, a given source may be either primary or secondary. A research paper on William James, the nineteenth-century philosopher, would treat R. W. B. Lewis's *The Jameses: A Family Narrative* as a secondary source, whereas a paper on Lewis, a well-known critic and biographer, would treat the same book as a primary source. Your assignment may require you to emphasize either primary or secondary sources or to use a combination of the two.

ELECTRONIC SOURCES, OR WEB SITES Web sites may be placed on the Internet by organizations, companies, or individuals for various reasons, most of which are promotional or self-serving to some degree. Even more than with books and periodicals you need to evaluate electronic sources critically. In addition to applying the criteria for evaluating print sources, you should judge a Web site by the following additional measures (see Figure 1.3).

Source or domain

The URL of a Web site will give you information about its domains, or affiliations. The top-level domain appears at the end of the address: .edu for colleges and universities; .org for a nonprofit organization; .gov for a government entity; .net for a private site. When the page site originates in another country, an abbreviation of that name appears, such as .jp for Japan, .ca for Canada, and .fr for France. A tilde ~ in the URL indicates that the site has been posted by an individual. The characters following http:// or www. give the name, sometimes abbreviated or truncated, of the institution or entity.

Responsibility for the site

A reliable Web site should indicate the author(s) of the text or visual material, which you should evaluate just as you would the author of a print form. In addition, look for the name and electronic address of the Web Master, a person responsible for creating and maintaining an electronic site. If you have questions about the site, contact the Web Master first.

Currency

To find out whether a site provides current information, look for the date it was created or the date it was last maintained. Also, try out some of the links to other sites. If some of those linked sites no longer exist (are "dead" rather than "live"), you will know that the site is not being kept current.

Purpose of the site

The advertising function of the Internet means that you have to be very skeptical about the information you find. Ask yourself why the site exists: to sell, to inform, to persuade, and so on. Individuals who post a bibliography on a subject may do it as a public service, or they may wish to promote themselves as authorities on the material. Businesses post sites to sell their products. The fact that most sites have motives not identical with your needs does not mean that they cannot be useful to you.

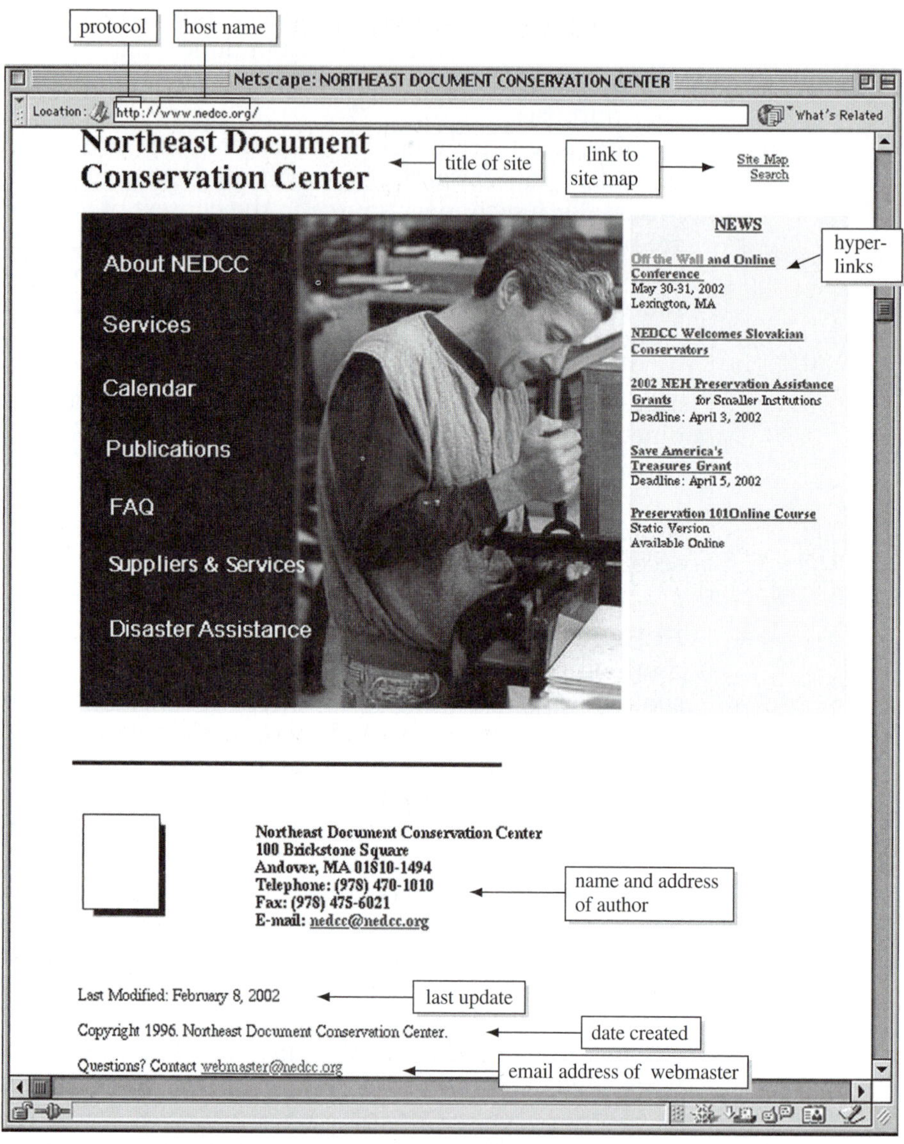

Figure 1.3. Sample of a web site, with annotations.

Technical features

Your ability to use a site depends heavily on the organization of that site. Instructions for navigating the site should be explained as simply and clearly as possible. The site should contain a site map, which lays out all of its branches in text form. The site should also prevent you from getting into dead ends with no way back to the home page. The graphics should function to facilitate your understanding of the material rather than to distract or confuse you. If you run into problems with the technical functioning of a site, look for another one. An incompetent design may indicate carelessness in matter of content. As with books, however, you can't always judge a Web site by its packaging.

■ Recording Information

As you look in indexes and other reference works, you will want to record information about the sources that seem relevant.

Required documentation

Record complete documentation for the source, preferably in the format recommended by the style sheet you intend to use for the final paper. Keep in mind that entries for bibliographies and lists of works cited require some or all of the following types of information for a book: the full name of the author; the title and any subtitle; the editor or translator, if any; the edition, if it is other than the first; the volume number if it is part of a multivolume work; the series name, if any; the city and state of publication; the publisher; the year of publication. For an article, you will require the name of the journal, the volume, the date of publication, and inclusive page numbers.

Form and Style provides instructions for using the note-bibliography system based on *The Chicago Manual of Style* (Chicago) and the parenthetical reference systems based on Modern Language Association (MLA) style and American Psychological Association (APA) style. Even though you may not find all the information you need for a particular bibliographic form in the index you consult, you can record the entry as the system indicates, leaving spaces for the missing elements as a reminder to locate them when you consult the source itself.

Electronic sources

For electronic sources, particularly information networks and online databases, you need data sufficient to allow your readers to recover material identical to whatever you consulted. Consequently, you will need even more information for an electronic source than for a book, which can be located easily. *The MLA Handbook* cautions that "in electronic research, as in print research, only the ability of readers to verify an author's use of a source can discourage the circulation of error."[1] If you believe that your sources will be difficult to find again, you may want to print them out. For information about citing electronic references, see the chapter for the style sheet you will follow in your final paper. For advice on more arcane matters of electronic citation, see Chapter 10, pp. 278–280, or refer to *The Columbia Guide to Online Style* by Janice R. Walker and Todd W. Taylor (New York: Columbia University Press, 1998).

Materials for recording documentation

The materials or medium you choose for recording documentation for your sources should allow you to rearrange, alphabetize, and delete entries. You may want to use index cards, software designed with a template for recording such information, or an alphabetized list in a word-processing file.

■ Understanding Information

To be able to organize and use the information you have found, you should devise a system for taking notes. If you leave the sources intact rather than separating the information out into note form, you are likely to follow the logic and development of each source rather than to impose your own organization on the material.

---

[1] *MLA Handbook for Writers of Research Papers,* by Joseph Gibaldi, 5th ed. (New York: Modern Language Association, 1999), xvii.

TAKING NOTES Taking notes is a process of assimilating and digesting the information you have gleaned in research. For these notes you may use any or all of several types of materials.

Note cards

The size of card you choose (three-by-five, four-by-six, or five-by-eight inches) might depend on the anticipated length of your notes or on personal preference. Whatever size you choose, use it consistently.

Computer software

Recording notes by computer has the advantage of allowing you to transfer quotations directly into your paper without having to recopy and thus possibly introduce errors. Of course, the data in your computer file must be correct if you are to avoid perpetuating errors. Some computer programs allow you to create and label note cards, a system that gives you the advantage of a flexible format for using the notes. Or you may wish to create a file for each source or each section of your paper. If you use this method, you can print out your files and cut them into pieces to be used as note cards.

Photocopied materials

Even though you will probably want to photocopy some materials in the library, you will still need to take notes on them. Having a photocopy of a work does not substitute for having a set of note cards: it is unlikely that you have studied the source as carefully as you would if you were taking notes. You may want to paste the relevant portions of a photocopy onto note cards or copy them into a computer file.

No matter which of these materials you select, you will follow the principles discussed below.

ORGANIZATION OF NOTES Before you begin to take notes, enter on the card or computer file the information you will need to link the note card to the appropriate bibliographical information. The last name of the author (and, if you have more than one entry for an author, the title) usually suffices. Some researchers number each bibliography entry and put the corresponding number on each note card, but using the author's name is more likely to be accurate. Check to be certain that you have recorded accurately the page number from which you are transcribing information. If you turn a page in the middle of a note, indicate precisely the point of division between the pages so that if you use only part of the note in the paper, you will know to which page in the source the note should refer. Also, before you put the note card aside, enter either the section of your outline or the area of your subject for which the information is relevant. Some researchers pencil in this comment so that they can make changes as their thinking develops.

FORMS OF NOTE TAKING You may record information in one of two basic forms: direct quotation or summary.

Direct quotation

A *direct quotation* is an exact copy of a portion of the original text. The quotation may encompass one or more words, phrases, clauses, complete sentences, or paragraphs. Take down a direct quotation when you think you may want to quote the passage or when the material meets one of the criteria for direct quotation discussed in Chapter 3 (see pages 61–62). Also, copy a direct quotation when you wish to have the material in your notes precisely as the author wrote it so that you can reread or verify it later. Before leaving the source, check direct quotations carefully so that, later, you can be confident of their accuracy.

Summary or paraphrase

The use of direct quotation in note taking helps ensure accuracy, but direct quotation can be a waste of time if you do not plan to use the quotations in the paper or if you merely copy information without understanding or digesting it. The use of summary or paraphrase rather than direct quotation forces you to comprehend as you read and leads naturally into the process of writing the paper. A *summary* is a brief synthesis of the original material in your own words. A *paraphrase* is a restatement of the author's ideas in about the same number of words. Writing a summary or paraphrase, then, requires you to identify the essential ideas and terminology in your source. An example of each appears below.

Note card with direct quotation

```
                               Musical Settings-Novels
                                              III. A.
Smith, Grover, ed.
p. 821
 Aldous Huxley to Leonard Bernstein, 4 Apr. 1957

" . . . I am writing to ask if you would be at all
interested in reading a dramatic version of my novel
Brave New World, which I have recently made, with a
view to a musical setting."
```

Note card with summary

```
                               Musical Settings-Novels
                                              III. A.
Smith, Grover, ed.
p. 821 Aldous Huxley wrote to Leonard Bernstein on
April 4, 1957, to ask him to consider setting a
"dramatic version" of Brave New World to music.
```

Precision in note taking

When you write a summary or paraphrase, you must be careful to avoid duplicating the author's wording. Changing an occasional word or reversing the order of phrases or sentences does not result in an adequate summary. A good method is to try to write a summary or paraphrase without looking at the source. After writing your version, look at the original and make a critical comparison, checking for any imitation of the original wording. If you find that you have used more than two consecutive words from the original (with the exception of articles and prepositions), place them in quotation marks. Carelessness in writing a summary can result in unintentional plagiarism. (See pages 59–62 in Chapter 3 for advice on avoiding plagiarism.) Even though the summary contains your own words, the ideas belong to someone else and must be so credited in your paper. Be as careful about recording the author's name and page numbers for a summary or a paraphrase as you would be for a direct quotation.

If you have large amounts of material to summarize, you might want to write your notes in outline form, either in an informal way or in a detailed, formal manner following the specific rules for outlining presented later in this chapter. Even when you outline, you should distinguish carefully between your own words and the words of the author.

You will want to strike a balance between taking enough notes to avoid having to return to your sources and taking repetitious or irrelevant notes. Judgment in this matter develops naturally as you learn more about your topic and as you master the process of writing a research paper.

Outlining the Paper

Some researchers begin with a tentative, or working, outline that guides the choice of research materials; others let the outline grow from their research and writing. If you develop an outline in advance, it should remain open to change as you read and take notes. Formulating and revising an outline throughout the processes of researching and writing can help you give your paper a logical and meaningful structure. After you have written a draft of your paper, check it against an existing outline or attempt to make an outline from the draft.

Creating a final outline involves making decisions about the thesis statement, the principle of organization, the type of outline, and the format of the outline.

▪ The Thesis Statement

The answer to the question with which you began your research, or the substantiated hypothetical statement, will eventually become the thesis statement, or controlling idea, for the paper. As your outline evolves and your research leads you in new directions, your thesis statement may change, and you should frequently consider revising it as your work progresses. You might even find that you have completely reversed your conclusions in the process of doing research.

The scope and precision of your thesis statement will vary depending on your field of study, the level at which you are writing, and the nature of the assignment. For an undergraduate research paper on a subject new to the writer, the thesis statement might well be broader than an appropriate thesis statement for a graduate paper. For the latter, a more knowledgeable and sophisticated approach to the subject would be required. The same would be true of a professional paper, which might delve into extremely specialized areas of the subject. Even when writing a very general paper, however, you might find a particular area of the subject on which to concentrate. You will want to get some idea from your instructor or adviser about the scope of conclusions you are expected to draw for any given assignment.

Your final thesis statement should cover all the points made in the paper. It need not enumerate each point, but you should not disconcert your reader by straying into an area of inquiry not suggested by the thesis statement. The thesis statement for the sample paper on pages 30–35, "Although electronic means of publication have some advantages, electronic texts are not likely to replace books," refers briefly to two major sections of the paper, the advantages of electronic texts and the disadvantages to electronic publishing, and it suggests the writer's answer to the question of the title, "Are Books Obsolete?" A paper beginning with this thesis statement should not conclude that books are obsolete; the writer who had come to that conclusion in the process of writing would have to revise the thesis and the rest of the paper accordingly.

▪ Principles of Organization

The organization of a paper often develops naturally in the course of research and during the writing of early drafts. Nevertheless, it is often instructive to try out various principles or patterns of organization with your material. Experimentation can help you find the pattern most appropriate to your material or can lead you to new insights. Among the most useful principles for structuring a research paper are chronology, comparison and contrast, spatial pattern, cause and effect, and analysis. These patterns of development are often used in combination, and they can be applied to individual paragraphs as well as to an entire paper.

CHRONOLOGY The chronological pattern explains each of the steps in a sequentially ordered process. The basic plan of this chapter, for instance, is chronological: The suggestions for writing a research paper begin with selecting a topic and progress step by step to proofreading the final copy. The chronological pattern is often appropriate for a paper describing a series of historical, political, or sociological processes or events.

COMPARISON AND CONTRAST The pattern of comparison and contrast presents the similarities and/or differences between two or more persons, places, or things. A logical development by comparison and contrast entails discussion of the same qualities of both subjects. For example, the statement that one politician was a poor public speaker and another had a good understanding of the legislative system does not provide a basis for comparison and contrast. Both the speaking ability of the two politicians and their understanding of political institutions should be discussed. Comparison and contrast are appropriate when a subject can best be understood by distinguishing it from others in its class.

SPATIAL PATTERN The spatial pattern develops the physical layout or geographical dimensions of a topic. It can guide the reader through a topic that includes several locations, such as the seasonal habitats of various animals, the movement of troops in the Vietnam War, or the concentration of heavy industry in the United States.

CAUSE AND EFFECT A cause-and-effect paper presents the events or forces that produced certain results, speculates about how things might have turned out if conditions had been different, or reports controlled experimentation to determine the factors important to a particular outcome. Cause and effect are difficult to determine, particularly in the social sciences, and valid work in this area should either control for or take into account as many factors as possible. Topics such as possible explanations for the decline in students' reading scores in the United States in the past decade or reasons for population shifts away from inner cities lend themselves to development by cause and effect.

ANALYSIS Some subjects can best be understood by an examination of their component parts. Analysis is the process of dividing a subject into its parts and classifying them. A research paper on the responsibilities of a hospital administrator might proceed by grouping the duties by types and discussing each type.

Major divisions of a paper

Your outline will develop naturally from the principle of organization you select. A paper involving comparison and contrast or cause and effect, for example, will usually have two major divisions. A paper organized chronologically, spatially, or analytically may have a number of major divisions. After you have identified the large segments of the paper, you can fill in the points to be made in each part.

Types of Outlines

Your working outline may consist of casual jottings, but the outline you present to your instructor either in the middle of your research or with your final paper should be formal and consistently developed. You may choose either a topic outline or a sentence outline, depending on your preference and that of your instructor.

TOPIC OUTLINE The entries in a topic outline are words, phrases, or clauses; that is, they are not complete sentences. The entries should be parallel; they all should take the same grammatical form. If you use a noun phrase for one entry, you should continue using noun phrases consistently. You may have to rework some of your entries to make them parallel, but paying attention to grammatical form often contributes to clear and logical thinking. (See the example topic outline on pages 23–24 and the discussion of parallelism on pages 23–24 and 84.)

SENTENCE OUTLINE The entries in a sentence outline are complete sentences. The process of writing a research paper involves writing sentences from the topics in the topic outline, in effect producing a sentence outline. A sentence outline, therefore, serves as a beginning for the paper and as a test of the logic of the outline. (See the example sentence outline on page 24.)

Outline Formats

The two basic formats for an outline are the number-letter sequence and the decimal pattern. With either format, logic requires that there be at least two items at each level or subdivision; that is, an A must not appear without a B and a 1.1.1 without a 1.1.2 because nothing can be divided into fewer than two parts. When you find that you have only one subdivision for a section, either restate the major heading to include the subdivision or search for another logical division for the heading. (See the sample outlines on page 23.)

Number-letter sequence

The number-letter sequence is shown in the following example:

```
 I. The two reasons for . . .
    A. The first reason . . .
       1. The women . . .
          a. They could . . .
             (1) The time . . .
             (2) The place . . .
          b. They could . . .
       2. The men . . .
    B. The second reason . . .
II. The reasons against . . .
```

Decimal outline

The sequence for a decimal outline proceeds as follows:

```
1. The two reasons for . . .
   1.1 The first reason . . .
       1.1.1 The women . . .
             1.1.1.1 They could . . .
                     1.1.1.1.1 The time . . .
                     1.1.1.1.2 The place . . .
             1.1.1.2 They could . . .
       1.1.2 The men . . .
   1.2 The second reason . . .
2. The reasons against . . .
```

▪ Parallelism in Outlines

Elements in an outline or list, as well as chapter titles, subtitles, and headings, should be parallel—that is, entries at the same level of subordination should take the same grammatical form. If you use a noun or noun phrase (such as "Effective Regulations") for one chapter title, the next chapter title should also be a noun phrase ("Adequate Screening" rather than, for example, "To Provide Adequate Screening," an infinitive phrase). Similarly, in a sentence outline, all entries at the same level should be complete sentences.

The entries in the following outline are not parallel. Entry I is a complete sentence, whereas entry II is an infinitive phrase; entry I.A is a noun phrase, whereas entry I.C is a sentence.

Topic outline with nonparallel entries

```
 I. Nuclear Opponents Cite Dangers
    A. Leakage
    B. Disposing of Nuclear Waste
    C. Groups Threaten Sabotage
II. To Protect against Nuclear Accidents
    A. Sound Design and Construction
    B. Monitoring Systems
    C. Correcting Problems with Automatic Devices
```

The entries in the following outline are parallel because they are all noun phrases:

Topic outline with parallel entries

```
  I. Dangers of Nuclear Power Plants
     A. Leakage of Radiation
     B. Disposal of Nuclear Waste
     C. Sabotage by Terrorist Groups
 II. Safety Features of Nuclear Power Plants
     A. Sound Design and Construction
     B. Monitoring Systems
     C. Automatic Correction Devices
```

You may use other constructions in an outline as long as each entry at the same level takes the same form. In the next outline, each entry is a complete sentence.

Sentence outline

```
  I. Ralph Waldo Emerson expounded a political theory close
     to anarchism.
     A. He believed that individuals should govern
        themselves.
     B. He believed that the state should not be concerned
        with property.
 II. Emerson disapproved of the educational system.
     A. He found fault with methods of instruction.
     B. He criticized the curriculum.
III. Emerson sought to abolish established religion.
```

In an outline with sentences at the first level (as above), you may choose to use noun phrases for the second and successive levels.

■ Logical Consistency in Outlines

The requirement for parallelism is not exclusively a grammatical one, but a logical one as well. Grammatical inconsistencies often signal problems in logic. Logical consistency requires that headings at the same level of an outline have approximately equivalent importance and refer to similar categories of ideas. For example, three headings designating historical periods and a fourth at the same level designating procedural difficulties would not be logically consistent. Moreover, each heading at a given level should represent the same degree of generalization and refer to approximately the same kind of information. The following set of headings is logically unbalanced:

Outline without parallel logic

```
  I. U.S. secondary schools during the nineteenth century
 II. Changes in secondary school programs in Pennsylvania
     from 1890 to 1930
III. Nature of secondary school curricular changes from 1930
     to 1970
 IV. Percentages of teenagers enrolled in high schools
```

The fourth heading is considerably narrower in focus than the others and calls for purely statistical information rather than interpretation. In addition, the scope of the inquiry changes from national in the first heading to local in the second.

Writing the Paper

Writing a research paper involves preparing a first draft, revising the draft as often as necessary, editing the draft, preparing the documentation and attending to other elements of the format, and proofreading.

Although to some extent you will approach these tasks in the order they are listed here, you should not expect to complete any of them until you have a finished copy. Each activity proceeds both linearly and recursively. Even as you proceed with writing your first draft, you will constantly be thinking back to the sentences and paragraphs you have already written and thinking ahead to the projected design of your entire paper. Similarly, throughout the writing process you may be preparing parts of the final format, such as the notes and bibliography.

▪ The First Draft

Exploratory writing

As you do research, you may want to write brief, exploratory pieces to develop your thinking. You may eventually incorporate them into your paper, or you may set them aside. Either way, because writing not only reflects thought but generates it, writing during all stages of research will help you refine your thesis statement and outline.

Writing on a word processor

Using a word processor has numerous advantages. It allows you to write as fast as your fingers can press the keys. The capacity to produce a great deal of prose quickly may help you overcome fear of the blank page and other impediments to getting started. Also, a word processor permits you to integrate several phases of your work. With most programs, you can activate two files at once, so that you can switch back and forth between your outline and your draft or between your notes and your outline. You can incorporate direct quotations into your draft by transferring material between files. If you have a windows program, you will be able to see two or more files on the same screen.

Nevertheless, even if they plan to use a word processor to type their papers, some writers prefer to draft their papers by hand. They find that they choose their words more carefully, and that they write more complex sentences and more coherent paragraphs with pen and paper. Also, some writers derive pleasure from writing with their favorite pen and on paper of a particular size or color. Whichever mode of drafting you choose, you should constantly monitor your writing process and scrutinize your writing, making changes in your tools and techniques to serve your work.

In using a word processor, keep in mind its mechanical requirements. Have every file backed up on diskette and on paper to avoid losing material if a power failure or disk error occurs, and allow enough time to deal with technical difficulties you may have at any stage, right through the final printing.

▪ Revision

Writing is a craft; and writers, like other craftspeople, should be prepared to cut, discard, and reshape their materials. Most workshops contain a clutter of scraps. Some of the scraps can be collected and reused; others are eventually swept away. Most artisans cherish such evidence of the progress of their work. Experienced writers have generally learned to do likewise. This is not to deny that revision is sometimes painful.

Revising on a word processor

The word processor makes revision immeasurably easier, most notably by eliminating the need for recopying multiple drafts. Not only can you add and delete words with the stroke of a key, but you can also block and move paragraphs and sections from one part of your paper to another. You can use the search feature to locate particular words or series of words, a good way to determine how you have previously used your terminology and how often you have repeated a particular word. A thesaurus, which permits you to see synonyms and antonyms, can help you find alternative words. Also, your printed copy will give you a view of your drafts that is different from the view that appears on the screen. Seeing your writing in different formats will help you to revise, which means to re-envision, by giving you an additional perspective on your work.

Although word processors facilitate revision, they can inhibit certain kinds of improvements, most importantly the integration of parts into a whole. Working on a screen that allows you to see only twenty-four lines at a time makes it difficult to keep the structure of the entire paper in mind. It is quite common for writers to rework a sentence or paragraph on the computer screen, only to find that it no longer fits logically into the paper. Any change in the position of a paragraph nearly always requires other revisions, such as changes in transitions and the reordering of sentences elsewhere in the paper. You can compensate for these problems by printing your document occasionally and making revisions on paper. When writing on a word processor, it is particularly important to have a detailed outline.

It is wise to keep all versions of your draft because you may find that you want to restore something you had deleted. Some writers keep each draft in a separate file organized by date; others keep a file of deleted paragraphs, sentences, or even single words for possible use in another part of the paper.

Questions for revision

The following questions can help you notice passages in your work that need revision:

- Does the thesis statement govern everything in the paper?
- Does the introduction prepare the reader for the paper?
- Are the paragraphs developed logically and arranged in a coherent sequence?
- Do any sections repeat or contradict other sections?
- Does the entire paper read smoothly, with transitions that carry the reader from one idea to the next?
- Does the paper address the appropriate audience?

After you have answered all these questions affirmatively, you can begin editing.

■ Editing

When you have a thoroughly revised draft ready for final typing, read through it at least once more, paying attention to every detail. Evaluate every sentence once again for clarity, check every paragraph for coherence, think about every choice of diction and sentence structure. In addition, look for mechanical errors in spelling and punctuation as well as for typographical errors. Chapter 4 discusses the problems that arise most often in editing a research paper.

Editing on a word processor

Many word-processing programs have features that you can use to help identify and correct errors. When you find an error, you can use the search command to retrieve other instances of this error and replace them with the correct form automatically. An adjunct to most word-processing programs is the spell checker, which identifies the misspelling of any word in its dictionary and allows you to add to the dictionary any words that you tend to misspell. Other programs can be used to identify problems with grammar, punctuation, usage, and wordiness.

When you use any of those features or programs, remember that the computer does not think; it only simulates thinking. The only misspellings that a spell checker can identify are errors in words that are in its dictionary. If you type the wrong word but spell it correctly—if you type *there* when you meant to type *three*—most spell checkers will not find the error. Error identification programs point out problems, but they cannot help you find the most effective way to revise your paper.

■ Format

Instructors in different disciplines have different requirements for the format of research papers. Most undergraduate papers, however, include the following parts in addition to the body, or text: a title page, an outline page, documentation (through parenthetical references in the text or through endnotes or footnotes), and a bibliography. Any given paper or instructor may require only some of these elements or additional ones. (See Chapter 2 for the elements of a thesis or dissertation and Chapter 6 for typing instructions for research papers, theses, and dissertations.)

TITLE PAGE The title page of a research paper should include the title of the paper, the student's name, the course and section, the instructor's name, and the date. (See the sample title page on page 30.) If your instructor does not require a title page, include this information on the first page of the text. (See page 32 for the first page of a sample paper without a title page.)

OUTLINE PAGE The outline page of a research paper presents a topic or sentence outline and sometimes includes the thesis statement. The numbers and headings on the outline page should not appear within the text of your paper. (See the sample outline on page 31.)

BIBLIOGRAPHY When your instructor or publisher does not specify a system of documentation, you probably will want to follow the requirements of *The Chicago Manual of Style* (detailed in Chapter 7), the most widely used documentation system. The type of bibliography most often requested for an undergraduate research paper is a list of the works that are referred to in the paper. If you read a work but did not cite it, that work is not included in your list. (See the sample bibliography page for a short research paper on page 35.) The introduction to Part II (pages 136–140) and Chapter 7 present information on preparing bibliographies according to the *Chicago Manual* system.

If you use the MLA or APA system, see the instructions for preparing a list of works cited on pages 220 through 223 for MLA, pages 269 through 270 for APA.

ANNOTATED BIBLIOGRAPHY An annotated bibliography includes a description, critique, or analysis of the source immediately following the citation. Creating an annotated bibliography can be helpful both to you and to readers. It permits you to present your opinion about the relevance or usefulness of the source. For readers it presents your attitude toward the source and provides a guide to their own research. See the sample annotated bibliography on pages 36–37.

DOCUMENTATION Each fact or opinion obtained from a source, whether quoted directly, summarized, or paraphrased, must be documented with a note or with a parenthetical reference. Notes may be in one of two forms: footnotes or endnotes. Footnotes are placed at the bottom of the page that contains the material they refer to. Endnotes are grouped together in a separate section at the end of the paper. (See the sample endnotes page on page 34.) Chapter 7 discusses the documentation of first and subsequent references in the note-bibliography format required by the Chicago system. For the parenthetical-reference format required by the MLA, see pages 214 through 220, and for that of the APA, see pages 246 through 251.

▪ Proofreading

Rereading the finished copy, or proofreading, can make the difference between a mediocre paper and an excellent one. Read your paper just one more time, even though you may be tired of it. Better yet, allow yourself enough time to set the paper aside for at least one day so that you can read it from a fresh perspective. Speed-reading techniques are not appropriate for proofreading; you need to read almost letter for letter. Careful proofreading will help ensure that the paper you submit does justice to the time, energy, and thought you invested in its creation.

ELEMENTS OF RESEARCH PAPERS

Sample Pages

This section provides sample pages from research papers illustrating principles of format and layout described in Chapter 1. The note and bibliography entries on these pages follow the *Chicago Manual* system. For sample pages showing MLA and APA parenthetical documentation, see Chapters 8 (pages 243–244) and 9 (pages 271–276), respectively.

A Title page for a research paper (optional) 30

B Outline page for a research paper (optional) 31

C First page of a research paper with endnotes and no title page 32

D Page of text using endnotes 33

E Endnotes page 34

F Bibliography page 35

G Annotated bibliography 36

H Bibliography divided by type of source 38

[5 inches]

Are Books Obsolete?: The Prospects for Electronic Texts

[3 lines of space]

Elizabeth Barnes

Professor Smith

English 1302.15

19 May 2002

[1 inch]

Title page for a research paper (optional)

[1 line of space]

Outline

[1 line of space]

Thesis Statement: Although electronic means of publication have many advantages for both readers and publishers, electronic texts are not likely to replace books.

I. The New Electronic Medium

II. Advantages of Electronic Texts

  A. For Publishers

    1. Publishing on Demand

    2. On-line Publishing

    3. Electronic Texts

  B. For Readers

    1. Instantaneous Access

    2. Capacity to Read the Text in Different Ways

    3. Elimination of Storage Problems

  C. For Authors

III. Drawbacks to Electronic Publishing

  A. For Publishers

  B. For Readers

  C. For Authors

IV. The Enduring Appeal of Books for Readers

  A. Portability

  B. Price

  C. Nostalgia

Outline page for a research paper (optional)

[1 inch]

Elizabeth Barnes

[1 line of space]

English 1302.15

[1 line of space]

Professor Smith

[1 line of space]

19 May 2002

[1 line of space]

Are Books Obsolete?: The Prospects for Electronic Texts

[5 spaces] [1 line of space]

Word processors have replaced typewriters in offices; the click of typewriter keys no longer resounds even in the newsroom. The computer has changed the way the word is produced, but so far it has had little effect on the way it is read. Recipients of business letters and subscribers to magazines read electronically processed words on the traditional printed page. The technology exists that could eliminate books as effectively as it has displaced typewriters. The book is not obsolete, however, nor is it likely to be. Although electronic means of publication have some advantages, electronic texts are not likely to replace books.

[5 spaces]

For publishers, electronic publishing has some alluring advantages. It holds out the promise of eliminating one of the most persistent problems of both publishers and booksellers, the overstock that is necessary to keep a large backlist in print and before the public.[1] The new technology for electronic publishing could allow for publishing on demand, the publication of books as they are ordered. This system would permit publishers to keep books in print indefinitely, even those that have a limited market, and it would reduce the storage and space problems that bookstores now face.[2]

First page of a research paper with endnotes and no title page

some disadvantages. It might even restrict the accessibility of information. The cost of the necessary equipment, even though it has been falling, could reduce the number of people with ready access to reading materials. While libraries have long lent books, it is unclear that they would be able to provide electronic texts to as large an audience. Also, if the proliferation of electronic databases on different systems is any guide, electronic texts might be published in different formats and for various systems. Because it would require a larger range of skills, reading would require more training. And because on-line publishing would of necessity be more centralized, Paul Starr suggests that it could actually undermine individual freedom to write and to read.

[10 spaces] [1 line of space]

> On-line publishing also has some sinister possibilities. In the hands of a totalitarian government, it could be used to monitor what citizens were reading. When it suited the regime, the texts of past newspapers, journals, and books could be permanently altered.[12]

[1 line of space]

These scenarios seem far-fetched, but it is sobering to remember that books might be destroyed more efficiently by pulling the plug on electronic texts than by throwing large numbers of copies on bonfires.

[5 spaces]

While the possibilities of electronic publishing seem to outweigh the risks, books probably will not become obsolete. Starr judges that "the printed page has such obvious advantages in ease of

Page of text using endnotes

[1 inch]

Barnes 11

[1 line of space]

Notes

[1 line of space]

[5 spaces]

1. Leonard Shatzkin, _In Cold Type: Overcoming the Book Crisis_ (Boston: Houghton Mifflin, 1982).

2. Paul Starr, "The Electronic Reader," in _Reading in the 1980s_, ed. Stephen Braubard (New York: Bowker, 1983), 149.

3. Robin P. Peek and Gregory B. Newby, _Scholarly Publishing: The Electronic Frontier_ (Cambridge, Mass.: MIT Press, 1996), 17.

4. Peek and Newby, 147-49.

5. Greg Durham, "Electronic Books and Print-on-Demand: Making Peace with the Digital Future," [electronic journal]; accessed 14 Aug. 2000; available from <http://www.authorlink.com/on909002.html>.

6. Shatzkin, 79.

7. Starr, 149.

8. Elizabeth I. Eisenstein, _The Printing Press as an Agent of Change_ (Cambridge: Cambridge University Press, 1979), 107.

9. Wendy Grossman, _From Anarchy to Power: The Net Comes of Age_ (New York: New York University Press, 2001), ix.

10. Eisenstein, 125.

11. Grossman, 157-59.

12. Starr, 155.

13. Eisenstein, 155.

14. Grossman, 25.

Endnotes page

[1 inch]

[1 line of space]

Bibliography

[1 line of space]

Crane, Gregory. "'Hypermedia' and Scholarly Publishing." Scholarly Publishing, Apr. 1990, 131-55.

Directory of Electronic Journals, Newsletters and Academic Discussion Lists. 7th ed. Washington, D.C.: Association of Research Libraries, 1997.

Durham, Greg. "Electronic Books and Print-on-Demand: Making Peace with the Digital Future" [online journal]; accessed 14 Aug. 2001; available at <http://www.authorlink.com/on909002.html>. 14 Aug. 2001.

Eisenstein, Elizabeth I. The Printing Press as an Agent of Change. Cambridge: Cambridge University Press, 1979.

Grossman, Wendy. From Anarchy to Power: The Net Comes of Age. New York: New York University Press, 2001.

Peek, Robin P., and Gregory B. Newby. Scholarly Publishing: The Electronic Frontier. Cambridge, Mass.: MIT Press, 1996.

Romano, Frank J. Delmar's Dictionary of Digital Printing and Publishing. Albany, N.Y.: Delmar, 1997.

Shatzkin, Leonard. In Cold Type: Overcoming the Book Crisis. Boston: Houghton Mifflin, 1982.

Starr, Paul. "The Electronic Reader." In Reading in the 1980s, ed. Stephen Braubard, 143-56. New York: Bowker, 1983.

Trend, David. Reading Digital Culture. Keyworks in Cultural Studies, no. 4. Malden, Mass.: Blackwell, 2001.

Bibliography page

[1 inch]

Smith 79

[1 line of space]

Annotated Bibliography

[1 line of space]

Daiute, Colette A. "The Computer as Stylus and Audience." College Composition and Communication 34 (May 1983): 134-45.

Daiute argues that computers can help writers overcome what she calls "psychological difficulties" in writing, such as the limits of short-term memory and the necessity of considering the reader's point of view.

Dobrin, David N. "Some Ideas about Idea Processors." In Writing at Century's End: Essays on Computer-Assisted Instruction, ed. Lisa Gerrard, 17-23. New York: Random House, 1987.

Dobrin argues that idea processors, programs such as ThinkTank that produce outlines, can help some writers to order their thoughts, but for most writers they limit creativity.

Leibowitz, Wendy R. "Technology Transforms Writing and the Teaching of Writing." Chronicle of Higher Education 26 Nov. 1999 [online version]; accessed 22 Dec. 1999; available from <http://chronicle.com/cbi2-bin/printable.cgi>.

Leibowitz interviews college professors about the bad habits their students seem to have acquired from writing on computers, such as overly conversational prose and neglect of global revision.

Perrin, Robert. "What Handbooks Tell Us about Teaching Writing with Word-Processing Programs." Computers and Composition 6 (Nov. 1988): 15-26.

Annotated bibliography

Perrin argues that handbooks should provide concrete advice about using a word processor to its best advantage. Perrin finds the following recommendations particularly instructive: do global searches for words likely to be overused; isolate all the topic sentences and check them against the outline; revise on hard copy; and keep hard copy of all drafts.

Schwartz, Helen J. "Teaching Writing with Computer Aids." College English 46 (Mar. 1984): 239-47.

Schwartz analyzes programs useful for teaching invention, organization, and revision in the composition classroom.

Teichman, Milton. "What College Freshmen Say about Word Processing." Perspectives in Computing 5 (1985): 43-48.

In response to a questionnaire prepared by Teichman, students listed the benefits and drawbacks of word processing. The most important advantages they cited were saved time, ease of revision, and a professional-looking copy. Among the disadvantages mentioned were the inconvenience of working in one place, preoccupation with the machine itself, and technical difficulties.

[1 inch]

Smith 111

[1 line of space]

Bibliography

[1 line of space]

Primary Sources

[1 line of space]

Collected Documents

Commager, Henry Steele, ed. Documents of American History. 2 vols. in 1. 5th ed. New York: Appleton-Century-Crofts, 1949.

MacDonald, William H., ed. Select Charters and Other Documents Illustrative of American History, 1606-1775. New York: Macmillan, 1899.

Whitmore, William H., ed. The Andros Tracts: Being a Collection of Pamphlets and Official Papers. 3 vols. Boston: n.p., 1868-74.

Diaries, Letters, and Narratives

Andrews, Charles McL., ed. Narratives of the Insurrections, 1675-1690. Original Narratives of Early American History. New York: Scribner's, 1915.

Bradford, William. Of Plymouth Plantation, 1620-1647. Ed. Samuel E. Morison. New York: Knopf, 1952.

Dreuilletes, Father Gabriel. "Narrative of a Journey to New England, 1650." In The Jesuit Relations and Allied Documents . . . 1610-1791, ed. Reuben G. Thwaites. Cleveland: n.p., 1898.

Dudley, Thomas. "Letter to the Countess of Lincoln." In Collections of the New Hampshire Historical Society. Concord: New Hampshire Historical Society, 1834.

Homes, William. "Diary of Rev. William Homes of Chilmark, Martha's Vineyard, 1689-1746." New England Historical and Genealogical Register 48 (1894): 446-53; 49 (1895): 413-16; 50 (1896): 155-66.

Usher, John. "Report on Northern Colonies, 1698." William and Mary Quarterly, 3rd ser., 7 (1950): 95.

Bibliography divided by type of source

2 Theses and Dissertations

In writing a thesis or dissertation, you will follow the same steps described in Chapter 1 for writing research papers. If you have not recently written a paper based on research, read through Chapter 1 to remind yourself of the basics. This chapter presents descriptions and models of the parts of a thesis or dissertation, along with procedures for preparing the entire manuscript.

A thesis or a dissertation contains three categories of materials: the preliminaries (front matter), the text (body) of the paper, and the reference materials (back matter or end matter). When the thesis or dissertation is bound in book form for library use or reproduced in other media such as microfilm or digital database, these elements are included. Before you produce the final copy of a thesis or dissertation, consult the university regulations on the required format.

Word-processing software can automatically perform some of the most time-consuming tasks involved in preparing the elements of a thesis or dissertation. Most new programs can create a table of contents and list of captions from your text; produce running heads and page numbers; integrate tables and figures into the text; indent and center headings; create footnotes and endnotes; and index the entire manuscript. To take full advantage of your software program, explore all its formating options and settings. Consult the accompanying manual for instructions about the features of the program or experiment with the function keys and the menus indicated on the screen with words or icons. If you cannot make your program produce pages corresponding to requirements, be sure to show sample pages to your adviser before generating the entire dissertation.

The Preliminaries (Front Matter)

The preliminaries, or front matter, of a thesis or dissertation consist of any or all of the following elements: abstract; approval sheet; title page; copyright page; table of contents; lists of tables, figures, and plates; clearance forms; acknowledgments; and preface. Not every thesis will include all these elements. They usually appear in this order, but your dissertation adviser may require another arrangement.

Page numbers for front matter take the form of lowercase roman numerals centered at the bottom of the page. All the preliminaries, except the abstract and the approval sheet, are counted as pages of your paper. All pages, except the title page and the copyright page, are numbered.

Abstract

Most universities require that a doctoral candidate submit an abstract, a concise descriptive summary of the dissertation. An abstract should explain the project rather than defend or evaluate it. It should begin with the most important information, which usually will be the conclusions or findings, followed by a brief but precise statement of the problem; a description of the research method and design of the study, if applicable; and the significance of your conclusions. The keywords and most important terminology, unabbreviated, should appear in the abstract; these facilitate access to the abstract by computer search and enable readers to decide whether to read the entire dissertation. Because the abstract is not part of the dissertation, it is neither numbered nor counted as a page.

To fulfill the requirement that the doctoral dissertation be available to other scholars, the graduate office generally sends a copy of the abstract to University Microfilms, which prints an abstract in *Dissertation Abstracts International (DAI)* for each dissertation available on microfilm. Abstracts published in *DAI* are limited to a maximum of 350 words. Abstracts from 1980 onward, as well as some complete dissertations, are now presented in electronic form by *Dissertation Abstracts (Digital Dissertations)*.

Abstracts for theses, articles, and short papers

Departments may require an abstract for theses and other types of reports. An abstract for a short paper is usually limited to one page. Abstracts for articles to be submitted to a journal of the American Psychological Association are limited to 120 words.

Approval Sheet

The approval sheet provides spaces for the signatures of the adviser, readers, department chairperson, graduate deans, and others indicating their acceptance of the work. Most institutions have a model for this page, and local requirements should always determine the format. Approvals are sometimes incorporated into the title page.

Title Page

Format of the title page

The first page of a thesis or dissertation is the title page. The graduate school office usually prescribes the form of the title page (see pages 52 and 53 for typical examples). The title page presents the title, the full name of the writer, and the submission statement, which includes the faculty or school, such as the Graduate School of Arts and Sciences or the School of Business Administration, and the institution, the degree sought (or granted), and the month and year in which the degree is to be (or was) granted. A particular institution may require different combinations of the elements shown in the samples, or it may require additional information, such as the writer's previous academic degrees.

Content of the title

The title is the part of your paper most readers will see first, and as a result it often determines whether or not they will begin reading your work. To avoid misrepresenting your paper, you should not settle on a final version of your title until you have completed the paper. In formulating or refining your title, you should make sure that it suggests the nature of your thesis statement and that it includes the principal words, concepts, and persons or things you discuss in the paper.

The title should be descriptive and comprehensive, but concise. A title like "The Tourist Industry in South Africa" would not sufficiently describe a research project on the hotel industry in Capetown. Even the title "The Hotel Industry in Capetown" would be too broad for a study of occupancy rates in Capetown hotels. If that were your subject, a title such as "Vacancy Rates in Capetown Hotels Analyzed by Month" would more accurately describe the content. Phrases like "A Critical Analysis and Evaluation of . . ." or "An Investigation of . . . " should be avoided when they are unnecessary. The following excessively long titles have been shortened considerably without eliminating any essential information.

Wordy title

AN EVALUATION OF THE IMPLEMENTATION PROCESS AND IMPACT
OF A PROGRAM TO EDUCATE TEACHERS IN QUITO, ECUADOR

Revision

THE IMPLEMENTATION AND IMPACT
OF A TEACHER-TRAINING PROGRAM IN QUITO, ECUADOR

Wordy title

A STUDY OF THE EFFECTS OF FOREIGN INVESTMENT
ON THE ECONOMIC GROWTH IN SPAIN
DURING THE PERIOD BETWEEN 1976 AND 2000

Revision

THE EFFECTS OF FOREIGN INVESTMENT
ON ECONOMIC GROWTH IN SPAIN, 1976–2000

Keep in mind that electronic databases cannot distinguish words used metaphorically from words used literally. An article on T. S. Eliot's poetic drama might colorfully, and accurately, be entitled "T. S. Eliot's Marriage of Poetry and Drama." However, the writer, aware that an electronic database would retrieve this title for a researcher interested in T. S. Eliot's marriage to Valerie Eliot, might consider a more literal title, such as "T. S. Eliot's Poetic Drama."

Two-part titles

Two-part titles, a title and subtitle separated by a colon, should be used to couple a pithy statement of your subject with an explanation that delimits or explains the title. Here are examples of the effective and ineffective use of two-part titles.

GOOD AND EVIL IN THE CLASSROOM:
A THEORY OF THE APPROPRIATE REPRESENTATION
OF MORALS AND ETHICS IN PUBLIC ELEMENTARY SCHOOLS

(The title states the subject dramatically and provocatively to emphasize the controversial nature of the topic. The subtitle tempers the tone and explains the parameters of this particular discussion of the subject. That is, the paper will present a theory, not a curriculum; the paper assumes that there are appropriate and inappropriate representations; and the paper will confine discussion to the public schools, rather than, say, the parochial schools, and the elementary level rather than middle or high school level will be discussed.)

The title below does not use the two-part format effectively.

AN INVESTIGATION OF MOTHERS' ATTRIBUTIONS AND AFFECTIVE RESPONSES TO PRESCHOOL CHILDREN'S PROBLEM BEHAVIOR: A GROUP COMPARATIVE STUDY

(The subtitle, "A Group Comparative Study," does not function to delimit the title; the words make "An Investigation" redundant. And despite its length, the title omits information, such as location of the group, that most prospective readers would want to know.)

Papers in the humanities often employ a quotation from the literary work or the theory under discussion, as in the following examples.

"ATTENTION MUST BE PAID": THE TRAVELING SALESMAN IN MODERN AMERICAN DRAMA

(The quotation, a well-known line from Arthur Miller's *Death of a Salesman*, signals one of the plays to be discussed and promises a sympathetic attitude toward the salesman, a figure often dismissed as insignificant in analyses of American life.)

▪ Copyright Page

The microfilming or digitizing of a dissertation is a form of print or electronic publication, respectively. Thus you need to follow the law regarding copyright, both to protect your own work and to ensure that your use of other people's work meets legal requirements.

According to federal law, you own the copyright for your thesis or dissertation from the time you write the work until you formally transfer the copyright to a publisher or to some other organization or individual. Before such transfer takes place, you control all the rights to your work, including the right to make and distribute copies of it (that is, to publish it).

Whether or not you put a copyright notice on the second page of your unpublished thesis or dissertation (see the sample copyright page on page 54), you are legally protected against the unauthorized use of your work. Depositing a thesis or dissertation in a library and microfilming it, however, are equivalent to publication, and the law requires a copyright notice in any published work in which a copyright is claimed. You are not obliged to register your copyright with the Library of Congress, but you should consider doing so. Registering is a public record of copyright ownership and a prerequisite for legal action in the event of inappropriate use of your material.

If your thesis or dissertation is to be microfilmed, University Microfilms will register the copyright for a fee. If your paper is not to be microfilmed, you can register the copyright with the Library of Congress by writing directly to the Copyright Office, Library of Congress, Washington, D.C. 20559.

Just as federal law safeguards your copyright in your thesis or dissertation, it safeguards the rights of other writers in their work. In using material from other sources, you must follow the guidelines of *fair use*, a legal concept interpreted in various ways. According to one rule of thumb, you may quote up to 150 words from a source, or two lines of poetry, for critical or evaluative purposes without obtaining permission from the copyright holder. In most cases, the copyright holder is the publisher (because the author has transferred the copyright to the publisher). Some publishers allow the quotation of 250 words without written permission; others allow up to 500 words.

When a quotation, even of fewer than 150 words, constitutes a substantial proportion of the source, you need to write to the copyright holder and request permission to quote. If you are in any doubt about whether the direct quotations in your thesis or dissertation qualify as fair use, consult your graduate school office or contact the publisher of the work you are quoting. Any permissions you receive should be acknowledged on the copyright page or in the acknowledgments section.

▪ Table of Contents

In a thesis or dissertation, the table of contents precedes all the sections it lists. The table of contents should list all elements of the preliminaries—the chapter (part or section) titles, the main headings and subheadings in the text, and the reference materials. The beginning page number for each section is indicated along the right-hand margin. The numbering of chapters and the wording, capitalization, and punctuation of titles and headings should be exactly the same as they are in the text. (See the sample table of contents on page 55.)

▪ Lists of Tables and Figures

A listing of tables and figures should follow the table of contents. Charts, graphs, maps, and illustrations of other kinds should be grouped and labeled as figures. All captions should appear in the listing exactly as they are in the text. When you have only two or three tables or figures within the text, local policy may permit you to leave them out of the table of contents.

Capitalization of captions

The traditional form for listing titles or captions of tables and figures calls for capitalization of the first letter of the first and last words and of all nouns, pronouns, adjectives, adverbs, and verbs. APA also capitalizes prepositions of more than five letters. Chapter 5 contains a full discussion of the presentation of tables and figures, with explanations and examples.

Clearance Forms

When human beings or animals are the subjects of experimental study or when the facilities of an institution are used, clearance forms may be necessary. These forms might include such information as the ethical standards followed and the principles for selecting the participants in a study. If the forms are short, they can be placed in the preliminaries. Any long or complex information on clearance should be placed in an appendix. The design of the experiment and the requirements of the institution dictate the nature of the clearance forms.

Acknowledgments

The acknowledgments section contains expressions of appreciation for assistance and guidance. The help given by advisers and readers does not require written acknowledgment, but the recognition of generosity with time and knowledge is a courtesy that is widely appreciated. Acknowledgments should be expressed simply and tactfully.

Preface

The preface, usually an optional section for a dissertation or thesis, might include brief comment on subjects such as the motivation for the study or methods of research. Substantial development of these issues and significant historical or background information belong in the text of the paper. The preface should be an adjunct to the paper rather than an essential part of it.

The Text (Body) of the Paper

The text, or body, of a thesis or dissertation begins with the first page of Chapter 1, which follows the preliminaries discussed above. Numbering in arabic numerals starts on this page with number 1; all pages are numbered, including chapter and section title pages. Position all page numbers one inch from the top of the page, flush with the right margin. Some institutions have different requirements for placement of page numbers on the first page of a chapter or section.

Organization of Chapters

Each topic calls for an organization appropriate to its own logic and to the discipline or field. Your research will determine the nature of the text, and your adviser will have suggestions concerning the design of your paper.

Formats for the body of the paper differ for the three general types of theses: (1) theses based on the collection of empirical data, (2) theses derived from critical analysis or philosophical inquiry, and (3) theses based on historical research.

THESES BASED ON THE COLLECTION OF EMPIRICAL DATA

Theses based on the collection of empirical data, that is, information derived from direct observation or experience, often follow a standard format. The chapters are usually divided into five categories, corresponding to the stages of research. Although these parts may be variously labeled, essentially they consist of an introduction, a review of the literature, a presentation of the method of the investigation, a report of the findings, and a summary discussion and interpretation.

Introductory chapter(s)

The introductory chapter(s) should contain the following:

1. An introduction to the subject, indicating the importance and validity of the problem chosen for study. The potential contribution of the study and the need for the research may also be explained here, and any necessary background information should be provided.
2. A clear and concise statement of the problem, together with an analysis of its delimitation or scope. An experimental study should be stated as one or more hypotheses (tentative statements of the relationship between variables), with, particularly in the case of a statistical study of variables, an accompanying null hypothesis (a statement of the absence of the hypothesized correlation). Other kinds of research problems may be posed in the form of questions. The schedule and procedures for gathering data should be explained.
3. A section that establishes the theoretical framework within which the investigation was conducted. This section usually includes basic assumptions of the study and definitions of terms.

Review of the literature

The review of related research and literature, usually a separate chapter, should give readers the context for your study. The review should not merely summarize a series of books and articles; rather, it should call attention to the most important previous work, identify the place of your work in relation to other research, and delineate areas of agreement and disagreement in the field. The review should evaluate and interpret existing research, not just repeat it. Organizing the review by topic rather than by author and avoiding unnecessary quotation can help you focus the review of research.

Method of the investigation

The chapter(s) devoted to the method of the investigation should discuss such matters as the nature of the sample and any control groups, the data needed to test the hypotheses or to answer the questions, the sources of data, and the procedures followed in gathering and analyzing the data. You may have sections devoted to such information as the participants, materials, and procedures. Your explanation should be sufficient to let other researchers attempt to duplicate your experiments for the purpose of verifying your results.

Results

A nonevaluative analysis of the results constitutes the heart of a thesis based on the collection of empirical data. The chapter(s) in this section should present the results of the investigation without interpretation or evaluation, reporting negative as well as positive results. This information should be explained in clear, coherent prose. If you wish to accompany your analyses with tables or figures, these should supplement the text rather than substitute for it. The body of the paper should be comprehensible even if the reader chooses not to consult the tables. (See Chapter 5 for information on presenting tables, figures, charts, and computer data.)

Discussion and interpretation

The final chapter(s) should be devoted to evaluation and interpretation of the data and to formulation of your conclusions. Also covered here, as appropriate, are the implications of the findings for revising the existing body of knowledge, the relation of the results to previous research, limitations of the study, and unexpected findings. Practical applications of the findings or speculation about further research might conclude this section.

THESES BASED ON CRITICAL ANALYSIS OR PHILOSOPHICAL SPECULATION No specified format governs theses based on critical analysis or philosophical speculation. Rather, they contain a number of common elements, either developed in separate chapters or interwoven in each chapter.

The introductory section usually places the study against the background of previous work in the field. The importance of the topic, its role in current controversy or developments, and the scholarly tradition in which the thesis belongs might be developed here. Although you want to acknowledge any studies that have influenced or guided your work, as well as those you may have reacted against, this section should not turn into a summary of the works in question. Instead, discussion of these works should always demonstrate their relationship to your topic. Although you will probably be critically evaluating theories advanced by other writers, your comments should remain fair and evenhanded. You need not demolish previous studies to give your own work validity.

The central chapters of such a thesis should present the results of your research and analysis. These results should be set forth clearly and systematically in order to convince readers that you have considered every facet of the topic and that the material uncovered by your research confirms your thesis statement. One of the challenges of writing these chapters is to present a good deal of information while continually keeping the central point of the thesis before the reader.

The interpretation or statement of the significance of the thesis may be integrated with the exposition of the findings or may be presented in the concluding chapter(s). The conclusion might include the implications of the work for the revision of previous interpretations, proof or disproof of assumptions or theories in the field, or new areas of inquiry opened by the study.

THESES BASED ON HISTORICAL RESEARCH Because papers based on historical research usually serve to present data about the past as well as to interpret it, organization of the paper depends largely on the kind and quantity of information the researcher is able to collect. The historical thesis thus follows no established format, but it usually contains several elements. (The elements of theses based on critical analysis, described above, may be useful for the historical paper as well.)

Commonly, the major portion of the historical thesis is devoted to reporting the findings, often in the form of telling a story about the event under study. Chronological organization is the most obvious, and very often the most useful, way of arranging historical information. However, this information might also be ordered by another logical principle, such as cause and effect, or divided or subdivided into categories such as persons, events, regions, or concepts. The introductory chapter(s) might be used to present the motive for the study, to detail the problems or deficiencies of previous scholarship, or to chronicle the difficulties and peculiarities of locating and retrieving the information in question. Whereas some historical theses may serve solely to present new information, others will attempt to explain a current situation in light of the past or to revise theories about the nature or significance of a sequence of events. This kind of interpretive material may be woven through the whole study or presented in the introductory or concluding chapter(s).

■ Chapter Titles and Headings

Chapter titles and headings emphasize the organization of your paper. Papers under twenty-five pages usually do not require divisions. In longer papers readers need signals to indicate the relationship of the individual parts to the whole. Titles and headings should be used to clarify the organization, not to conceal incoherent development or insufficient transitions. The title of a chapter should indicate clearly and concisely the contents of the chapters and its relationship to the complete paper.

Headings may be used to divide a long or complicated chapter. Headings function just as an outline does, and the same principles of parallelism and logic of division apply here. Every division of a subject must yield at least two subdivisions, and all headings at the same level should be parallel grammatically and logically.

Headings for a dissertation

The five generally accepted levels of headings are shown below. Most research papers and dissertations do not require all these levels of headings. With fewer than five levels, you need not begin with a head of the highest level and proceed consecutively; instead you may select headings appropriate for your purpose or institutional requirements. The number of levels of headings may vary from chapter to chapter, depending on the logic of organization in each.

1. CENTERED UPPERCASE LETTERS

2. Centered Uppercase and Lowercase Letters

3. Centered, Underlined Uppercase and Lowercase Letters

4. Flush Left, Underlined Uppercase and Lowercase Letters

5. Indented five spaces, underlined lowercase ending with a period. The paragraph begins at the end of the heading.

Divisions beyond the third level should be avoided. If fourth-level headings are necessary, they should take the form of enumerated paragraphs. At least one paragraph of text should be placed between a heading and its first subheading.

The first two levels of headings are appropriate for titles of dissertations, parts of long papers, and titles of short papers.

1. TITLE OR MAJOR DIVISION OF LONG PAPER

2. Title of Short Paper or Chapter of Long Paper

The next three levels divide the body or text of the paper.

3. First Level within the Text

4. Second Level within the Text

5. Third level within the text.

When fewer than five headings are required, the suggested choices and sequences are the following: for one level of heading, level 2 only; for two levels of headings, levels 2 and 4; for three levels of headings, levels 2, 4, and 5; and for four levels of headings, levels 2, 3, 4, and 5.

APA headings

APA uses the same design and sequence of headings, but the three lower-level headings are italicized rather than underlined.

1. CENTERED UPPERCASE LETTERS

2. Centered Uppercase and Lowercase Letters

3. *Centered, Italicized Uppercase and Lowercase Letters*

4. *Flush Left, Italicized Uppercase and Lowercase Letters*

5. *Indented five spaces, italicized lowercase ending with a period.* The paragraph begins at the end of the heading.

When fewer than five headings are required, they should be selected and arranged according to the guidelines above.

Reference Materials (Back Matter, or End Matter)

The reference materials for a thesis or dissertation may include an appendix or appendixes, a glossary, endnotes, a bibliography, and an index.

▪ Appendix

An appendix should be used for materials that supplement the text but are not appropriate for inclusion in it. Original data, summary tabulations, complicated mathematical proofs, descriptions of equipment, very lengthy quotations, supporting legal decisions or laws, supplementary illustrative materials, special computer programs, computer printouts, and pertinent documents not readily available belong in an appendix.

Questionnaires with their letters of transmittal and the verbatim comments of respondents should also be included in an appendix. The use of appendixes for lengthy tables and other such material prevents the text from becoming unduly bulky.

The material in the appendix may be subdivided according to logical classifications. List each appendix by letter and title, if any, in the table of contents.

▪ Glossary

A *glossary* (a list of definitions of terms and concepts) is usually not necessary for a dissertation because such a work is directed toward a professional audience. For other types of papers, a glossary may be desirable if the typical reader might not be familiar with the terminology. See the glossary at the end of this book for a sample format.

▪ Notes

If you use the note-bibliography format, you will have footnotes appearing throughout the paper or you will have a section of endnotes. Even if you use parenthetical documentation, you are likely to want to include some informational or bibliographical notes in a section at the end of the paper.

A thesis or dissertation to be microfilmed should use footnotes rather than endnotes so that the reader will not have to turn the film back and forth to follow the notes. Notes should be numbered consecutively throughout each chapter, beginning with 1 for the first note in each chapter. A research paper or report that is not to be microfilmed may use endnotes. (See page 34 in Chapter 1 for a sample endnotes page.)

▪ Bibliography, List of Works Cited, or References

Papers based on research should have a bibliography, works cited, or references section listing the sources of information. See the introduction to Part II for a discussion of the various types of documentation, and see Chapters 7, 8, and 9 for specific formats.

▪ Index

A dissertation or unpublished report rarely includes an *index* (an alphabetical listing with page numbers of subjects treated in the work). If an index is required, it follows all the other reference material. (See the index at the end of this book.)

ELEMENTS OF THESES AND DISSERTATIONS

Sample Pages

This section contains sample pages showing various formats and layouts for the different elements of theses and dissertations.

A Title page, Form A 52

B Title page, Form B 53

C Copyright page 54

D Table of Contents page 55

E List of tables 56

F Chapter title page (dissertation text with footnotes) 57

[2 inches]

THE IMPLEMENTATION AND IMPACT

OF A TEACHER-TRAINING PROGRAM IN QUITO, ECUADOR

[3 inches]

by

[1 line of space]

John William Herbert

A dissertation

[1 line of space]

submitted in partial fulfillment

of the requirements for the degree of

Doctor of Philosophy in the School of Education

University of New Mexico

May 2002

[1 inch]

Title page, Form A

[2 inches]

THE EFFECTS OF FOREIGN INVESTMENT

ON ECONOMIC GROWTH IN SPAIN, 1976-2000

[2 inches]

A Dissertation

presented to

the Faculty of the Graduate School

University of the Pacific

[3 inches]

In Partial Fulfillment

of the Requirements for the Degree

Doctor of Philosophy

by

Jennifer Christine Smart

December 2002

[1 inch]

Title page, Form B

[1 inch]

Copyright page

[1 inch]

Table of Contents

[1 line of space]

Page

List of Tables iv

List of Figures vi

Chapter

1. Introduction 1

   Theoretical Formulation 3

   Purpose 6

   Problem 7

   Method and Procedures 8

2. Background of the Study 11

   Review of Research 11

   Agency Setting 19

   Description of the Study Sample 21

3. Analysis of the Data 23

4. Findings and Interpretations 30

Appendixes

A. Sample Schedule 42

B. Summary Tables--Study Sample 43

C. Family Profile Scale 45

Bibliography 47

 [position 1 inch from bottom of page]

Table of Contents page (only chapter titles and first-level heads are included here; see pages 131–132 for contents format showing first-, second-, and third-level heads)

Tables [**or** TABLES]
[1 line of space]

Table — Page

1. Mean Error Scores for L-L and L-M SES Dyads for Concrete and Abstract Stimuli 30

2. Mean Number of Critical Attributes Communicated per Dyad 32

3. Mean Number of Critical Attributes Communicated by Encoders: Spontaneously and upon Request of Decoder 33

4. Mean Number of Critical Attributes Communicated by Encoders: Spontaneously 35

5. Mean Number of Critical Attributes Communicated by Encoders: Upon Request of Decoder 36

6. Mean Number of Critical Attributes Communicated by Decoders 38

7. Mean Number of Decoder Requests for Additional Information: Specific and Nonspecific 39

8. Mean Number of Decoder Requests for Additional Information: Specific 41

9. Mean Number of Decoder Requests for Additional Information: Nonspecific 42

10. Frequency of Encoding Styles Employed by L-L SES and L-M SES Dyads 44

[1 inch]

List of tables

[1 inch]

25

[1 line of space]

CHAPTER 2

[1 line of space]

The Relationship of Writing and Reading Abilities

[1 line of space]

E. D. Hirsch's concept of cultural literacy developed in part from his study of writing abilities. In The Philosophy of Composition, Hirsch argued that writing is a skill and that successful teaching of writing requires only isolating the principles that allow students to master the skill. In that utopian book, he suggested that the literacy problem might be solved within ten years if teachers and researchers could agree on the right set of principles:

[10 spaces] → The maxims should be sound ones, having a wide application. They should be explained persuasively, and in a form the student can apply directly to his own prose. They should be limited in number, and grouped according to their relative importance for their typical audience. The book should encourage the student to believe that he can master the elements of the craft and make future progress on his own.[1]

Hirsch abandoned this formalistic approach when his numerous studies of high school students convinced him that their writing revealed a lack of common knowledge rather than ignorance of such maxims.[2]

Convinced of the need for a shared reading background, Hirsch

[1 line of space]

———————— [1½-inch rule]

[1 line of space]

1. E. D. Hirsch, The Philosophy of Composition (Chicago: University of Chicago Press, 1977), 168.

[1 line of space]

2. E. D. Hirsch, "Cultural Literacy," American Scholar 52 (spring 1983): 159-69.

Chapter title page (dissertation text with footnotes) in *Chicago Manual* format

3 Quotations

You may use material from your sources in either direct quotations (verbatim, or word for word, enclosed within quotation marks) or indirect quotations (paraphrased, without quotation marks). With either mode of quotation, you must indicate the source, either with a superscript (raised number) in the text that refers to a note, as *Chicago Manual* recommends, or with a parenthetical reference in the text, as the MLA and APA documentation systems recommend.

This chapter provides information about the general principles of direct and indirect quotation applicable to all of these style sheets; any differences among them are indicated with multiple examples. The first set of indirect and direct quotations is shown with footnotes in *Chicago Manual* format and with parenthetical documentation in both MLA and APA systems. Subsequent examples show only the footnote format, but you can easily adapt it to MLA or APA by inserting the appropriate parenthetical documentation and eliminating the superscript.

Documentation of direct and indirect quotations in no way diminishes the originality of your work. To the contrary, documentation permits your reader to survey the range of materials on which you have based your conclusions, to verify your interpretations of sources, to place your work in a tradition of inquiry, and to locate further information. Your contribution consists of imposing order on the sources, of drawing your own conclusions, and of making a case for your interpretation of the information.

You must document any fact or opinion that you read in one of your sources, whether you first discovered the idea there or you have assimilated it so thoroughly that it seems to be your own. Some exceptions to this rule are facts that are common knowledge (for example, that John Hancock signed the Declaration of Independence), facts that can be verified easily and do not differ from one source to another (for example, that Madrid is the capital of Spain), and well-known sayings or proverbs (for example, Theodore Roosevelt's aphorism, "Speak softly and carry a big stick"). Under most circumstances, these kinds of materials do not need to be documented. In contrast, material available in one source or in a limited number of sources (for example, a statistic about the population of Iran or the birth rate in Italy) should usually be documented. Statistics other than those you have compiled yourself should be attributed to the source. Such attribution not only gives appropriate credit but also protects you if the information proves to be wrong.

Understanding and avoiding plagiarism

Plagiarism, a word derived from the Latin for kidnapping that now means a form of intellectual dishonesty, results from inaccurate or incomplete attribution of material to its source. Plagiarism includes submitting work done by another person or purchased from any course; failing to document ideas found in sources, print and electronic, with appropriate notes and bibliographical references; and failing to enclose borrowed phrases or sentences within quotation marks. Whether intentional or unintentional, plagiarism can bring serious consequences, not only academic, in the form of failure or expulsion, but also legal, in the form of lawsuits. Plagiarism is taken seriously because it violates the ethics of the academic community.

Ideas, as well as the expression of those ideas, are considered to belong to the person who first puts them forward. Therefore, when you incorporate in your paper either ideas or phrasing from another writer, whether you quote directly or indirectly, you need to indicate your source accurately and completely.

Indirect Quotation (Summary and Paraphrase)

Use indirect quotation whenever you do not have a compelling reason for choosing direct quotation (see pages 62–63 for guidelines). Direct quotation should be used sparingly; in most cases it should be reserved for primary sources and the most significant secondary sources. Indirect quotation calls less attention to itself than does direct quotation and thus allows your readers to concentrate on your argument.

When you quote indirectly, use your own words and sentence structure (see pages 18–19 for the distinction between summary and paraphrase). Avoid imitating the original syntax and repeating phrases even as brief as two or three words. Use quotation marks to designate any significant words or phrases you borrow from the original. A paraphrase used as an indirect quotation should represent the original source accurately, without the distortions of imprecise or mistaken paraphrase, altered emphasis, or significant omissions.

DOCUMENTING INDIRECT QUOTATION Even when you have restated a passage in your own words, you must indicate that you encountered the information in your reading. That is, you must document the source of the idea or information in a note or in a parenthetical reference within the text.

The several versions of indirect quotation of the two passages below demonstrate the difference between paraphrasing that relies so heavily on original wording or sentence structure that it constitutes plagiarism, even if documentation is included, and paraphrasing so thorough that it does not require quotation marks but should nevertheless be documented.

Original #1

Like electrical energy, capital will not be generated if the single key facility that produces and fixes it is not in place. Just as a lake needs a hydroelectric plant to produce usable energy, assets need a formal property system to produce significant surplus value. Without formal property to extract their economic potential and convert it into a form that can be easily transported and controlled, the assets of developing and former communist countries are like water in a lake high in the Andes—an untapped stock of potential energy.[1]

Plagiarism

`Just as a lake requires a plant to generate energy, assets require a system to give value to property.`

(Borrowed sentence structure—plagiarism even if documented)

Plagiarism

`To create significant surplus value, a formal property system is required.`

(Borrowed wording without quotation marks—plagiarism even if documented)

The sentences below correctly use documentation to give credit for the ideas even though the passage has been restated.

Chicago Manual *documentation of indirect quotation*

`In many developing countries land resembles untapped water in that neither can be used without a mechanism to translate potential power into actual power.`[1]

MLA documentation

`In many . . . into actual power (Soto 2).`

APA documentation

`In many . . . into actual power (Soto, 2000, p. 48).`

Subsequent examples in this chapter show only documentation with footnotes in *Chicago Manual* format

You may combine direct and indirect quotation, a technique that allows you to condense the original while preserving particularly significant wording or the author's tone.

Paraphrase of paragraph with quoted phrase, documented

`In the absence of a "formal property system," land and other assets cannot be converted into capital.`[1]

Original #2

This distinction [Eudora] Welty draws between leading a sheltered life and a daring life, between living cautiously and thinking adventurously, runs not only throughout *One Writer's Beginnings* but also throughout Welty's body of work. While she points out their marked differences, Welty simultaneously emphasizes the blurring of these two categories: out of the sheltered life comes its seeming opposite, the daring life. Welty makes it clear that her daring thinking is absolutely dependent on the nurturing care that her protected life provides.[2]

Plagiarism

`Eudora Welty makes a distinction between a cautious life and an adventurous life.`

(Imitated sentence structure—plagiarism even if documented)

1. Hernando de Soto, *The Mystery of Capital: Why Capitalism Triumphs in the West and Fails Everywhere Else* (New York: Basic Books, 2000), 48.

2. Carol Ann Johnston, *Eudora Welty: A Study of the Short Fiction* (New York: Twayne, 1997), 4.

```
Eudora Welty maintained that a person who leads a sheltered
life can do daring deeds.
```
(Borrowed wording—plagiarism even if documented)

Paraphrase not requiring quotation marks

```
Eudora Welty believed that a person who leads a protected
life can be capable of bold thoughts and deeds.2
```

Correct use of quotation marks and documentation

```
Eudora Welty regarded her own "sheltered life" as a source
of her "daring thinking."2
```

Subsequent examples in this chapter show documentation with footnotes in *Chicago Manual* format only. To save space, illustrations of indented material will be single-spaced even though you may be asked to double-space such indentions in your papers.

Direct Quotation

Direct quotation presents material from a source word for word. Direct quotation is appropriate when you wish to summon the voice of an authority, to preserve the source author's original wording, or to emphasize the accuracy of your borrowing from the source.

Authority

Direct quotation provides authority for controversial positions or statements requiring expertise in fields other than your own. For example, if, in a thesis on higher education, you wish to substantiate a conclusion about the implications of a university's open-admissions policy for the region's economy, a quotation from a prominent economist or a local business-person could be effective. Or if you wish to buttress your assertion about the significance of a historical trend, you might show that a respected historian drew a similar conclusion from an analogous set of facts.

Original wording

When an author has stated an idea so inventively or forcefully that you cannot do it justice in a paraphrase, you should quote directly to lend color and power to your work. It would be difficult to improve on J. H. Plumb's way of stating the contrast between thriving, artistic Florence and declining, war-torn Milan. "If Florence belonged to Minerva, Milan belonged to Mars."[3] Direct quotation is also appropriate when you want to give your reader the flavor of the original. Malcolm X's sentence concerning the African-American nationalist Marcus Garvey communicates the leader's importance to the community better than a paraphrase might. "I remember seeing the big, shiny photographs of Marcus Garvey that were passed from hand to hand."[4]

Accuracy

For statements in which accuracy is extremely important, direct quotation assures the reader that you have presented the information

---

3. J. H. Plumb, *The Italian Renaissance: A Concise Survey of Its History and Culture* (1961; reprint, New York: Harper Torchbooks, 1965), 63.

4. Malcolm X with Alex Haley, *The Autobiography of Malcolm X* (New York: Grove, 1966), 6.

accurately. Materials you might consider quoting are laws, mathematical formulas, and complex theoretical formulations.

When you use a direct quotation in your text, you must reproduce the language of the source exactly, following the internal punctuation, spelling, emphasis, and even the errors found in the original.

Length of direct quotations

Direct quotations should be kept as short as possible. It can be tempting to insert a quotation and thereby let someone else do some of your writing, but by yielding to this temptation, you evade some of your responsibility. Direct quotations should be pared down to the absolutely essential portions.

When very long quotations—more than one-half page of text—seem out of place in the body of your paper yet are essential to the paper as a whole, place them in an appendix and refer the reader to this appendix.

Fair use

When deciding how much direct quotation to use in a dissertation that will be microfilmed or a thesis that will be deposited in a library (both considered published materials), you need to take into account the concept of *fair use*. You may need to secure the permission of the publisher or the copyright holder for some quotations. (See pages 42–43 in Chapter 2 for more information on fair use.)

Short Quotations

Brief quotations of prose

Direct quotations of prose that do not exceed forty words (about four typewritten lines) should be run into the text and enclosed in double quotation marks. Separate the quotation from your own prose with a comma and quotation marks and punctuate the sentence as it would be if the quoted material were part of your own writing.

```
Scheper-Hughes explains that the people of rural Brazil,
whom she calls "foresters," "live by their wits, not by the
book."5
```

Brief quotations of poetry

Direct quotations of poetry consisting of two full lines or less should be run into the text. Use a slant line with a space on each side between lines of the poem. Retain the capitalization of the original, even though the excerpt combines with the surrounding text to form a grammatical whole.

```
In his "Hymn to Intellectual Beauty," Shelley personifies
the immaterial, spiritual world: "The awful shadow of some
unseen Power / Floats though unseen amongst us."
```

Emphasizing a brief quotation

For the purpose of emphasis, you may choose to indent brief passages of prose or poetry.

5. Nancy Scheper-Hughes, *Death without Weeping: The Violence of Everyday Life in Brazil* (Berkeley: University of California Press, 1992), 91.

■ Extended Quotations

A direct quotation of more than forty words (about four typewritten lines of prose or two lines or more of poetry) should be set off from the text by indention and double-spaced. Set-off quotations are not enclosed in quotation marks.

For dissertations and theses, single-spacing may be preferred because it more closely resembles a printed format.

PROSE Set-off blocks of prose should be indented. The most effective introduction for a set-off quotation is usually a grammatically complete sentence.

The style sheets have different policies regarding the amount of indention and punctuation of the introductory sentences.

Chicago Manual indentation

Chicago Manual recommends indenting a set-off quotation five spaces or one-half inch from the left margin, with five additional spaces or one-half inch to indicate paragraphing in the original. When the introduction is a complete sentence, it concludes with a period. When the introduction to a set-off quotation includes a formal introductory word, such as *the following* or *in this way*, it closes with a colon.

Raymond Williams explains that the word career has all but lost its original meaning.

[5 spaces]

> Career is now so regularly used to describe a person's progress in life, or, by derivation from this, his profession or vocation that it is difficult to remember, in the same context, its original meaning of a racecourse and a gallop--though in some contexts, as in the phrase "careering about," these survive.
>
> Career appeared in English . . .[6]

MLA indentation

MLA indents set-off blocks of prose ten spaces or one inch from the left margin, with three additional spaces to indicate paragraphing in the original. All introductions to the quotation should be complete sentences and should end with a colon. MLA does not indicate indention of the original material when only one paragraph is quoted.

Raymond Williams explains that the word career has all but lost its original meaning:

[10 spaces]

> Career is now so regularly used to describe a person's progress in life, or, by derivation from this, his profession or vocation that it is difficult to remember, in the same context, its

6. Raymond Williams, *Keywords: A Vocabulary of Culture and Society*, rev. ed. (New York: Oxford University Press, 1983), 52–53.

original meaning of a racecourse and a gallop--
though in some contexts, as in the phrase
"careering about," these survive.[6]

When the set-off quotation spans two or more paragraphs in the original, indicate all original paragraphs with additional spaces.

[3 spaces]
[10 spaces]

Career is now so regularly used to describe a
person's progress in life, . . .
   Career appeared in English . . .

APA indention

APA indents set-off material five spaces or one-half inch, with five additional spaces or one-half inch to indicate paragraphing in the original. Introductory sentences should end with a colon. When a set-off quotation spans two or more paragraphs in the original source, the first paragraph is not indented, but second and subsequent paragraphs are indented an additional five spaces.

Raymond Williams explains that the word career has all but

lost its original meaning:

[5 spaces]

Career is now so regularly used to describe a person's
progress in life, . . .
   Career appeared in English . . .

[5 spaces]

Quotations from letters

Quotations from letters should be treated like any other long prose quotation—that is, introduced and formatted in keeping with the other quotations in your paper. If you quote the salutation and date, position them precisely as they appear in the original.

POETRY Set off quotations of more than two lines, introducing them as the syntax of your sentence requires. Indent poetry ten spaces from the left margin; indention may be five spaces when the line would otherwise have to be broken. Lines of poetry extending beyond one typescript line should be indented ten spaces, with the rest of the line indented an additional three spaces on the next line. Alignment, spacing, and punctuation within the set-off quotation should follow the original as closely as possible.

Runover lines

In "Song of Myself," Walt Whitman uses the diction and

rhythm of natural speech.

[10 spaces]

A child said What is the grass? fetching it to
   me with full hands;

[3 spaces]

How could I answer the child? I do not know what
   it is any more than he.
I guess it must be the flag of my disposition,
   out of hopeful green stuff woven.

Placement of partial lines

When a quotation from a poem begins in the middle of a line, place the first word approximately where it appears on the page in the original, as the placement of the following lines from Keats's "Endymion" illustrates.

```
                    When yet a child
I oft have dried my tears when thou has smil'd.
Thou seem'dst my sister: hand in hand we went
From eve to morn across the firmament.
```

Alignment

Align quotation marks at the beginning of a line under the capital letter of the preceding line, as indicated in this quotation from Wordsworth's "Anecdote for Fathers."

```
At this my boy hung down his head,
He blushed with shame, nor made reply;
And three times to the child I said,
"Why, Edward, tell me why?"
```

Original spacing

Reproduce the spacing of a poem as accurately as possible, as in this typed version of the beginning of Robert Herrick's "The Pillar of Fame."

```
 Fame's pillar here, at last, we set,
   Out-during Marble, Brass, or Jet,
       Charmed and enchanted so,
        As to withstand the blow
            Of     overthrow:
```

Parenthetical documentation

Follow the above guidelines for spacing, but include documentation within parentheses after the final punctuation mark, as in this quotation from Elizabeth Barrett Browning's "Sonnets from the Portuguese."

```
How do I love thee?  Let me count the ways.
I love thee to the depth and breadth and height
My soul can reach, when feeling out of sight
For the ends of Being and ideal Grace. (27.1-4)
```

(Parenthetical references should be abbreviated, as in this citation of sonnet 27, lines 1 through 4. If the divisions of a work are not well known, identify them in a note for the first of the quotations in your text.)

DRAMA For quotation of dialogue, indent the names of the characters, italicized, five spaces. If the names are long, you may abbreviate them after the first reference. Place a period after each name, and leave two spaces before the speech. Indent successive lines ten spaces. Place stage directions, italicized and enclosed by brackets, approximately as they appear in the original.

Chicago Manual format

```
In a flashback, Arthur Miller demonstrates that the Loman
family has a memory of better times:

[5 spaces]
     [Linda enters, as of old, a ribbon in her hair,
     carrying a basket of washing.]
     Linda.  [with youthful energy] Hello, dear!
     Willy.  Sweetheart!
     Linda.  How'd the Chevvy run?
     Willy.  Chevrolet, Linda, is the greatest car ever
[10 spaces]  built. [to the boys] Since when do you
             let your mother carry wash up the stairs?7
```

MLA format

For quotation of dialogue, indent the names, in full capital letters, ten spaces. Place a period after each name, and leave one space before the speech. Indent each successive line an additional three spaces.

```
Like their father, the Loman sons have unrealistic dreams:

[10 spaces]
          BIFF. Listen, why don't you come out West with
[3 spaces]   me?
          HAPPY. You and I, heh?
          BIFF. Sure, maybe we could buy a ranch.  Raise
             cattle, use our muscles. Men built like we
             are should be working out in the open.
          HAPPY. The Loman Brothers, heh? (Death of a
             Salesman, act 1)
```

EPIGRAPHS An *epigraph* is a quotation that precedes the text of a chapter or book. An epigraph usually serves to introduce, to summarize, or to comment upon the material that follows. The relevance of the epigraph should be clear to the reader, even at the outset, and its significance should be amplified after a reading of the work it prefaces. There is no standard length for an epigraph, except that the passage should be pared down to the essential portion. Indenting or centering substitutes for quotation marks. Give the name of the author and the title of the source, marked by two hyphens or a dash, below the quotation. When an author is widely known, further bibliographical information is optional. If biographical information for the epigraph of a dissertation or book is required, place it in the preface or introduction, not in a note. For an essay or article, you may identify the epigraph in a note.

Preceding a dissertation or book, epigraphs are normally blocked and centered on an otherwise blank page, with the designation of the source placed flush right.

---

7. Arthur Miller, *Death of a Salesman* (1949; reprint, New York: Penguin, Viking, 1977), act 1.

The critical power is of lower rank than the creative.

--Matthew Arnold,
"The Function of Criticism at the Present Time"

Epigraphs at the beginning of a chapter are most often placed flush right, but they may also be centered or placed flush left, as taste and policy dictate.

Fair seed-time had my soul, and I grew up
Fostered alike by beauty and by fear.
--William Wordsworth, The Prelude

or

The world is too much with us: late and soon,
Getting and spending we lay waste our powers.
--William Wordsworth, "The World is Too Much With Us"

(Because the first line is the same as the title, it may be omitted, particularly for readers knowledgeable about Wordsworth or poetry.)

DIRECT QUOTATIONS IN NOTES Informational notes may contain direct quotations. All quotations should be run in with the text of the note and enclosed in quotation marks. If the quotation is longer than one paragraph, begin each paragraph at the left margin without indention. Place quotation marks at the beginning of each paragraph and at the beginning and end of the entire selection. Quoted material in notes should follow the spacing used throughout.

1. On other issues the Supreme Court handed down these decisions in 1989. "Ruling unanimously in a copyright case (Community for Creative Non-Violence v. Redi, No. 88-293), the Court held that freelance artists and writers retain the right to copyright what they create as long as they were not in a conventional employment relationship with the organization that commissioned their work.

"The court unanimously refused to narrow the scope of the Federal racketeering law. The decision, H.J. Inc. v. Northwestern Bell, No. 87-1252, left the law, originally aimed at organized crime, as a powerful weapon in private civil lawsuits" (Linda Greenhouse, "The Year the Court Turned Right," New York Times, 7 July 1989, A10).

▪ Introducing Direct Quotations

BRIEF QUOTATIONS An introduction to a direct quotation should provide a smooth transition between your own words and those of the author you quote. The name of the author (the full name the first time; the last name only thereafter) and the author's profession, affiliation, or the title of the work you are quoting (the first time you quote; thereafter only if significant) should accompany the quotation. Notice the way G. Beato integrates quotations into the following paragraphs while maintaining authorial control over the argument.

> The documents and records that remain accessible over the long term are likely to offer a different view of their creators than earlier paper-based archives have of theirs. "We can look at a Hemingway manuscript or a Tennessee Williams manuscript and see cross-outs and changes," says Jean Ashton, director of Columbia's Rare Book & Manuscript Library. "But with the new technologies, the whole process of creation has become less visible." Theoretically, digital archives can offer an even greater level of detail than paper-based ones, but that proposition hinges on the currently dubious assumption that people actually use Microsoft Word's "Mark Revisions" capabilities (or the equivalent), save successive drafts of their documents, or even hold onto e-mail for more than a few weeks.
>
> At least a few people do these things, of course. One of them is Columbia historian Anders Stephanson, who suggests that e-mail may restore much of the historical record that the telephone has eliminated. "When people stopped writing letters," he comments, "historians lost an invaluable set of sources. Now, at least, we have in theory a remarkable amount of writing; though most of it might disappear, it might still probably be more than we had in the age of the telephone. This assumes, admittedly, that some people at least think as 'archivally' as I do." Alas, the computer makes it just as easy to discard information as it does to save it. Consider, for example, the mystery surrounding the first e-mail message, which was sent in 1964. Because no one saved it, no one knows exactly who sent it. (M.I.T., Cambridge University, and the Carnegie Institute of Technology are the three sites of suspects.)[8]

In your reading of scholarly materials you will notice many paragraphs that end with quotations, often long ones. Despite the widespread practice and temptations of ending a paragraph with a quotation, try to avoid it. You leave your reader with someone else's voice and argument instead of your own. Try to find a way to incorporate the quotation into the middle of your paragraphs. If you cannot do so without fabricating a redundant or useless sentence, leave the quotation at the end of your paragraph, but be certain that you provide a transition from the quotation to your own line of discussion at the beginning of the next paragraph.

Your introduction should also accurately indicate your attitude toward the source and your reason for using the quotation. It should specify the relationship between your argument or ideas and those of the source,

8. G. Beato, "Does the Past Have a Future?" *21stC: The World of Research at Columbia University,* 3 (Spring 1998), 9.

indicating, for example, whether you disagree or agree with the source or whether the source differs from another source that you have cited.

In his magisterial history of the fall of Rome, Edward Gibbon begins to set up the narrative as a tragedy with his opening statement that "in the second century of the Christian era, the Empire of Rome comprehended the fairest part of the earth, and the most civilized portion of mankind."[9]

(This introduction could serve as the first reference to Gibbon's work: it provides the author's complete name, mentions the work being cited [by allusion to the content] and with the word "magisterial" indicates that the writer approves of the quoted statement.)

"In the second century of the Christian era, the empire of Rome comprehended the fairest part of the earth," in Gibbon's estimation, as well as "the most civilized portion of mankind."

(This introduction assumes that Gibbon has already been introduced, that the reader knows that the work in question is his *Decline and Fall*, and that in general the writer finds it a reliable source.)

Introductions to direct quotation should not distort the content of the quotation. Notice how a change in the introduction alters the meaning of a quotation:

George Orwell, the English essayist and novelist, explains that "Dickens's criticism of society is almost exclusively moral."[10]

(The introductory word explains and the characterization of Orwell's career as literary suggest that Orwell analyzes Dickens's attitudes toward society with the empathy of a writer rather than as a critic of his politics.)

Although the sentence reads smoothly, the researcher has misrepresented the source, in which Orwell goes on to criticize Dickens for merely portraying societal problems without making any suggestions for change. The following introduction more accurately represents Orwell's intention in making the same statement quoted above:

George Orwell, the English political activist, complains that "Dickens's criticism of society is almost exclusively moral."[10]

(The introductory word *complains* and the characterization of Orwell's career as political suggest that Orwell condemns Dickens's concentration on morals to the neglect of politics.)

---

9. Edward Gibbon, *The Decline and Fall of the Roman Empire*, vol. 1 (New York: Modern Library, 1961), 1.

10. George Orwell, "Charles Dickens," in *A Collection of Essays* (New York: Harcourt Brace, 1946), 51.

EXTENDED QUOTATIONS Introductions to extended quotations that are indented should be punctuated according to their grammatical form. An introduction that is a complete sentence containing a formal introductory word or phrase, such as *following, thus,* or *in this way,* usually ends with a colon.

```
Deborah Tannen characterizes women's use of speech as

follows:
```

[5 spaces]

```
     For most women, the language of conversation is
     primarily a language of rapport: a way of establishing
     connection and negotiating relationships. Emphasis is
     placed on displaying similarities and matching
     experiences.11
```

Informal introductions

An introduction that does not contain a formal introductory word and that is a complete sentence should close with a colon (MLA and APA) or with a period (*Chicago*).

Chicago Manual

```
Deborah Tannen distinguishes women's use of speech from

men's.
```

[5 spaces]

```
     For most women, the language of conversation is
     primarily a language of rapport: . . .11
```

MLA

```
Deborah Tannen distinguishes women's use of speech from

men's:
```

[10 spaces]

```
          For most women, the language of conversation is
          primarily a language of rapport: . . . 11
```

APA

```
Deborah Tannen distinguishes women's use of speech from

men's:
```

[5 spaces]

```
     For most women, the language of conversation is
     primarily a language of rapport: . . . 11
```

An introduction that is an incomplete sentence—a phrase or a clause—should end with the punctuation that would be necessary if the introduction and quotation were run together as one sentence.

11. Deborah Tannen, *You Just Don't Understand: Men and Women in Conversation* (New York: Ballantine, 1990), 77.

```
James Moffett finds that when people try to talk about

abstraction,
```
[5 spaces]
```
    they resort finally to talking about how people,
    especially children, learn.  It is hard to avoid
    an analogy between stages of information processing
    that go on in all of us all the time, and developmental
    stages of growth.  A curriculum sequence based on such
    an analogy, however, needs to be carefully qualified.12
```
(The sentence begins, "Whenever I ask people to define abstraction for me, they . . .")

When the juncture between your sentence and the quotation does not require punctuation, omit it even when you indent the quotation.

```
Awareness of audience is essential to successful

communication because
```
[5 spaces]
```
    all utterances are to some degree determined by a
    complex of contextual factors including who is talking,
    who is being addressed, what is being talked about, and
    others.  If speakers did not take these factors into
    account, all kinds of communicative misfires would
    result.13
```
(The original sentence begins with the words "To sum up, all utterances . . .")

■ Punctuating Direct Quotations

Quotations should combine grammatically as well as logically with your own sentences and paragraphs. To do this, you will need to use punctuation—capital letters, quotation marks, end punctuation, ellipses, and brackets—to indicate the exact way the quotation appears in the original source.

CAPITALIZATION In writing that does not involve textual criticism or legal cases, you may capitalize according to the requirements of your own sentence without indicating the change. That is, you may change an initial capital letter to lowercase or an internal lowercase letter to a capital, provided that you do not alter the meaning.

MLA format requires that original capitalization be retained or indicated with the use of brackets.

Alteration of original capitalization

You may use lowercase for the first letter (except for proper nouns), regardless of the way it appears in the original, if the quotation forms a grammatical whole with the sentence that encompasses or introduces it, as in this example.

12. James Moffett, *Teaching the Universe of Discourse* (Boston: Houghton Mifflin, 1968), 23.

13. Elizabeth Closs Traugott and Mary Louise Pratt, *Linguistics for Students of Literature* (New York: Harcourt Brace Jovanovich, 1980), 12.

Harrison E. Salisbury has observed that "every war propels some obscure city or town into the limelight," pointing out that the identities of Guernica, Coventry, and Stalingrad emerged largely in connection with wars.[14]

(In the original, *every* is the first word in the sentence.)

Capitalize the first letter, regardless of how it appears in the original, if the quotation is treated as a grammatical whole—that is, if the quotation is formally introduced as a direct quotation or is set by itself as a complete sentence.

William James asks, "How <u>can</u> things so insecure as the successful experiences of this world afford a stable anchorage?"[15]

(The original sentence reads, "To begin with, how . . . ?")

You may lowercase the first letter of either a run-in or a set-off quotation, even when it is capitalized in the original, as the grammar of your sentence requires.

H. D. F. Kitto explains that

> a sense of the wholeness of things is perhaps the most typical feature of the Greek mind. . . . The modern mind divides, specializes, thinks in categories: the Greek instinct was the opposite, to take the widest view, to see things as an organic whole. The speeches of Cleon and Diodotus showed precisely the same thing: the particular issue must be generalized.[16]

(The sentence in the original begins with *A*. The ellipsis points indicate the omission of a sentence.)

H. D. F. Kitto explains that "a sense of the wholeness of things is perhaps the most typical feature of the Greek mind."[16]

Retaining the original capitalization

When for any reason you think it necessary to retain the original capitalization, you may do so in one of several ways. First, and usually best, you may change your introduction to a form that does not require a change. The quotation from Kitto above might be introduced to indicate that the original sentence begins with the words "A sense."

---

14. Harrison E. Salisbury, *Behind the Lines—Hanoi* (New York: Bantam, 1967), 84.
15. William James, *The Varieties of Religious Experience* (New York: Collier, 1961), 120.
16. H. D. F. Kitto, *The Greeks* (Baltimore: Penguin, 1951), 169.

H. D. F. Kitto defines the Greek mentality in these terms:

[5 spaces]

A sense of the wholeness of things is perhaps the most typical feature of the Greek mind. . . .[16]

Or, if it is particularly important to indicate the original capitalization, as in quoting literary works, classical works, philosophical writings, or legal texts, use the capital letter even if it does not fit your sentence.

Kant postulates that

[5 spaces]

Time is nothing but the form of inner sense, that is, of the intuition of ourselves and of our inner state. It cannot be a determination of outer appearances: it has to do neither with a shape nor position, but with the relation of representations in our inner state.[17]

or

Kant postulates that "Time is nothing but the form of inner sense, . . ."[17]

Use of brackets, MLA format

You may also indicate a capital letter in the original source by enclosing the lowercase letter in brackets, or vice versa.

H. D. F. Kitto explains that "[a] sense of the wholeness of things is perhaps the most typical feature of the Greek mind."[16]

Kitto asserts, "[T]he Greek instinct was the opposite, to take the widest view."[16]

QUOTATION MARKS Enclose direct quotations run into the text in double quotation marks. Quotation marks should be placed outside a comma or period and inside a colon or semicolon.

Oscar Wilde wrote that "unselfish people are colourless"; however, most would agree with William Gladstone that "selfishness is the greatest curse of the human race."[18]

---

17. Immanuel Kant, *Critique of Pure Reason*, trans. Norman Kemp Smith, unabridged ed. (New York: St. Martin's, 1963), 77.

18. Oscar Wilde, *The Picture of Dorian Gray* (New York: Harper and Row, 1965), 68; William Gladstone, speech delivered at Hawarden, 28 May 1890.

In the case of an exclamation point or question mark, the quotation marks are placed outside when the mark belongs with the quoted material and inside when the mark belongs with the text.

```
What does Hamlet mean when he tells the players "to hold as

'twere the mirror up to nature"?19
```

(The question mark belongs with the writer's sentence.)

```
Hamlet asks himself, "Am I a coward?"20
```

(The question mark belongs with the quotation.)

Quotations within run-in quotations

If a portion of the original was enclosed in double quotation marks, change them to single quotation marks in a run-in quotation, as in the following example where the author of the original quoted the phrase "pushing on open doors."

```
Because the French vetoed the European Defense Community,

"the United States was no longer 'pushing on open doors,'

and afterwards Washington conducted itself far more

cautiously."21
```

When quotation marks within single marks are needed, use double marks, then single marks, and so on, alternating the marks as necessary.

Quotations within set-off quotations

When a set-off quotation contains an excerpt that was enclosed in double quotation marks in the original, retain the double quotation marks, as shown below.

```
Marshall McLuhan points out that the development of print

led to the concept of perspective:
```

[5 spaces]

```
     As the literal or "the letter" later became
     identified with light on rather than light through the
     text, there was also the equivalent stress on "point of
     view" or the fixed position of the reader: "from where
     I am sitting."22
```

19. William Shakespeare, *Hamlet*, in *The Riverside Shakespeare,* ed. G. Blakemore Evans (Boston: Houghton Mifflin, 1974), act 3, scene 2, lines 21–22.

20. *Hamlet* 2.2.571.

21. William Diebold, Jr., *The United States and the Industrial World: American Foreign Economic Policy in the 1970's* (New York: Praeger, 1972), 26.

22. Marshall McLuhan, *The Gutenberg Galaxy: The Making of Typographic Man* (1962; reprint, New York: Signet, 1969), 138.

END PUNCTUATION The punctuation used at the end of a quotation depends on the context into which the quotation is placed. A period in the original, for example, may be changed to a comma or omitted to produce a grammatically correct sentence. If any distortion of the author's original meaning occurs through such an omission, indicate the original punctuation with an ellipsis (see pages 75–78).

Original

Every man bears the entire form of human nature.[23]

When Montaigne wrote, "Every man bears the entire form of human nature," he advocated studying the self rather than others.[23]

Montaigne asserted that "every man bears the entire form of human nature": on the strength of this philosophy, he turned from public affairs to introspection.[23]

End punctuation that must be retained

Question marks and exclamation marks must accompany the quotations in which they appear. Either of these strong marks of punctuation can take the place of a period. The exclamation mark cannot be excluded even when a colon or semicolon indicates the end of an independent clause or a complete thought.

"Give me liberty, or give me death!": Patrick Henry thus stated his challenge to British rule.

The following sentence, though not exclamatory, ends with the exclamation mark of the quotation.

Patrick Henry proclaimed, "Give me liberty, or give me death!"

End punctuation with parenthetical documentation

For variations in end punctuation with parenthetical documentation and placement of superscripts after quotations, see Chapters 7, 8, and 9.

OMISSIONS FROM QUOTED MATERIAL (ELLIPSES) In some circumstances, as the previous sections explain, you may omit a capital letter or end punctuation from a direct quotation. In addition, you may omit footnotes or endnotes and the numbers indicating them. Otherwise, indicate all omissions from quoted material with three ellipsis points, which are periods

23. Michel de Montaigne, "Of Repentance," in *Selected Essays*, trans. Blanchard Bates (New York: Modern Library, 1949), 285.

with one space on either side. The quoted material should read clearly and grammatically without the deleted portion, and the deletion should not alter the meaning or logic of the sentence. The following guidelines apply to the use of ellipsis points.

Omission at the beginning of a sentence

Ellipsis points are not needed at the beginning of a run-in quotation. If you wish to indicate the original capitalization, do so with a capital letter or brackets (see page 73).

Omission at end of sentence

Ellipsis points indicate the omission of the end of a sentence only when another sentence of quotation follows immediately. An ellipsis is not necessary in the cut quotation below.

Original

> A foolish consistency is the hobgoblin of little minds, adored by little statesmen, philosophers and divines.[24]

Cut version

```
Emerson advocated the courage to change one's mind when he
said that a "foolish consistency is the hobgoblin of little
minds."24
```

Internal omission

Indicate omission of an internal part of a direct quotation with ellipsis points, separated from the text and from each other by one space, as in the example below.

Original

> In the western farm states the Granger movement, organized in 1869 as The Patrons of Husbandry, was able to force regulatory legislation through some state legislatures.[25]

Cut version

```
    According to Margaret G. Myers, "the Granger movement
. . . was able to force regulatory legislation through some
state legislatures."25
```

(The original commas are not necessary when the phrase is omitted.)

Ellipsis with original end

When you wish to retain the original punctuation at the end of either a cut or a full sentence, the appropriate mark of punctuation substitutes for the period preceding the ellipsis points.

Original

> Ilse smiled scornfully. "What's it to you? Just because Papa Kremer put us in the same row? You're not jealous of him?"[26]

Cut version

```
Then Ilse taunts Hans: "What's it to you? . . . You're not
jealous of him?"26
```

---

24. Ralph Waldo Emerson, "Self-Reliance," in *The American Tradition in Literature*, ed. George Perkins et al., vol. 1, 6th ed. (New York: Random House, 1985), 846.

25. Margaret G. Myers, *A Financial History of the United States* (New York: Columbia University Press, 1970), 226.

26. André Schwarz-Bart, *The Last of the Just*, trans. Stephen Becker (New York: Atheneum, 1981), 225.

Original

From the boy's face one might suppose that sacred emblem to be, in his eyes, the crowning confusion of the great, confused city;—so golden, so high up, so far out of his reach.[27]

Cut version

```
"From the boy's face one might suppose that sacred emblem
to be, in his eyes, the crowning confusion of the great,
confused city; . . . so far out of his reach."27
```

Omission of sentences

When another sentence follows either a complete sentence or a cut sentence that is grammatically complete, place a period at the end of the sentence, without an intervening space, and add three ellipsis points. A complete sentence must precede the four dots, and a complete sentence must follow them.

Original

The Maya world was made up of three layered domains: the starry arch of heaven, the stony Middleworld of earth made to flower and bear fruit by the blood of kings, and the dark waters of the Underworld below. To say that the Maya considered these to be three distinct regions, however, is to give a false impression, for they believed all dimensions of existence were interrelated. Furthermore, all three domains were thought to be alive and imbued with sacred power, including the sky, which was represented by a great crocodilian monster. This Cosmic Monster made the rains when it shed its blood in supernatural counterpoint to the royal sacrifices on the earth below.

The Underworld was sometimes called Xibalba, but it is perhaps closer to the original Maya understanding to think of Xibalba as the parallel unseen Otherworld into which the Maya kings and other shamans could pass in ecstatic trance. Like the world of human beings, Xibalba had animals, plants, inhabitants of various kinds, and a landscape with both natural and constructed features. At sundown Xibalba rotated above the earth to become the night sky.

The human plane of existence, like the Otherworld, was a sacred place. The Maya conceived of the human world as a region floating in the primordial sea. Sometimes they represented the earth as the back of a caiman and sometimes as the back of a turtle. The four cardinal directions provided the fundamental grid for the Maya community and for the surface of the world. But for the Maya, the principal axis of the Middleworld was the path of the sun as it moved from east to west on its daily journey. Each direction of the compass had a special tree, a bird, a color, gods associated with its domain, and rituals associated with those gods. East was red and the most important direction since it was where the sun was born. North, sometimes called the "side of heaven," was white and the direction from which the cooling rains of winter came. It was also the direction of the north star around which the sky pivots. West, the leaving or dying place of the sun, was black. South was yellow and was considered to be the right-hand or great side of the sun. In the Maya conception east, not north, should always be at the top of maps.[28]

27. Charles Dickens, *Bleak House* (New York: Bantam, 1983), 253.

28. Linda Schele and David Freidel, *A Forest of Kings: The Untold Story of the Ancient Maya* (New York: William Morrow, 1990), 66.

Cut version

```
   Schele and Freidel explain that for the Mayas "the
Underworld was sometimes called Xibalba. . . . At sundown
Xibalba rotated above the earth to become the night sky."28
```

Omission of entire paragraph(s)

Indicate the omission of one or more paragraphs in a prose quotation with an ellipsis at the end of the paragraph immediately preceding the omission.

```
Schele and Freidel describe the Mayan belief in a
sacramental universe.

          All three domains were thought to be alive and
          imbued with sacred power, including the sky.
          . . . Sometimes they represented the earth
          as the back of a caiman and sometimes as the
          back of a turtle.28
```

(The ellipsis indicates both a cut sentence and a cut paragraph. The place of *Sometimes* at the margin of the indention indicates that it does not begin a paragraph in the original.)

Omission of line(s) of poetry

Show the omission of one or more lines of poetry with a full line of ellipsis points equal in length to the longest line of the poem, as in this example from Alexander Pope's "An Essay on Criticism."

```
'Tis with our judgments as our watches: none
Go just alike, yet each believes his own.
. . . . . . . . . . . . . . . . . . . . . . . . . . . .
Authors are partial to their wit, 'tis true,
But are not critics to their judgment too?
```

ADDITIONS TO DIRECT QUOTATIONS (BRACKETS) Except for necessary changes of beginning capitalization and end punctuation, direct quotations should not be altered. However, if you believe that a reader may find a quotation unclear or may miss the point you are trying to make by using the quotation, you may insert explanatory material within the quotation, enclosing it in brackets. Such an addition is called an *interpolation.*

Clarifying original source

```
"No society in which these liberties [liberty of conscience,
liberty of pursuits, and freedom to unite] are not, on the
whole, respected, is free, whatever may be its form of
government."29
```

Correcting errors

An error in a quotation should be designated in brackets immediately following the error. You may indicate your awareness of an error with the

29. John Stuart Mill, *On Liberty,* ed. David Spitz (New York: Norton, 1975), 14.

word sic (meaning "thus" in Latin) or with a correction. When the correction would be obvious to your readers, as in most spelling or typographical errors, use sic.

Correction with sic

```
John Doe explained, "The results of the 1988 experiment were
quite amasing [sic]."30
```

When the nature of the error might not be readily apparent, supply the correction in brackets.

Correction in brackets

```
Doe added, "The affects [effects] of radiation exceeded our
estimates."30

Doe advised that "Smith completed her experiments in 1987
[1986]."30
```

Unless you particularly want to call attention to the inaccuracy or carelessness of a source, you may want to try to avoid quoting sentences with errors.

Indicating source of italics

Indicate the source of italics with an explanatory phrase in brackets when the source might be misinterpreted. Note the following example:

[5 spaces]

```
     This is the story of an adolescent whose needs are not
     understood by his father, who thinks his son is stupid.
     The son will not develop himself as the father thinks
     he should, but stubbornly insists on learning instead
     what he [italics in original or original emphasis]
     thinks is of real value. To achieve his complete
     self-realization, the young man first has to become
     acquainted with his inner being, a process no father
     can prescribe [italics mine or emphasis mine] even if
     he realizes the value of it, as the youth's father does
     not.30
```

(The bracketed material has been interpolated.)

Clarifying pronoun reference

If the referent of a pronoun in a quotation might be ambiguous or if the pronoun refers to a noun in a previous sentence that is not quoted, supply the noun in brackets.

```
"The scientist refers to it [a datum] as an observation."30

"This ["The Three Languages"] is the story of an adolescent
whose needs are not understood by his father."31
```

30. John Doe, letter to author, 19 May 1989.

31. Bruno Bettelheim, *The Uses of Enchantment: The Meaning and Importance of Fairy Tales* (New York: Vintage, 1977), 100.

4 Style and Mechanics

Precision in expressing your ideas is as essential as accuracy in taking notes and documenting your sources. If your paper is to extend knowledge in your field, you need to communicate your ideas to as wide an audience as possible. For this purpose you need to follow the conventions of style and mechanics readily understood and widely accepted in the academic community.

This chapter surveys the issues of style and mechanics you are most likely to confront when writing a research paper. For other issues in the areas of grammar, usage, and mechanics, you should have at hand and consult frequently a dictionary, a thesaurus, a handbook of grammar, and a textbook on composition and rhetoric. If you are required to follow a local or professional documentation system, you will want to refer to it also.

Style

As you know well in the case of clothes or music, the same object, such as a dress or a symphony, can be made in many different styles. Style in prose is the *way* you present your ideas. All the choices you make while writing—of words, sentence structure, and paragraph length, for example—create the style of your paper. Style is not just decoration. In the words of William Safire, a well-known commentator on language, "Style in writing is not elegance in phrasing; it should marshal argument and prose to move or persuade."[1] Style, then, is not mere decoration; it cannot be separated from meaning. Most of your writing for the academic community, particularly your research papers, will require formality of style.

---

1. William Safire, "Stylish Books and Koobs," On Language, *New York Times Magazine,* 20 Aug. 1995, p. 18.

▪ Diction

Just as you vary your vocabulary in different conversational situations, so you will alter your diction, or word choice, to suit each writing project. The diction in a research paper should be formal rather than colloquial. Slang generally has no place in a research paper, nor does the relatively imprecise diction of casual conversation. Each word should convey your meaning as exactly as possible. Do not use quotation marks to indicate that you do not really mean what the word means. When you need specialized vocabulary or jargon to accomplish your purpose, define your terms clearly the first time you use them and make sure that you keep the definitions consistent throughout your paper. Avoid using jargon when you do not need it.

▪ Tone

The tone of your paper is the attitude you project toward your subject. In most cases, the tone in research papers should be serious, rather than, for example, ironic or casual. Humorous, casual, or conversational approaches are usually inappropriate for research papers. Furthermore, they are usually ineffective because they contradict the expectations for research writing. Given that your purpose is to promote understanding of your subject, you will not want to use a tone that can easily be misinterpreted.

Your attitude toward previous researchers in your field should be respectful, even when you disagree with their conclusions. When you find previous work on a subject inadequate, confine your critique to the content rather than extending it to an attack on the author.

▪ Voice

Even the most formal paper can have a voice, the quality of prose that indicates the presence of a human speaker. Voice conveys your relationship or connection to the ideas you present. Voice is generally more pronounced in creative writing than in academic writing. In genres such as the personal essay, the writer's voice may be used to divulge much of the meaning. For most research papers you will not want to foreground your personality, but at the same time you need not expunge all evidence of your presence. Your voice can certainly convey your interest and enthusiasm for your endeavor.

Personal pronouns and voice

You do not need to use first-person pronouns to give your papers a voice. Most research papers should be written in the third person, that is, with nouns or third-person pronouns (*he, she, they,* or *it*) as subjects of the sentences. Using a first-person pronoun (*I, me, my, mine*) to call attention to the fact that a statement is your opinion often weakens the assertion by implying uncertainty. The reader assumes that statements in your paper, unless otherwise attributed, are your opinion and represent your point of view. At the same time, you should not use impersonal labels such as "the researcher" or "the writer," which tend to remove you entirely from your paper. Also, there is no need to avoid personal pronouns by inappropriately assigning agency to inanimate objects. A glossary can appropriately be said to define terms and a chart can illustrate relationships, but they cannot argue or defend a proposition.

The first-person pronoun is appropriate when you relate a personal experience, such as your own process of research, or when you wish to call particular attention to your opinion as distinguished from the views of others. In papers that call for personal responses to texts, ideas, or situations (some kinds of literary criticism and anthropological studies, for example), you will want to use first-person pronouns.

The plural first person, the editorial "we," should not substitute for "I," but it may be used to refer to a group of researchers that includes you. Whatever choice of pronouns you make for the text, you may freely use the first person in the preface and acknowledgments.

Because your reader will assume that you are addressing him or her, second-person pronouns (*you, your*) usually do not belong in a research paper. Commands (implied second person, as in "Observe that . . . ," the subject of which is actually *you*) should be avoided. These constructions of direct address sometimes have a place in creative writing and informal papers.

▪ Economy

In creative writing you may repeat or multiply words just for the sound of them. Academic research writing is judged on a different standard, however: economy of expression. In general, you should use as many words as you need, but no more than you need, to accomplish your goal. Writers often inflate their prose during the drafting stage as a means of keeping their momentum, but any excessive verbiage should be eliminated during revision. Look for the filler phrases that can be replaced with one or two words, such as `with regard to`, `in the matter of`, `based on the fact that`, `at this point in time`, `in the process of being`, and `by way of`. Also, watch for redundancy, or duplication, in phrases such as `progressively improve`, `gradually decrease`, `completely unanimous`, `necessary requirement`, and `brief summary`.

▪ Verb Tense

Cast verbs in the tense or tenses appropriate to the time of the events under discussion. A few general guidelines apply.

Literature

Narrate events in literary works in the present tense to indicate that multiple experiences of reading serve to repeat the action.

```
After passing up the opportunity to kill the kneeling

Claudius, Hamlet enters his mother's bedchamber, where he

kills Polonius.
```

A description of the author's actions in creating a literary work generally takes the present tense.

```
Shakespeare takes many of his plots from historical

chronicles.
```

Theory or philosophy

The past tense is appropriate for discussions about works of theory or philosophy.

```
Descartes distinguished three classes of ideas:

adventitious, fictitious, and innate.
```

The present tense may also be used in such discussions to indicate that a given work continues to present the same ideas.

```
Descartes distinguishes three classes of ideas: . . .
```

Research results

When you report the results of research, use the past tense to describe the result of a particular experiment. Use the present tense for generalizations or conclusions.

```
Scores on standardized grammar tests did not correlate with

the ability to write.
```

(Reporting the results of a particular study)

```
Scores on standardized grammar tests do not correlate

with the ability to write.
```

(Generalization based on one or more studies)

Review of literature

In a review of literature, you may use either the past tense or the past perfect tense in summarizing findings.

```
Researchers demonstrated that . . .

Researchers have demonstrated that . . .
```

■ Sentence Structure

Grammatical correctness is not the sole attribute of a good sentence: A good sentence reinforces your meaning through its structure and pace. Explore the full range of possibilities for expressing the logical relationships of ideas in a variety of sentence structures, including compound and complex sentences and parallel constructions. Because meaning cannot be separated from its expression in language—that is, content is inseparable from style—weak or inappropriate sentence structure often reveals faulty logic or undeveloped thought. Thus, careful attention to your sentences can help you refine your ideas.

ACTIVE AND PASSIVE VOICE In the active voice, the actor is the subject of the sentence, whereas in the passive voice, the object or receiver of the action is the subject. Active voice is a stronger, more vigorous construction than passive voice. Sentences should be active except when you specifically want to emphasize that the subject was acted upon, as in "The Lindbergh baby was kidnapped," or when either you do not know the subject or it is irrelevant, as in "The votes were not tallied until midnight." Otherwise, the passive voice results in evasion ("My sweater got left at school") or bureaucratic impersonality ("Trespassing laws will be enforced"). Changing a sentence from passive to active can result not only in the use of a stronger form of the verb but also in the elimination of wordiness, as in this example:

The Worldly Philosophers was written by Robert Heilbroner.

Robert Heilbroner wrote The Worldly Philosophers.

INTRANSITIVE VERBS Reliance on intransitive verbs, verbs that do not take objects, produces weak prose. In particular, the expletive constructions of these verbs—*there are, there is, it is*—result in weak, wordy sentences. You can avoid these constructions by determining the subject of the sentence and supplying a transitive verb.

Original It was in the Poetics that Aristotle analyzed Greek tragedy.

Revision Aristotle analyzed Greek tragedy in the Poetics.

▪ Parallelism

Elements in a list or series, including chapter titles and headings, should be parallel—that is, entries at the same level of subordination should take the same grammatical form. If you use a noun or noun phrase for one chapter title, the next chapter title should also be a noun phrase rather than, for example, an infinitive phrase (see pages 23–24 for examples of parallelism in outlines). In a sentence, all elements in a series linked by a coordinating conjunction (such as *and, but, for*) or by correlative conjunctions (conjunctions that cannot be used alone, such as *not only . . . but also; either . . . or*) should be grammatically parallel.

Adjectives in a series that is not parallel For twenty-nine years Robinson Crusoe lived on an island that was small, fertile, and without any inhabitants.

Correction For twenty-nine years Robinson Crusoe lived on a tiny, isolated, and unpopulated island.

Lack of parallelism with correlative conjunctions

```
Congress not only passed the bill but overrode the
president's veto.
```

Correction

```
Congress not only passed the bill but it also overrode the
president's veto.
```

▪ Coherence

A coherent paper presents ideas in an orderly sequence and makes the logic behind the organization apparent to readers. Try to visualize yourself taking readers step by step through your paper, pointing out all the important features as they follow your instructions for reaching your conclusion. Sentences and paragraphs should begin with a reference to the theme or topic developed in the previous paragraph and by the end should have presented readers with some new information. At the beginning of the next paragraph use a word or phrase from the conclusion of the previous paragraph to remind readers that they have reached a new level of understanding and now should be ready to move forward with your argument.

Transitional expressions

Once you have organized your paper logically, you can use transitional expressions as signals to demonstrate the relationships between your sentences and among your ideas. Transitional expressions are words or phrases that indicate contrast (*but, however*), comparison (*similarly, just as*), the introduction of additional information (*also, likewise, in addition*), the presentation of examples (*for example, for instance*), and conclusions (*in short, in conclusion, therefore*). Such words or phrases do not substitute for organizational and logical development. Clear statements of purpose and the demonstration of logical relationships within each paragraph, section, and chapter provide the most effective coherence.

When you have problems making a coherent transition to a paragraph or section, consider whether the section belongs somewhere else in the paper or should be omitted. When you have trouble identifying the key topics or relationships between ideas, you may have failed to develop the topic sufficiently in previous discussion, neglected to anticipate an idea, or announced topics that you left undeveloped.

▪ Unbiased Language

Most journals and professional organizations have adopted policies requiring that the language in their publications be unbiased—that it neither demean nor exclude any person or group. Linguists now understand that some previously acceptable vocabulary has the effect of portraying persons derogatorily or confining them to one segment of their identity. You need to be particularly careful about words that designate gender, sexual orientation, race, ethnicity, disability, and age, especially when such identification is gratuitous, or unnecessary for your purpose. Avoiding biased language usually demands only minor editing, and most writers consider the goal worthy enough to justify some inconvenience and an occasional infelicity.

Gender bias

Here are a few of the strategies for revising to avoid gender bias. First, change a sentence using the generic masculine pronoun from singular to plural.

`A doctor should know the ethics of his profession.`

Revision `Doctors should know the ethics of their profession.`

Although informal usage now permits linking a singular noun with a plural pronoun, as in "Everyone should hand in their worksheets," this construction is not acceptable in formal written usage.

Substitute the phrase *he or she* or, as some writers prefer, *she or he*, for *he* used generically.

`If he is to succeed, a new teacher requires intelligent supervision.`

Revision `If he or she is to succeed, a new teacher requires . . .`

Because this double pronoun is cumbersome, avoid using it repeatedly, or find a way to edit out the pronoun altogether.

Alternative revision `To succeed, a new teacher requires intelligent supervision.`

Use gender-neutral designations for professions and positions: `firefighter` instead of `fireman`; `humanity` rather than `mankind`; `work force` rather than `manpower`.

Ethnic and racial bias

When numerous designations exist, use the one preferred by the particular racial or ethnic group you are discussing: e.g., `Black` or `African American`; `Latino, Hispanic,` or `Chicano`.

Avoid specifying racial or ethnic group when the identification is not relevant. When you identify a group, avoid implying that race or ethnicity is the most important quality: rather than `the prize-winning Puerto Rican writer, the prize-winning writer who portrays her native Puerto Rico`; rather than `the heroic African American pilot`, simply `the heroic pilot`.

Bias toward persons with disabilities

Avoid equating the person with his or her disability: rather than the `schizophrenic, the person with schizophrenia`.

Avoid emotionally charged words in favor of more neutral language: instead of `the heart attack victim, the person who had a heart attack`.

Guides to avoiding bias

The various professions have published their recommendations for eliminating linguistic bias and stereotyping in writing.

American Psychological Association. *Guidelines for Nonsexist Language in APA Journals; Guidelines for Avoidinq Racial-Ethnic Bias in Language; Guidelines for Nonhandicapping Language in APA Journals; Avoiding Heterosexual Bias in Language* (all available from the American Psychological Association, Publications Office, 750 First Street, NE, Washington, D.C. 2002-4242).

Frank, Francine Wattman, and Paula A. Treichler. *Language, Gender, and Professional Writing: Theoretical Approaches and Guidelines for Nonsexist Usage*. New York: Modern Language Association, 1989. Explains and provides remedies for gender bias.

International Association of Business Communicators. *Without Bias: A Guidebook for Nondiscriminatory Communication.* 2nd ed. New York: Wiley, 1982. Deals with ways to avoid discrimination in employment and personnel practices.

Schwartz, Marilyn, and Association of American University Presses. *Guidelines for Bias-Free Writing.* Bloomington: Indiana University Press, 1995. Deals with gender, race, ethnicity, citizenship, nationality, religion, disabilities, medical conditions, sexual orientation, and age.

Mechanics

Correctness in mechanics, which include grammar, punctuation, and other technical matters, is essential to effective communication. This section deals with those areas of mechanics that relate most directly to a research paper. Unless otherwise specified, all guidelines here apply to papers written according to the *Chicago Manual,* MLA, and APA style sheets.

▪ Spelling

When you are in doubt about the spelling of a word or when variant spellings exist, consult a standard dictionary, such as *The American Heritage Dictionary* or *Webster's New Collegiate Dictionary.* Select the preferred American spelling, and use it consistently throughout your paper. For the correct spelling of proper names not found in a dictionary, refer to an authority such as a biographical dictionary or an encyclopedia. If you decide to use an uncommon spelling (such as an archaism or an Anglicism), specify the reason for your decision in a note. When you find a misspelled word in a passage that you wish to quote directly, enter the word exactly as you find it and indicate that the error is not yours by adding `sic` (Latin for "thus") in brackets immediately after the word.

▪ Abbreviations

Avoid abbreviations in the text of a research paper. Exceptions to this general rule include abbreviations of social titles such as `Mr.`, `Messrs.`, `Mrs.`, `Ms.`, and their foreign equivalents; professional and honorary titles such as `Dr.`, `Prof.`, `Rev.`, and `Hon.` preceding proper names; identifications such as `Esq.` (to designate an attorney), `Ph.D.`, `S.T.B.` (Bachelor of Sacred Theology), `Sr.`, and `Jr.` following proper names; familiar abbreviations of names of countries (`the former USSR`), cities (`St. Louis`), and organizations (`UNESCO`, `YWCA`); abbreviations or acronyms now accepted as words (`IQ`, `AIDS`); abbreviations for units of time, such as `a.m.`, `p.m.`, `A.D.`, `B.C.`; and abbreviations of Latin terms when they appear within parentheses (`e.g.`, `i.e.`). In technical writing, abbreviations of units of measurement such as `mm`, `cc`, `ft`, and `in` should be used. Names of states, reference works, universities, publishers, and books of the Bible should be spelled out in the text unless you designate an alternative, either in the text or in a note: (Oxford English Dictionary, hereafter OED). Consistently use any abbreviations that you select.

Abbreviations in notes and appendixes

The general warning against abbreviations does not apply to material included in notes, appendixes, bibliographies, and, most particularly, tables and figures, where abbreviations are not only permissible but often preferable and where the accepted style, especially in the sciences and mathematics, allows exceedingly abbreviated forms.

Hyphenation

Hyphens are used to create compound words. Compounds that function as nouns may be open (school year), hyphenated (self-concept), or closed (schoolroom). The current trend discourages use of the hyphen; generally, it is dropped when a compound becomes common. Words designating new areas of endeavor offer good examples of rapid change in policy on hyphenation. The compound word *on-line,* while still the preferred form in some dictionaries, will probably close to *online,* just as the compound *psycho-analysis,* standard usage in the first half of the twentieth century, changed to *psychoanalysis.*

Some hyphenated compounds are permanent, or hyphenated regardless of increased usage or placement in the sentence, whereas others are temporary, or hyphenated when they precede a noun but not when they follow it. Keep in mind that there are occasional exceptions to the rules for permanent and temporary compounds and that you may find an instance where you need to add a hyphen to ensure readability.

Permanent hyphenated compounds

1. Prefixes followed by a capitalized word: pro-American, post-World War II.
2. Prefixes followed by a numeral: post-1980, pre-1900.
3. Prefixes followed by an abbreviation: pre-AIDS.
4. Prefixes followed by a hyphenated compound: pro-city-state.
5. Compound adjectives with *self-, half-, quasi-,* and *all-*: self-serving, half-brother, quasi-legal, all-powerful.
6. Compounds that create repetition of the same vowel that could be misread: co-opt, de-emphasize.
7. Compounds that might be misunderstood or misread: re-sign (meaning to sign again, to distinguish it from the word resign), re-form (to form again), pro-life, pro-choice.
8. Fractional numbers written out: one-fourth, two and two-thirds. In APA format, common fractions, when used as nouns, are not hyphenated: one third of the participants, three quarters of a pound.
9. Adjectival phrases that are commonplace: stick-in-the-mud, over-the-hill.
10. Compound nouns with *self-, great-* (relatives), *-in-law,* and *-elect*: self-concept, great-grandfather, sister-in-law, president-elect.

Temporary hyphenated compounds

1. Compound of an adjective or participle plus a noun: `nineteenth-century poet`, but `poet of the nineteenth century`; `second-floor apartment`, but `apartment on the second floor`; `dining-room table`, but `table in the dining room`.
2. Compounds with the prefix *full*: `full-height basketball hoop`, but `hoop at full height`.
3. Compounds with the adverbs *well, ill, better, best, little, lesser,* and *least* before an adjective or participle: `the better-qualified candidate`, but `the candidate better qualified`.
4. Phrases ending with a preposition: `a spelled-out number`, but `a number spelled out`.

Unhyphenated compounds

The following combinations of words generally do not require hyphenation:

1. A compound with an adverb ending in *-ly*: `broadly conceived plan`, `widely read book`.
2. A compound with a comparative or superlative adjective: `better built mousetrap`, `higher priced goods`.
3. Foreign phrases used as adjectives: `a priori argument`, `ad hoc committee`.
4. Uncapitalized words following these prefixes: *after* (`aftershock`); *anti* (`antibiotic`); *bi* (`bilingual`); *bio*; *co*; *counter*; *equi*; *extra*; *infra*; *inter*; *intra*; *macro*; *mega*; *meta*; *micro*; *mid*; *mini*; *multi*; *neo*; *non*; *over*; *post*; *pre*; *pro*; *proto*; *pseudo*; *re*; *semi*; *socio*; *sub*; *super*; *supra*; *trans*; *ultra*; *un*; *under*. When the repetition of the final letter of one of these prefixes and the first letter of the subsequent word would double the *i*'s or *a*'s, as in `anti-intellectual`, or would create an unrecognizable word, hyphenate it.

Division of words at end of line

Hyphens also indicate the division of a word at the end of a line of type-Hyphenated compounds should be broken only at the hyphen. See page 123 for information on dividing words and lines in typescripts. APA format does not permit divided words in typescripts.

■ Italics

Italic is a typeface in which the letters slant to the right. *This sentence is printed in italic type.* In theses, dissertations, and manuscripts that are to be typeset, indicate italic with underlining even if your computer can produce italics. `The underlining of this typed sentence tells a typesetter that the sentence should appear in italics`. APA journals now require italics rather than underlining in articles to be submitted for publication. Given the ease with which italics can be inserted with most computer software, it seems likely that italics will be used more widely. *Form and Style* will follow current advice in the latest *Chicago Manual* and MLA style sheets in using underlining for the purposes explained below.

Emphasis or clarification in your text

Italics may be used to provide emphasis in your text or in direct quotations. Also, italics can serve to indicate the correct reading of a word when it might be misunderstood. These uses of italics should be kept to a minimum because an overabundance of emphasized words reduces the impact of them all, as in this sentence.

`An hour into the marathon he was in second place, and she was in last place. Yet she eventually won the race.`

Emphasis within direct quotation

When you use italics to add emphasis within direct quotations, indicate your alteration of the original with a note enclosed in brackets: `[my emphasis]` or `[emphasis mine]`. Similarly, if you want to point out that the original contains italics, you may do so within brackets: `[original emphasis]` or `[italics in original]`. For a detailed discussion of making additions to quotations, see pages 78 to 79 in Chapter 3.

Words as words

Italicize references to words as words, letters as letters, and terms you will define for your reader.

`She spelled the word laxiflorous.`
(Word as word)

`That word begins with a capital A.`
(Letter as letter)

After you have introduced the definition of a technical term, you need not continue to italicize.

`The term virgule means slanted line or slash mark. Use a virgule to separate lines of poetry.`
(Term to be defined)

Foreign words and phrases

Foreign words and phrases should be underlined except when they have become Anglicized, or accepted as English words. If the word is familiar in ordinary language, chances are good that it is no longer italicized: `à la carte, Spanish peseta, per se, joie de vivre`. Examples of foreign words that are italicized include `mabinogi`, `omphalos`, and `peripeteia`. Because the status of foreign words changes continually, you will need to consult a current dictionary when you are not certain about whether to italicize a word.

Genera and species

Italicize the Latin names for the genera and species of plants and animals: `Ananas comosus (pineapple); Canis familiaris (dog).`

▪ Titles of Works

The guidelines below for designating and punctuating titles apply to titles included within your own writing and in notes and bibliography or lists of works cited for *Chicago Manual* and MLA formats. APA style has different rules concerning punctuation of the reference list (see Chapter 9), but within the body of your paper you should use the punctuation illustrated below, except where noted. Where underlining is shown here, APA requires italics instead.

TITLES IN ITALICS The titles of the following types of works should be italicized or underlined in your typescript.

Book: Descartes' Error: Emotion, Reason, and the Human Brain
Pamphlet: Regional Dances of Mexico
Journal: Critical Inquiry
Newspaper: St. Louis Post-Dispatch
Play: The Cherry Orchard
Long poem: The Prelude
Magazine: Atlantic Monthly
Film: Breakfast at Tiffany's
Ballet: Swan Lake
Opera: Don Giovanni
Record album, tape, or CD: Sgt. Pepper's Lonely Hearts Club Band
Painting: View of Toledo
Sculpture: Pietà
Musical composition identified by name (rather than by key or type of work): Pastoral Symphony
Legal case: Brown v. Board of Education
Name of vehicle: HMS Mauretania; space shuttle Atlantis

Marks of punctuation

Underline all marks of punctuation and spaces in a title. If a title appears at the end of a sentence, do not underline the final period. Similarly, do not extend italics to an end punctuation mark.

In defining his field of study, he referred readers to Comparative Literature as Academic Discipline: A Statement of Principles, Praxis, Standards.

TITLES IN QUOTATION MARKS The titles of the types of works listed below should be put in quotation marks.

Article in a journal: "Ageist Language in Psychological Research"
Article in a magazine: "Civil Liberties in Cyberspace"
Article in a newspaper: "Regents Name New President"
Article in an encyclopedia: "Huntington, Collis Potter"
Article in a compilation: "The Narrative Quality of Experience"
Short story: "The Pit and the Pendulum"
Short poem: "Fern Hill"
Song: "I Dream of Jeannie"
Chapter in a book: "Emergence of the Polis"
Lecture: "Résumé Writing and Effective Interviewing"
Unpublished thesis: "The Ambiente of Latin America in Five Novels by Graham Greene"

TITLES WITHOUT UNDERLINING OR QUOTATION MARKS The titles of sacred works, series, editions, and societies and words referring to the divisions of a book are neither underlined nor put in quotation marks.

Sacred writings: `Holy Bible, Mark, New Testament, Koran`
Series: `New Accents, The Brain, Approaches to Teaching Masterpieces of World Literature`
Editions: `Library of America, Norton Critical Edition`
Societies: `American Psychological Association, Association of American Petroleum Geologists`
Divisions of a book: `foreword, preface, introduction, appendix, glossary, chapter, act, volume, scene`

TITLES WITHIN TITLES Titles may include another title. On this matter *Chicago Manual* and MLA differ, as noted below. For APA, which does not make any recommendation, follow the more traditional form, *Chicago Manual.* Underline any end punctuation that belongs with the title, such as quotation marks, but not a period that concludes a sentence or bibliography entry.

When a title enclosed in quotation marks appears within an italicized title, retain and underline the quotation marks.

`Coleridge's "Kubla Khan"`
("Kubla Khan" is a short poem included here as part of the title of a book.)

When a title ordinarily enclosed in quotation marks appears within another title that is also ordinarily placed within quotation marks, change the interior quotation marks to single quotation marks.

`"A Reading of Coleridge's 'Kubla Khan'"`
("Kubla Khan" is a short poem mentioned in the title of an article.)

An underlined title that appears within a title in quotation marks remains underlined.

`"A Principle of Unity in Woolf's To the Lighthouse"`
(*To the Lighthouse* is a novel mentioned in the title of an article.)

When a title that is ordinarily underlined appears within another underlined title, MLA recommends leaving it without underlining or quotation marks.

`Imagery in Woolf's To the Lighthouse`
(*To the Lighthouse* is the title of a novel mentioned in the title of another book.)

Chicago Manual style prefers putting all interior titles, whether normally underlined or quoted, within quotation marks. The included titles of a novel and a short poem would be identical.

Imagery in Woolf's "To the Lighthouse"

Imagery in Coleridge's "Kubla Khan"

▪ Capitalization

The prose in a research paper should follow standard rules and conventions for capitalization.

Capitalization of titles in body of text

Capitalize the first and last words in titles and all other words with the exception of articles (*a, an, the*), coordinate conjunctions (*but, or, for, nor, yet, so*), prepositions (*to, at, before, between,* etc.), and the word *to* in an infinitive. Always capitalize the first and last words of a title or subtitle, the first word after a colon, and both elements of a hyphenated compound. Original capitalization may be changed to conform to these rules, but original spelling should not be changed.

Capitalization in APA format

APA capitalizes all words of four letters or more.

```
The Bias-Free Word Finder: A Dictionary of Nondiscriminatory
   Language

Across the River and into the Trees

The Ship Sails On

How to Succeed in Business without Really Trying

APA: How to Succeed in Business Without Really Trying

Emily Dickinson: The Mind of the Poet

University of Toronto Quarterly

"On Actors and Acting"

"The Lotus-Eaters"

"Thesis to Book: What to Get Rid Of"
```

Capitalization in reference lists and bibliographies

APA style capitalizes titles within the text according to the above guidelines, but in reference lists, APA capitalizes only the first word of the title, the first word after a colon or dash, and proper nouns (see Chapter 9, pages 250–251, 254). *Chicago Manual* and MLA observe the following guidelines in documentation and in the text.

Divisions of your paper

References to divisions of your own paper may be capitalized when they substitute for a title and are followed by a number or letter.

Chapter 7   Section 3   Appendix C

General references to a division are not capitalized.

the final chapter   this section   the preface   the glossary

Divisions in sources

References to divisions of sources are not capitalized: chapter 7 in Morrison, volume 3 of Pelikan's history. Tables and figures are capitalized, but not elements of them: column 3 in Smith's Table 7, note 5 in Figure 3.

Headings within the text

Headings in your text are capitalized according to the principles for capitalization of titles, except for the fifth level, in which only the first word is capitalized (see pages 47–48).

Headings in tables

In headings for tables, capitalize only the first word and proper nouns.

Words in foreign languages

Every foreign language has its own rules for capitalization of titles and names. See *The Chicago Manual of Style,* the *MLA Handbook for Writers of Research Papers,* or a dictionary for the language in question.

■ Numbers

In formal nonscientific writing, numbers from one to one hundred and numbers that can be expressed in one or two words—for example, seventy-five, three thousand, fifteen, and seven billion—should be spelled out. In addition, large round numbers may be spelled out even if they require more than two words. The word and connects a digit in the hundreds to a digit in the tens, as in two hundred and fifty, but is omitted above the hundreds, as in three thousand fifty or two million two hundred thousand. For large numbers you may also combine numbers and words: 7.5 million inhabitants.

In APA format, numbers one through ten are spelled out, except in the cases of mathematical calculations, statistics, or numbers grouped for purposes of comparison. Numbers above ten should always be written in numerals.

Numbers expressed in numerals

Use numerals for dates, times, ages, and precise sums of money; page, street, serial, and telephone numbers; fractions accompanied by a whole number, decimals, and percentages; quantities combined with abbreviations and symbols; numbers to be calculated; and scores and points on a scale.

Sentences should not begin with numerals, including dates. If a sentence must begin with a number, spell the number out, but whenever possible, rewrite the sentence.

Original Five hundred and seventeen people visited the gallery last week.

Revision Last week 517 people visited the gallery.

Punctuation of numbers

Numbers consisting of four or more digits have commas at the thousands and millions points. The exceptions are page numbers, street numbers, serial numbers, numbers to the right of the decimal point, and four-digit dates. In dates of five digits, insert a comma to mark the thousands.

Built in 1916, the elementary school at 10916 Main Street had a play area comprising 4,729 square feet of concrete and 57,128 square feet of lawn. Maintenance of the yard cost $56,157 last year.

The illustration is on page 1078.

The fossil dates from 9000 to 10,000 B.C.

He recorded the serial number as 77266319.

Pi is 3.14159265.

Fractions

A fraction should be spelled out in the text when it is not accompanied by a numeral: two-thirds of the population; a two-thirds majority; 2 3/4 pounds of apples. (APA does not hyphenate fractions used as nouns: two thirds of the population, but a two-thirds majority.) When you have a key or symbol that condenses a fraction into one space, use it: ¼, ½, ¾. For other fractions, use a slanted line without spacing to separate numerals: 2/3, 27 5/8.

Decimals and percentages

Numbers with decimal points and percentages are written in numerals. The word percent (spelled as one word) accompanies the number. In formal nonscientific writing, the percent symbol (%) should be used only in tables and figures; in scientific or technical papers, the percent symbol follows a numeral. In the absence of a number, the word percentage is used.

Sales have increased 37 percent this year, but the percentage increase was greater than last year's.

The current rate of inflation is 2.3 percent.

APA recommends using the percent symbol with all numbers, except at the beginning of a sentence.

The current rate of inflation is 2.3%.

Numbers in mathematical and statistical calculations

Textual reference to numbers derived from mathematical and statistical calculations, including those taken from figures and tables, should be in the form of numerals, even if the numbers might otherwise be written out.

Only 2 of the 30 tests were valid.

A ratio of 12:1.

A winning margin of 5,000 votes.

Numbers with abbreviations or symbols

Numbers accompanied by abbreviations or symbols are expressed in numerals: 6 ft, 27 mm, $9.99.

Dates in the text may be written in one of two ways. *Chicago Manual* and MLA prefer day-month-year order without commas.

`On 22 July 1999 the group met for the first time.`

APA prefers month-day-year order, with the year set off by commas.

`On July 22, 1999, the group met for the first time.`

When you refer to a month or season and a year, do not set off the year in commas.

`In January 2000 the mayor declared several snow days.`

`Summer 2001 had record heat waves.`

B.C. and A.D. The abbreviation `B.C.` (meaning "before Christ") follows the year. The abbreviation `A.D.` (*anno Domini* in Latin, or "in the year of our Lord") precedes the year. The designations `B.C.E.` ("before the Christian [or common] era") and `C.E.` (Christian [or common] era) follow the year.

`Agriculture changed little between 1900 B.C. and A.D. 1400.`

`Agriculture changed little between 1900 B.C.E. and 1400 C.E.`

MLA omits the periods in these abbreviations: `AD, BC, BCE, CE.`

Inclusive page numbers When citing inclusive pages, enter only the final two digits if all other numbers remain the same: 121–48, 300–07, 1813–16, 23976–78. Enter any numbers that have changed: 2989–3016, 23976–4801. Never use fewer than two digits, except for numbers below ten: 5–8, 1–2, but not 501–2. For numbers below one hundred, enter both digits even if the number in the tens place remains the same: 47–48, 55–69, 70–71.

Inclusive pages: APA In parenthetical notes and bibliographical entries, APA recommends entering complete page numbers both before and after the hyphen: 121–148, 300–307, 1813–1816, 23976–23978.

Inclusive years In references to inclusive years, give only the final two digits when the century remains the same: 1975–78, 1939–45, 1901–09, 155–82, 711–17. When the century changes, include the entire set of digits: 1890–1950, 400–1000, 1700–1900, 1994–2004.

Ordinal numbers Ordinal numbers designate place in a series: 1st, 2nd, 3rd, 4th, 5th, 6th, and so on. Variants for *second* and *third* are `2d` and `3d`. Although *Chicago Manual* gives preference to these variants, *Form and Style* uses the traditional and more common `2nd` and `3rd`.

Plurals of numbers Make numerals plural by adding an *-s* without intervening space or punctuation: 1920s, the '60s, his 30s. Plurals of numbers written out as words follow the rules for other words: his thirties, the nineteen twenties, trillions, at sixes and sevens.

Roman numerals Current usage discourages roman numerals in all types of writing. They are acceptable for designating individuals in a series, such as Henry VIII, Philip II, and John Smith III; in standard terminology, such as DSM IV; in numbering outlines; and in numbering preliminary matter in a dissertation or book. Otherwise, use arabic numerals.

Enumeration

You may wish to give some items special emphasis by designating them in a series with numerals or lowercase letters. When the list of items is short enough to be run smoothly into the text, identifying numerals are enclosed in parentheses.

The steps in writing a research paper include (1) choosing a topic, (2) preparing a working bibliography, (3) outlining the paper, (4) collecting information, and (5) writing the paper.

For a research paper that includes numbers or statistics, designate items with letters to avoid confusion.

When the length or number of items listed would create a cumbersome or confusing sentence if the list were run into the text, set off the list. When the items to be listed are complete sentences, use the following format:

The authors made the following recommendations for keeping European markets open:

1. Companies must step up their strategic planning in Europe. (The paragraph may continue.)

2. Business leaders outside Europe must realize that there is strength in numbers. (The paragraph may continue.)

3. Non-European companies must enlist their governments' help at the highest levels. (The paragraph may continue.)

If the listed items are words or phrases that are a grammatical part of the lead-in statement, they should be punctuated as a series and a period should be put at the end of the last item.

The syllabus for the seminar included sessions on

a. new systems of discourse,

b. the rhetorical inheritance,

c. literacy, and

d. measurement of writing ability.

If you need to include an outline within the text, the outline should follow the conventional format and sequence (see pages 22–23). When items enumerated in an outline are longer than one line, align the second and succeeding lines with the first word in the line above.

```
I. Carol Gilligan attempts to distinguish the moral
   development of women from that of men in In a Different
   Voice.
   A. Gilligan defines male morality as "the morality of
      justice."
   B. Gilligan describes female morality as "the morality
      of care."
```

Editing and Proofreading

Your paper should be accurate in every way, including style and mechanics. After you have revised your paper, paying attention to the interaction of content and style, you should edit it thoroughly, making corrections in mechanics and grammar, consulting reference books when necessary, and proofreading carefully.

Because writers are often too close to their work to view it objectively, an effective way to measure your audience's reaction is to read the paper to someone else. Reading the paper aloud to yourself can also be helpful. The passages over which you hesitate or stumble may need revision. Finishing the final draft a few days ahead of your deadline will give you an opportunity to improve your paper. You will be able to read and proofread and then set the paper aside so that you can return to it with a fresh perspective and a keen eye for rough spots and errors.

5 Tables and Figures

Tables and figures (the general name for any illustrative material, including graphs, maps, diagrams, and photographs) can buttress your argument by revealing complex relationships in a way that prose alone often cannot. Tables provide precise numbers and values and can place these in relationship to each other more effectively than prose. By providing a graphic perspective quickly, figures can effectively serve as a useful prelude to a more precise or detailed explanation in your text.

Many word-processing programs incorporate functions for the creation of tables and charts. If your word-processing program does not include the functions you need, you can choose among numerous varieties of other software to integrate with your word-processing software. In some cases you may have to or want to create some figures by hand.

Regardless of the medium you use to produce tables and figures, the same principles apply to introducing and presenting them in your paper. First, any table or figure included within your text or in an appendix must be mentioned in the text. If you leave readers on their own to figure out the relationship between a table and your argument, they might draw a conclusion different from the one you intended. Second, tables and figures should not contain more elements than are required to make your point. With large quantities and types of data you may need to construct more than one table. Tables and figures that contain duplicate information should usually be combined.

Tables

The data from which you draw your inferences and conclusions should be presented clearly and precisely. When you want readers to know the precise numbers or quantities you used to reach your conclusions, you need to include the raw data. Large quantities of statistics or numerical data usually should be formatted in the form of a table.

Not all statistics need be organized into a table, however. If you can have three or fewer statistics, you may present them within the text. For example, you would not tabulate the following numbers: "The 607 delegates, representing seventeen nations, voted 402 to 205 in favor of the resolution." Data that include 4 to 20 numbers may be presented as an informal table within the text.

Informal table, typed

```
Support for the candidates did not divide along gender

lines, as these results of an informal poll indicate:

                  Men      Women      Total

For Smith         17       16         33

For Brown         14       15         29

Total             31       31         62
```

Alternatively, you may create such a table with the Table function in your software or with another program, such as Excel or Lotus.

Computer-generated table:

Table 1. Sample Table with Two Variables on Each Axis

	Men	Women	Total
For Smith	17	16	33
For Brown	14	15	29
Total	31	31	62

When you have more variables or wish to demonstrate several kinds of relationships, computer software can organize it quickly and do many of the calculations.

Small tables

Tables small enough to fit on part of a page may be incorporated in your text. Complete paragraphs should precede and follow such illustrative material, as they do throughout this chapter.

Extensive data

Large sets of numbers belong in an appendix. Readers who wish to follow your verbal argument or focus on your conclusions should not be distracted by long expanses of statistics. Extensive data supporting your conclusions, particularly when you have compiled them yourself, should be available in an appendix.

▪ Relationship Between Tables and Text

The prose introduction to a table should explain how the data support your thesis. In addition, it should explain any principles governing the table and state the significance of the data.

A table should be constructed so that it can be read and understood without reference to the text. For those readers who wish to study only the statistical data, tables should be organized logically and explained fully in a caption, or title. Likewise, the text should be so complete that readers can follow the argument without referring to the tables. You should incorporate into the body of the paper enough analytical and summary statements derived from each table to provide coherent support for your conclusions.

Textual references to tables

Tables should be placed as close as possible to the discussion of the facts or data in the text. If a table appears within the two or three pages following the first reference to it, only the number of the table need be given in the text ("Table 3 shows . . . "). Tables that are farther away from their initial mention in the text should be referred to by the table number and page number ("Table 4 on page 13 shows . . . " or "Table 4 in Appendix B shows . . . "). Avoid using imprecise and potentially confusing phrases such as "in the following table" and "in the table above."

▪ Captions

Each table must have a caption, or title. A caption should not repeat material from the table column headings, and it should not contain abbreviations, even if you use them within the table. Also, the caption should not be an interpretation of the data presented in the table; rather, the caption should be a clear, concise description of the subject matter of the investigation or experiment in which the data were collected. Captions should take the form of phrases, not sentences.

Concision in table captions

Avoid excessively wordy or repetitive captions.

`Table 1. Results of a Survey of Butler College Students Concerning the Kinds of Computers They Used From 1990 to 2002`

Revised `Table 1. Computers Used by Butler College Students, 1990-2002`

Use participial constructions rather than relative clauses.

`Table 2. Numbers and Nationalities of International Students Who Attended American College and Universities, 1991-2001`

Revised `Table 2. International Students Attending American Colleges and Universities, 1991-2001`

Your table of contents should list all tables by the same number and caption you use within the text or in appendixes.

Place the caption above the table, flush with the left margin. The caption for a table begins with the word `Table` followed by its number, followed by a period, one space, and the caption. The rules for capitalization of all titles apply to captions for tables (see pages 93–94). The caption should not have end punctuation.

`Table 7. Distribution of U.S. Tax Dollars among Local, State, and Federal Governments, 1946 and 2000`

APA style

APA places the number of the table on a separate line, flush left, and begins the first line of the caption two spaces below, with one space between subsequent lines.

```
Table 7

Distribution of U.S. Tax Dollars Among Local, State, and
Federal Governments, 1946 and 2000
```

(APA capitalizes all words of four letters or more; in this caption APA capitalizes *among*, whereas *Chicago Manual* and MLA do not.)

▪ Numbering

Tables should be numbered with arabic (not roman) numerals in the order of the first mention in the text. They may be numbered consecutively through the entire paper or through individual chapters. If numbered by chapter, tables should be double-numbered. Table 3.7 designates the seventh table in Chapter 3; Table 4.1 the first table in Chapter 4. This system is particularly useful when you have numerous tables. In appendixes with multiple tables, confine the numbering to each appendix: Table B.2 designates the second table in Appendix B; Table C.3 designates the third table in Appendix C.

▪ Columns and Rows

The numbers and words arranged vertically in a table are called columns, and those running horizontally are called rows.

HEADINGS Each column should have a brief, descriptive heading that explains the nature of the information that follows below. You may use abbreviations in column headings if the meaning is obvious. When you need to abbreviate technical terms, use a footnote to explain the reference. Capitalize only the first word and any proper nouns in headings, and do not use end punctuation.

Center any subheading for a column within parentheses below the heading. If you need two or more levels of heads, use decked heads, as shown below. Two or more decked heads for columns are positioned beneath a spanner head, a head spanning the width of the columns. Use a horizontal rule to separate the spanner and column heads.

Table 2. Salary of Employee Compared to Satisfaction with Work Environment

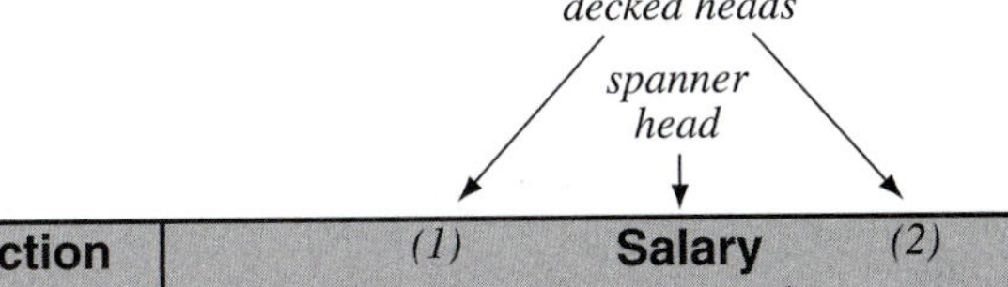

Satisfaction	(1) Salary Less than $21,000		(2) $21,000 or more		Total	
	No.	%	No.	%	No.	%
More Satisfied	13	29.5	74	60.7	87	52.4
Less Satisfied	31	70.5	48	39.3	79	47.6
Total	44	100.5	122	100.0	168	100.0

When a table consists of numerous columns or when you need to refer to specific columns frequently, you may number the columns from left to right, as above.

Horizontal rules

RULES (LINES) IN A TABLE Double horizontal rules, closely spaced, or a wide, bold single rule, should mark the top of the table. A single horizontal rule goes below the column headings—at least one-half space below the heading so as not to look like underlining—and a double rule or wide, bold single rule indicates the end of the table. When a table continues on to a second page, the bottom rule appears only at the end of the table, not at the end of each page.

Vertical rules

Vertical rules are optional, except when you need them to separate columns. APA does not use vertical rules.

▪ Footnotes for Tables

Tables may require footnotes to document the source of the data or to provide explanatory information.

Independent notes for each table

Each table should have an independent, self-contained set of footnotes, regardless of whether it appears within the text or in a separate section. Footnotes should be placed at the end of the table, even if the text of the paper uses endnotes.

General notes for entire tables

A note that applies to the table as a whole or to the title of the table is indicated by the word Note (italicized in APA style) followed by a period. The first and succeeding lines of the note should appear flush with the left margin, double-spaced, two spaces below the table. If you do not have the space for that format, you may use a reduced type size or single-spacing. Introduce a note containing bibliographical information with the word Note (italicized or underlined in APA format), followed by a period. Introduce the documentation of the source with the word From, not italicized or underlined, without end punctuation, followed by a reference to the source formatted according to the style sheet you are following.

Notes to specific items

Designate a note to a specific item, such as a particular heading or statistic, with a superscript. Lowercase letters or standard reference symbols, rather than numbers, should be used as superscripts when the table contains numbers.

Lowercase letters should begin with a and proceed alphabetically, as in superscript [a] and superscript [b]. When superscript letters might be confusing, as in tables consisting of mathematical or chemical equations, standard reference symbols should be used. The customary order of symbols is asterisk (*), dagger(†), section mark (§), two asterisks (**), two daggers (††), and so on. When tables run over more than one page, the list of symbols should be repeated on each page.

Placement of notes in tables

Superscripts should proceed in order across each row of the table from left to right: that is, across the first row, across the second row, and so on from the top of the table to the bottom, just as you would read the lines in a book.

When you have several types of notes, you should number and group them by type in the following order: (1) general notes, (2) specific notes, and (3) probability-level notes.

Place all notes flush against the left margin without indention. You may want to consider the left side of the table as the left margin, even though it may differ from margins within the text.

You may place each note on a separate line, if you have space, or run them consecutively, leaving one space after the period for each note before the superscript for the next note.

▪ Large Tables

Tables created with computer software can be reduced or turned vertically, as space indicates. If a table cannot be fitted onto one page, divide the table into two (or more) parts and label each part with the same table caption, followed by a comma and the word `continued`. Repeat the headings and subheadings on each page. For research papers that are presented or bound with single rather than facing pages, you need to be certain that your reader can comprehend the second page of a table without having to flip back and forth.

Many of the newer software programs include functions that automatically create table divisions and column headings. When activated, a command such as "Heading Rows Repeat" in Microsoft Word breaks the table across pages and repeats the column headings at the top of each page.

Figures

The term *figure* refers to any kind of graphic representation or illustration, whether in the text or in an appendix. Figures include graphs, charts, drawings, diagrams, maps, photographs, blueprints, and some kinds of computer printouts. If you plan to use such illustrative materials, be sure that you possess or have access to the skills and materials required to produce them.

Some software programs include functions for generating some kinds of figures and graphics and inserting them into your text. The greater the number of computer-generated graphics, the more computer memory required and the greater storage space consumed by the document. Make certain that you have enough memory on your computer to accommodate all the graphics you will need.

Figures enable you to demonstrate the relationships among three or more dimensions of data on the two-dimensional space of a piece of paper. They should be designed and used as visual representations of your evidence. You should take full advantage of figures, in new or old media, to reinforce or enhance your argument in the text, but such illustrations should not be treated as ends in themselves. You should have no more of them than you require, and each of them should be as compact and uncluttered as possible. If you use color in a figure, be certain that it works to clarify your information.

■ Graphs

Line, bar, area, and volume graphs effectively convey quantitative and proportional data. Like other figures, they illustrate relationships, and they should be designed to convey information that cannot fully be communicated in prose. If you create a graph one way and find that it does not clarify your point, or worse, that it obscures it, try using another kind of graph to present the material.

Newer word-processing and spreadsheet programs offer a library of options for graph presentation. A writer may create a spreadsheet, develop the graphical representation of the data contained in the spreadsheet, and import the table or the graph into the word-processing document. Several techniques for data and graph importation exist, such as copying graphical elements from one document and pasting them into another, and creating a hotlink, an automatic shift to another document. When a spreadsheet is hotlinked to your word-processing document, changes in the spreadsheet will automatically be transferred to the appropriate figure in the text.

LINE GRAPHS Line graphs are appropriate for demonstrating trends: their increase, decrease, fluctuations, or constancy. Line graphs show the difference between one or more elements in relation to some other variable. They are particularly suitable for plotting values, which are placed along either the left- or right-hand side of the graph, over the time intervals designated on the bottom of the graph. The line indicating the trend should be bolder than other lines in the figure.

When you want to plot two or more elements against each other, you may group the lines into a grouped-line chart, which when it contains three or more lines is called a spaghetti chart. Represent each additional line differently, using long dashes, short dashes, dots, or different colors to distinguish them. Your most important trend line should be bold or distinctive enough to stand out against the rest, and it should be more prominent visually than other lines in the graph. (See sample page 106.)

When you have too many trend lines for a coherent grouped line graph or when you want to emphasize each one against the principle trend, you may want to create several line graphs, with each line plotted against the most significant one for your argument.

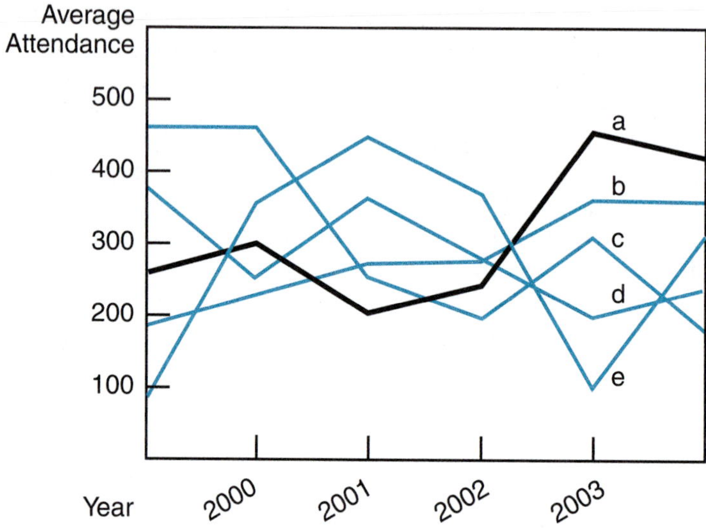

Figure 4. Sample of overly-complicated spaghetti chart.

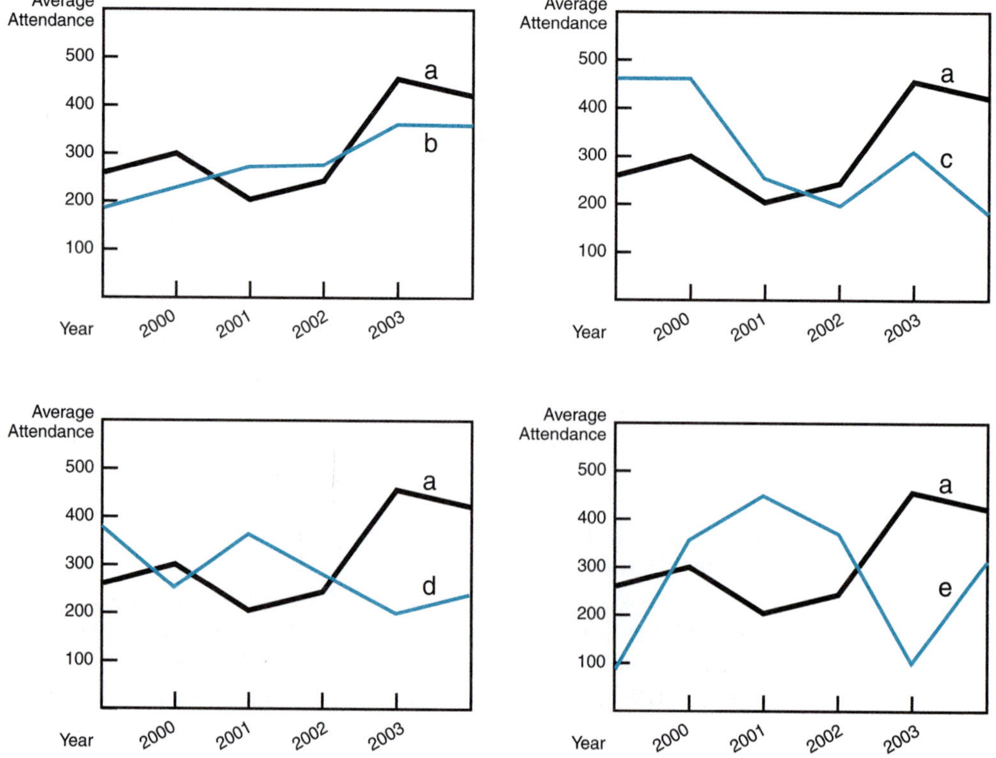

Figure 5. Sample of elements in spaghetti chart separated for clarity.

PIE CHARTS A pie chart works well for comparing the components of a whole. The full circle indicates the total, or 100 percent, and the sizes of the pieces within it indicate percentages of the whole. With a pie chart the reader can see the relationships of each part to the other parts and to the whole. Because the reader should be able to grasp the relative sizes quickly, the pie chart does not work well with more than six or seven components. You may be able to reduce the number of pieces in the pie by grouping some components that are not individually significant for your argument. Arrange the components clockwise, starting at the top with the most important and progressing clockwise to the least important. You may also want to shade one or more segment, extract one segment from the whole, or leave one piece missing, whichever works best for your purpose.

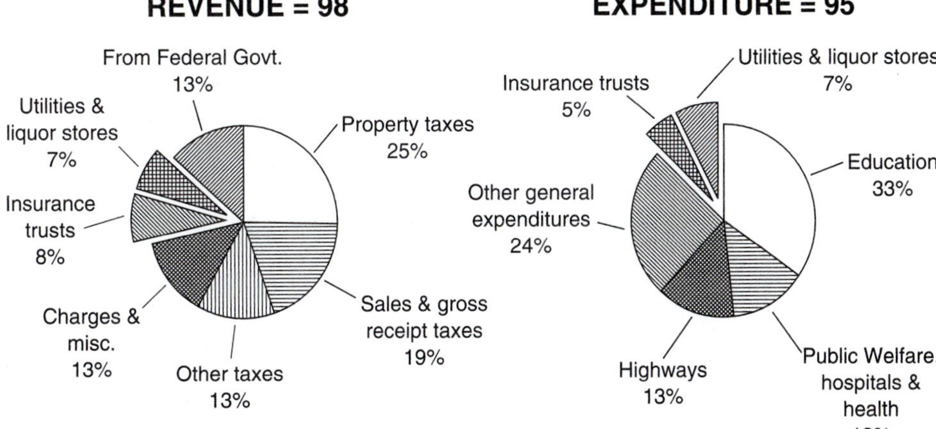

Figure 6. Pie charts with segments separated for emphasis.

Figure 2.4. Distribution of state and local government revenue and expenditure in 1966 (in billions of dollars).

APA-style caption

Figure 2.4

Distribution of state and local government revenue and expenditure in 1966 (in billions of dollars).

BAR GRAPHS Bar graphs illustrate comparisons of more than one total for individual entities. Shading or colors can be used to distinguish the segments of bar graphs.

Horizontal bars work for comparing labeled items, such as industries, persons, universities, or nations. The bars should be wider than the space between them. Because bars are not suited to indicating precise values, you may round off numbers and fractions when they make little difference on the bar scale. Horizontal bars usually accommodate headings better than vertical bars.

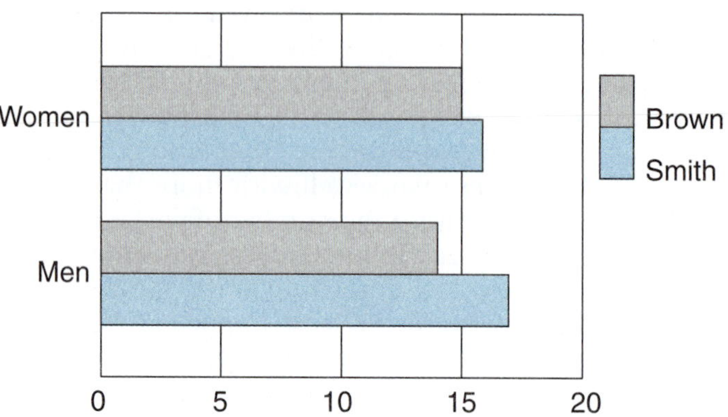

Figure 6. Example of simple horizontal bar graph.

Vertical bars work best to show changes in the relationship of two or more elements over time or some other series. Groups of vertical columns may be grouped, joined, or overlapped to emphasize their similar relationship to the point of reference on the bottom scale. With two or more vertical bars grouped at each interval, you will need to distinguish them clearly from one another so that the reader can identify each one quickly (see page 113).

Variations on the vertical bar graph include columns segmented to show how several components contribute to the makeup of the whole. The entire bar represents 100 percent, and the segments represent a percentage of the whole (see page 112).

The step-column bar graph, which presents bars without intervening spaces (as in Figure 6 above), can be effective to demonstrate relative quantities and dramatic changes.

PRESENTATION OF NUMERICAL DATA IN GRAPHS The following conventions govern the presentation of numerical data in graphs and charts. When limited space or some other obstacle makes use of the convention awkward, make sure your system is readily comprehensible.

1. Scales of numerical value should read from left to right and usually from bottom to top.
2. If one or both scales have a zero point, it should be indicated, even if a break in the continuity of the scale must be drawn.
3. Scales that are based on percentages should indicate clearly the basis of comparison.
4. Scale values should be placed toward the outside of the figure; normally, this is to the left of the vertical scale and below the horizontal scale.
5. The exact numerical data from which a graph is produced should be included either in the figure or in an accompanying table.
6. A key or legend must be included when symbols or distances are not otherwise explained.

ILLUSTRATIONS Graphics may be created with digital cameras, scanners, and graphic software such as Adobe Photoshop. With newer word-processing programs, graphic elements may be saved in any of several graphic formats, including .tiff, .pic, .jpg, and .gif, all of which are ways of compressing information in digital form. When one wishes to use the graphics for a print document, the .tiff or .pic format usually provides higher quality than do the .jpg and .gif formats. If the document will later be converted to a Web page, the graphics should be saved in either .jpg or .gif formats.

There still may be times when you will want to present an illustration, such as a photograph or map, in its original paper form. Such illustrations should be mounted on paper at least as heavy as that you use for printing. Use rubber cement or, to avoid making permanent marks on the illustration, a dry-mounting technique.

▪ Relationship between Figures and Text

A figure should be constructed and labeled so that it may be read and understood without reference to the text. Also, the text should be so complete that readers can follow the argument without referring to the figures. The prose introduction to a figure should elaborate and explain the ways it relates to your argument. Incorporate into the body of the paper enough analytical and summary statements derived from each figure to provide a coherent support for your conclusions.

Textual references to figures

Figures should be placed as close as possible to the discussion of the material illustrated. If a figure appears within the two or three pages following the first reference to it, only the number of the figure need be given in the text ("Figure 3 shows . . . "). Figures that are farther away from their initial mention in the text should be referred to by the figure number and page number ("Figure 4 on page 13 shows . . . " or "Figure 4 in Appendix B shows . . . "). Avoid using imprecise and potentially confusing phrases such as "in the following figure or "in the figure above."

Captions for figures

Each figure must have a descriptive caption, or title, which should be a clear, concise phrase (not a sentence). Avoid excessively wordy or repetitive constructions such as "Graph representing."

Place the caption below the figure, flush with the left margin. The caption begins with the word `Figure` followed by its number, followed by a period. Capitalize only the first word of a figure caption, and follow the caption with a period. The caption may be followed by one or more explanatory sentences that guide the reader to interpreting the illustration.

Numbering

Like tables, figures should be numbered with arabic (not roman) numerals. Label all illustrations—whether maps, photographs, graphs, or other materials—as figures. Figures may be numbered consecutively through each chapter or throughout the entire paper, but not through the appendixes. Alternatively, figures, like tables, may be double-numbered by chapter. Figure 1.1 would be the first figure in Chapter 1; Figure 2.2 would be the second figure in Chapter 2.

▪ Notes for Figures

Figures may require notes to document the source of the data or to provide explanatory information.

Independent notes for each figure

Each figure should have an independent, self-contained set of notes, regardless of whether it appears within the text or in a separate section. Notes may be placed either at the bottom of the figure, or if space permits, within the figure. Such notes should not interfere or overlap the figure. Keep them short and use a modern sans-serif typeface, one without extensions on the ends of letters, like this Century Gothic. You may reduce the type size as long as it remains readable.

General notes for entire figure

A note that applies to the entire figure should be placed below the figure. Use a numerical superscript and begin the note without any intervening space. The first and succeeding lines of the note should appear flush with the left margin, double-spaced, two spaces below the figure. If you do not have the space for that format, you may use a reduced type size or single-spacing. Introduce a note containing bibliographical information with the word `From`, either italicized or underlined, with the reference to the source immediately following.

TABLES AND FIGURES

Sample Pages

A Vertical bar graph with segmented columns 112

B Vertical bar graph with paired columns 113

C Grouped-line graph 114

D Two short tables on a page with text 115

E Map with superimposed arrows and labels 116

F Photograph with elements designated 117

G Long table divided into two parts, with headings repeated 118

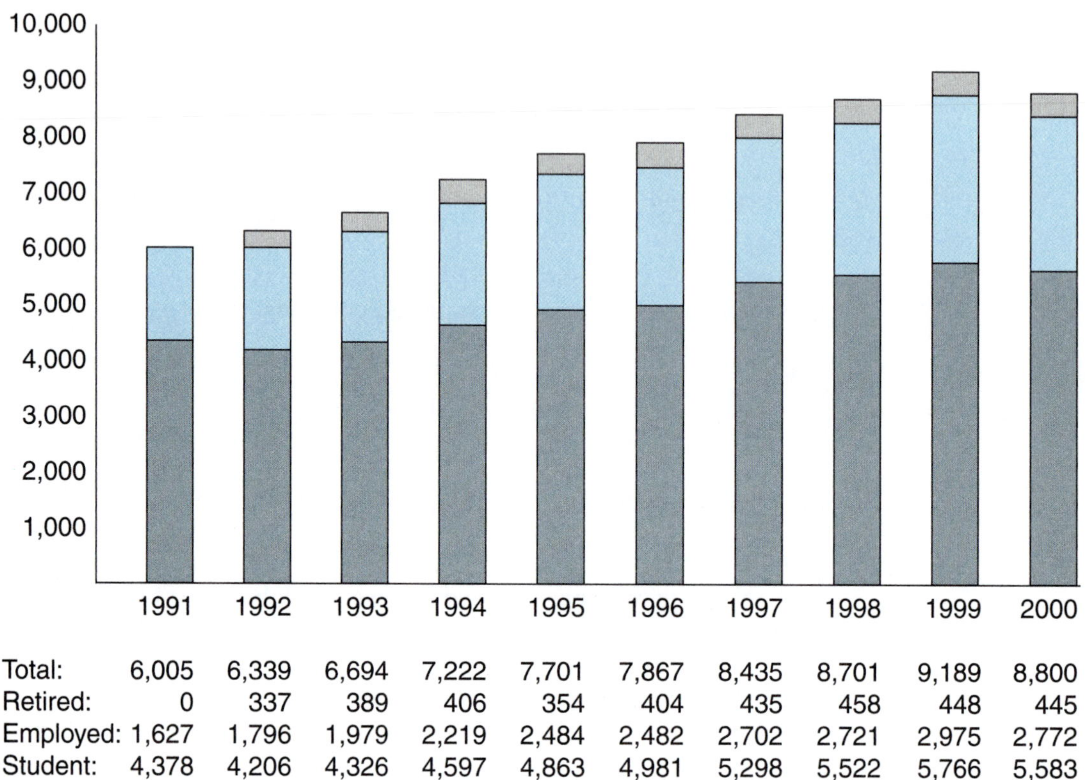

	1991	1992	1993	1994	1995	1996	1997	1998	1999	2000
Total:	6,005	6,339	6,694	7,222	7,701	7,867	8,435	8,701	9,189	8,800
Retired:	0	337	389	406	354	404	435	458	448	445
Employed:	1,627	1,796	1,979	2,219	2,484	2,482	2,702	2,721	2,975	2,772
Student:	4,378	4,206	4,326	4,597	4,863	4,981	5,298	5,522	5,766	5,583

Figure 6. Sample vertical bar graph with segmented columns.

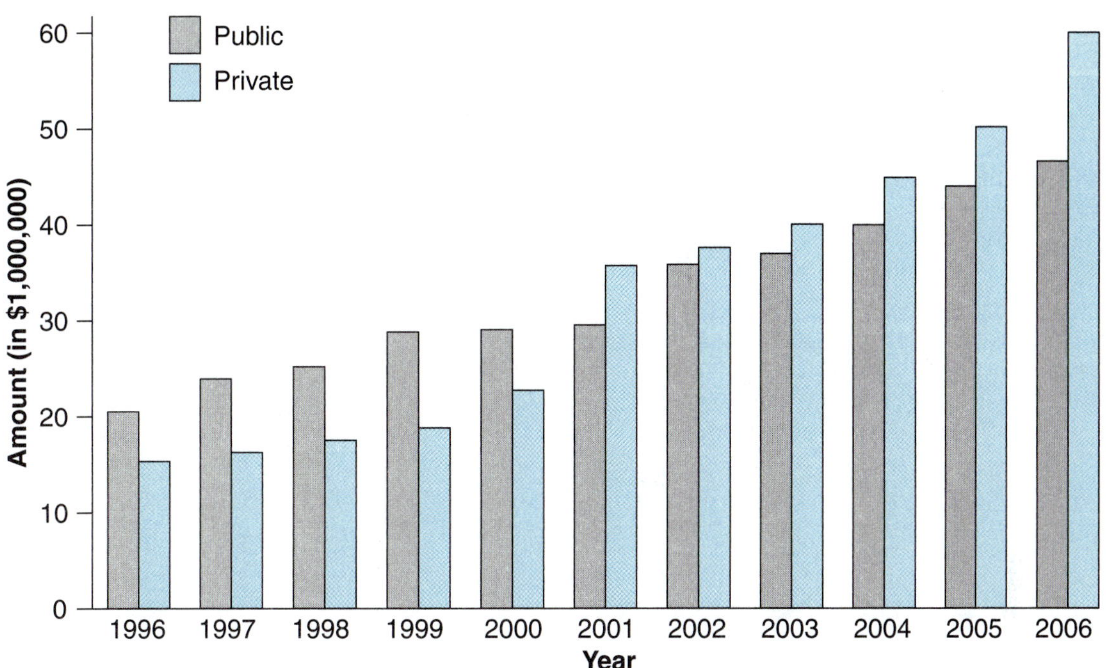

Figure 7.2. Amounts of scholarship aid to students at Bennett University from public and private sources, 1996-2006.

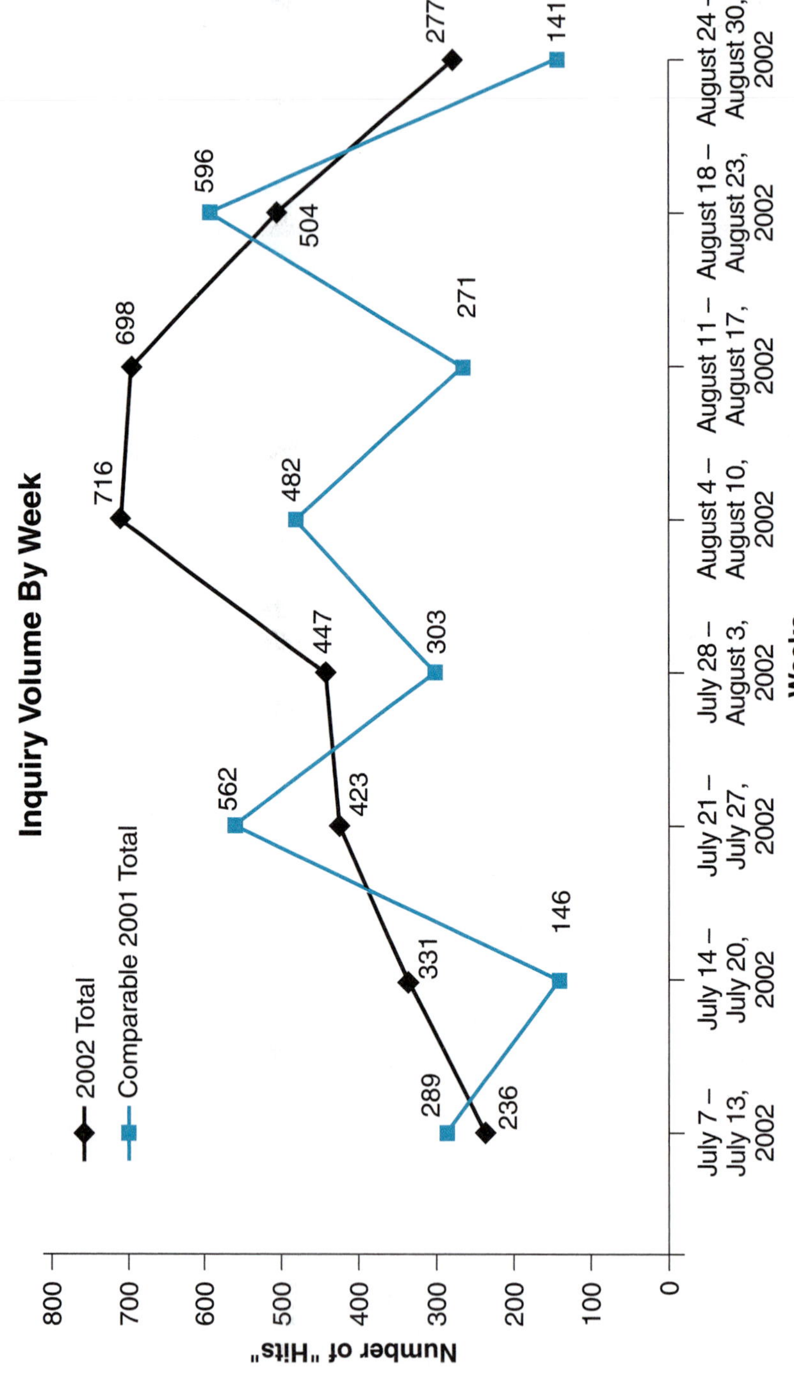

Figure 5.3. Volume of "hits" to Butler and Smith homepage <www.ButlerandSmith.com> July 7, 2002–August 30, 2002 compared to the same period in 2001.

Grouped-line graph

Table 3

A Comparison of DAT Subtest Scores and Ninth-Grade Semester Grades for Algebra

DAT subtest	N	r	Percentage of efficiency	Mean	S.D.
Verbal reasoning	129	.31[a]	4.61	25.85	8.46
Numerical ability	132	.51[a]	13.40	19.10	7.06
Abstract reasoning	124	.29[a]	4.00	34.00	8.44
Space relations	123	.20[b]	2.02	47.85	19.94

[a]Correlation significant at the .01 level.

[b]Correlation significant at the .05 level.

Table 4 shows correlations of the Differential Aptitude Test subtest scores with grades in Spanish. The correlations of .57 (Verbal Reasoning), .43 (Spelling), and .58 (Sentences) were significant at the .01 level.

Table 4

A Comparison of DAT Subtest Scores and Ninth-Grade Semester Grades for Spanish

DAT subtest	N	r	Percentage of efficiency	Mean	S.D.
Verbal reasoning	74	.57a	17.15	22.10	8.46
Spelling	68	.43a	9.72	44.95	22.53
Sentences	72	.58a	18.54	26.80	13.17

[a]Correlation significant at the .01 level.

Two short tables on a page with text

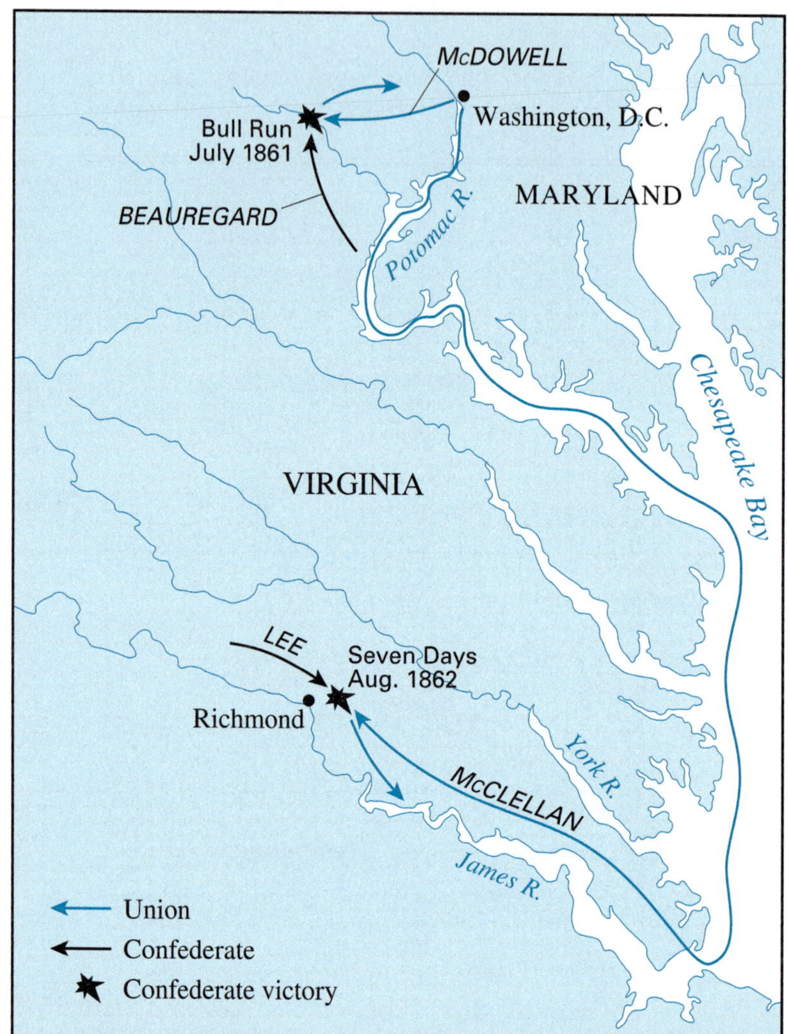

Figure 7. Region in which Union armies aggressively used water routes.

Source: Mary Beth Norton, *A People and a Nation,* 5th brief ed. (Boston: Houghton Mifflin, 1999), 278.

Map with superimposed arrows and labels

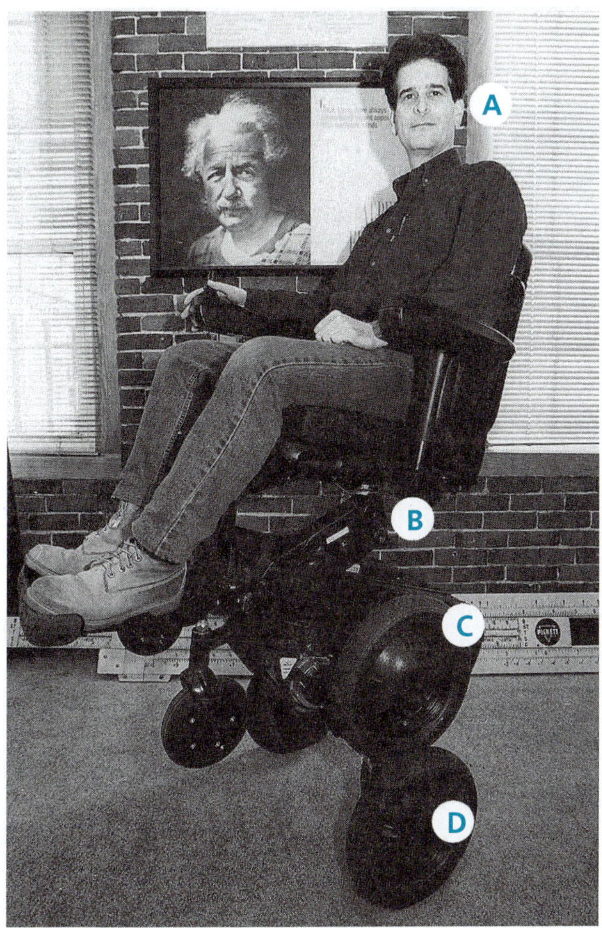

Figure 6. Ibot all-terrain wheelchair.

A User rises to eye level with standing person.

B Seat rises (shown in raised position).

C Three-computer redundancy protects against electronic failure.

D Chair balances on two wheels.

Table 8. Total Fall Enrollment in Degree-granting Institutions, 1999

(in thousands)

Attendance status, and type and control of institution	Total			Undergraduate			First-professional			Graduate		
	Total	Men	Women	Total	Men	Women	Total	Men	Women	Total	Men	Women
Total	**14,791**	**6,491**	**8,301**	**12,681**	**5,559**	**7,122**	**303**	**165**	**138**	**1,807**	**766**	**1,041**
Full-time	**8,786**	**4,026**	**4,761**	**7,735**	**3,516**	**4,219**	**271**	**147**	**124**	**781**	**363**	**418**
Part-time	6,005	2,465	3,540	4,946	2,044	2,903	33	19	14	1,026	403	623
Total 4-year	**9,199**	**4,103**	**5,095**	**7,089**	**3,172**	**3,917**	**303**	**165**	**138**	**1,807**	**766**	**1,041**
Full-time	6,642	3,057	3,585	5,591	2,547	3,044	271	147	124	781	363	418
Part-time	2,556	1,046	1,510	1,498	625	873	33	19	14	1,026	403	623
Total 2-year	**5,593**	**2,387**	**3,205**	**5,593**	**2,387**	**3,205**	-	-	-	*	*	*
Full-time	2,144	969	1,176	2,144	969	1,176	-	-	-	*	*	*
Part-time	3,448	1,419	2,030	3,448	1,419	2,030	-	-	-	*	*	*
Public, total	**11,309**	**4,941**	**6,368**	**10,110**	**4,431**	**5,679**	**123**	**64**	**59**	**1,077**	**446**	**630**
Full-time	6,224	2,852	3,372	5,660	2,581	3,079	117	61	56	447	210	238
Part-time	5,085	2,090	2,996	4,450	1,850	2,600	6	3	3	629	237	393
Public 4-year	**5,970**	**2,670**	**3,300**	**4,771**	**2,160**	**2,611**	**123**	**64**	**59**	**1,076**	**446**	**630**
Full-time	4,293	1,984	2,309	3,729	1,713	2,015	117	61	56	447	210	238
Part-time	1,677	686	991	1,042	446	596	6	3	3	629	237	392
Public 2-year	**5,339**	**2,272**	**3,068**	**5,339**	**2,271**	**3,068**	-	-	-	*	*	*
Full-time	1,931	868	1,063	1,931	868	1,063	-	-	-	*	*	*
Part-time	3,408	1,404	2,005	3,408	1,404	2,004	-	-	-	*	*	*
Private, total	**3,482**	**1,549**	**1,932**	**2,571**	**1,128**	**1,443**	**180**	**101**	**79**	**730**	**320**	**441**
Full-time	2,562	1,174	1,388	2,075	935	1,141	154	86	68	334	154	180
Part-time	919	375	544	496	194	302	27	15	11	397	166	231
Private 4-year	**3,229**	**1,434**	**1,795**	**2,318**	**1,013**	**1,305**	**180**	**101**	**79**	**730**	**320**	**411**
Full-time	2,349	1,073	1,276	1,862	834	1,028	154	86	68	334	154	180
Part-time	879	360	519	456	179	277	27	15	11	397	166	231
Private 2-year	**253**	**116**	**137**	**253**	**116**	**137**	-	-	-	-	-	-
Full-time	213	101	112	213	101	112	-	-	-	-	-	-
Part-time	40	15	25	40	15	25	-	-	-	-	-	-
Not-for-profit, total	**3,052**	**1,334**	**1,718**	**2,183**	**932**	**1,251**	**179**	**101**	**78**	**690**	**301**	**388**
Full-time	2,207	994	1,214	1,752	769	983	153	86	68	302	139	163
Part-time	844	340	504	431	163	267	26	15	11	388	162	226

Long table divided into two parts, with headings repeated

Table 8, cont.

(in thousands)

Attendance status, and type and control of institution	Total			Undergraduate			First-professional			Graduate		
	Total	Men	Women	Total	Men	Women	Total	Men	Women	Total	Men	Women
Not-for-profit, 4-year	**2,989**	**1,308**	**1,682**	**2,120**	**9,06**	**1,215**	**179**	**101**	**78**	**690**	**301**	**388**
Full-time	2,160	972	1188	1705	747	958	153	86	68	302	139	163
Part-time	829	335	494	416	158	257	26	15	11	388	162	226
Not-for-profit, 2-year	**62**	**26**	**36**	**62**	**26**	**36**	**-**	**-**	**-**	**-**	**-**	**-**
Full-time	47	22	26	47	22	26	-	-	-	-	-	-
Part-time	15	5	10	15	5	10	-	-	-	-	-	-
For-profit, total	**430**	**215**	**215**	**388**	**196**	**192**	**1**	**1**	*	**41**	**18**	**22**
Full-time	355	180	175	323	166	157	1	*	*	31	14	17
Part-time	75	35	40	66	31	35	1	*	*	9	4	5
For-profit 4-year	**239**	**126**	**113**	**198**	**107**	**91**	**1**	**1**	*	**41**	**18**	**22**
Full-time	189	101	88	157	86	71	1	*	*	31	14	17
Part-time	50	25	25	41	21	20	1	*	*	9	4	5
For-profit, 2-year	**191**	**89**	**101**	**191**	**89**	**101**	**-**	**-**	**-**	**-**	**-**	**-**
Full-time	166	79	87	166	79	87	-	-	-	-	-	-
Part-time	25	10	15	25	10	15	-	-	-	-	-	–

– Not available.
* Less than 500.
Note. Data are for 4-year and 2-year degree-granting higher education institutions that were eligible to participate in Title IV federal financial aid programs. Detail may not sum to total due to rounding.
U.S. Department of Education, National Center for Education Statistics, Integrated Postsecondary Education Data System (IPEDS), "Fall Enrollment" survey, and unpublished data. (March 2001).
http://nces.ed.gov/pub2001/proj01/tables/tableE1.asp. Accessed on January 31, 2002.

Second page of long table, with headings repeated

6 The Finished Copy

This chapter provides information about turning the final draft of your research paper into a finished copy that will be acceptable to your instructor or institution or to the publication to which you submit it.

The Final Draft

Before you begin to think about producing the finished copy, you should have a completely accurate, thoroughly polished final draft. You will save time in the long run if, from the outset of the research and writing processes, you observe the format requirements for front and back matter, headings, margins, indention, notes and bibliography, placement of documentation, spacing, and so on.

Advisers of theses and dissertations often wish to approve the final draft and some sample pages before you begin to prepare the finished copy.

Equipment and Supplies

The equipment you need to produce the finished copy includes a word processor and printer with appropriate software. In addition, you should have a supply of paper that will suffice to allow you to print out sections, correct them by hand, and then print them again, if necessary.

Computer printer

You will want to use a printer that produces clean, clear copy in letter-quality type. Dot-matrix printers, now almost entirely supplanted by letter-quality printers of various types, including ink-jet and laser, may not be acceptable, particularly for a dissertation that will be photocopied rather than set into type.

Type size and typeface

The preferred type size for the text of research papers and dissertations is twelve spaces or letters to the inch. Ten spaces to the inch is the smallest acceptable size.

Most software now permits you to choose from a wide array of typefaces. Unusual typefaces—extra-large, or ornate—should not be used for theses or dissertations, and they rarely are acceptable in reports written for academic credit. Choose a standard font, such as Courier or Times New Roman.

Software If you plan to produce tables or figures on your computer, you need appropriate software that may be integrated into a word-processing program or installed as a separate program on your computer. Also, you may need software with functions that enable you to print symbols or foreign language characters. If you want to submit your paper on a disk, CD, or as an e-mail attachment, format it in the computer language requested by your reader or translate it into a universal language, such as ASCII, the American Standard Code for Information Interchange, or text only. For information on preparing a manuscript to be submitted electronically, consult *Chicago Guide to Preparing Electronic Manuscripts for Authors and Publishers* (Chicago: University of Chicago Press, 1987) or *Handbook for Academic Authors,* by Beth Luey (New York: Cambridge University Press, 1995), chapter 11.

Special symbols Any symbol not available on your software or printer should be neatly handwritten in black ink.

Toner cartridge Particularly when you anticipate a rush to finish (you nearly always have less time at the end than you expect), be sure you have a backup toner cartridge on hand. Even though printers often give hints that the cartridge is running out of ink, with lightened areas or streaks, you may not have time to find a replacement.

Paper Use a good-quality bond, of twenty-pound weight and eight and one-half by eleven inches in size, for both the original copy and the photocopies of your research paper.

Copies Keep a current paper copy of your electronic documents, as well as a backup copy on disk. Even though the constant updating may be a nuisance, it can protect you from loss of work that can result from such events as power outages or computer errors and failures. Any copies submitted with the original should be photocopies. All pages of each photocopy should be identical in weight, color, and texture of paper.

Spell checker Make certain that you have spelled everything correctly, either by referring to a standard dictionary or by using a spell checker on your computer, or both. Use of a spell checker helps detect typographical errors as well as misspelled words; however, most checkers do not pick up the error if you type the wrong word, such as *their* for *there*, but spell it correctly. Once you have located an error in a computer-generated text, you can use a "find-and-replace" function, available in most word-processing programs, to search for and correct all instances of the mistake. Remember that your spell checker may use conventions other than those required by your style sheet.

Printing Your Paper

This section discusses formatting conventions for the elements of theses and dissertations. To follow the spacing requirements outlined here, you may have to change some of the default settings on your software. When you cannot make the computer behave as you would like, consult your adviser about using an approximation of the required format.

Numbering of Pages

Activate the function for numbering pages starting with the first page. Use the setting that positions numerals in the upper right-hand corner one inch from the top of the page, flush with the right margin. If you are typing double-spaced material, you can simply press the Enter or Return key to provide the required one full line of blank space between the numeral and the first line of text.

MLA format

MLA recommends using a running head, or header, composed of the last name of the writer followed by one space followed by the page number, without any intervening punctuation (`Jones 2` or `Smith 273`), one-half inch from the top of the page. One line of space separates the header from the first line of the text, which sits approximately one inch from the top of the page.

APA format

For the running head, APA recommends a shortened version of the title, up to a maximum of fifty spaces, including spacing, punctuation, and page number, as in

```
Equality of Access  5
```

for the fifth page of a paper entitled "Equality of Access in Public Higher Education." Place the header one inch below the top margin and leave one line of space between the header and the first line of text.

Preliminary matter in research papers

In a research paper, the title page and outline should not be numbered or counted as pages. The first page of the text of a research paper is page one.

Front matter in theses and dissertations

In a thesis or dissertation, front matter, such as the abstract and the approval sheet, should not be numbered or counted as part of the thesis or dissertation. The title page and copyright page should be counted but not numbered. Use lowercase roman numerals for front matter. For the text, begin the numbering again in arabic numerals, which should run consecutively through the text and continue through the back matter. Center page numbers for front matter one inch from the bottom of the page. Leave at least one line of space between the last line of the front-matter text and the page number.

Articles for APA journals

APA numbers the title page and all succeeding pages with continuous arabic numerals.

Spacing

Follow whatever policies on spacing you select throughout your paper. Conventions and requirements for spacing exist not to create additional hurdles but to make your paper readable.

MARGINS Margins should measure a minimum of one inch on all sides. Place page numbers and running heads one inch from either the top or bottom of the paper, except in MLA format, where you should place them one-half inch from the top. For a dissertation to be bound for library use, follow university requirements for spacing of the text.

Justify the left-hand margin of your text, but not the right-hand margins. That is, words should not be spaced out so that the right margin is even.

Justification often leaves irregular, unattractive spacing that interferes with reading and distorts the spacing of the documentation.

INDENTION Indent the first line of a paragraph five spaces. Bring all subsequent lines to the left margin.

For indention of set-off quotations, see pages 63–65.

CENTERED MATERIAL Any material to be centered on a page, such as first-level headings and set-off poetry, should be centered between margins, not between the edges of the page. Most computer programs allow you to center a line automatically either before or after entering the words.

DIVISION OF WORDS, NUMBERS, AND LINES OF TEXT When you need to divide a word, place the break between syllables. Most word-processing programs have a function that will hyphenate words automatically.

Because there are numerous situations in which you should not hyphenate words in a text even if the break is correct with respect to the syllables, you may wish to turn off the hyphenation function for the entire paper.

At the end of a line, one-letter and two-letter divisions, such as *a-ble*, *a-tone*, *de-velop*, *consecrat-ed*, or *entire-ly*, are not acceptable. The word should be written on one line, or another division point should be used: *conse-crated*, for example. Compound words should be divided between the elements that make up the compound: *volley-ball* rather than *vol-leyball.* Break hyphenated compounds only at the hyphen. When the appearance of a part of a word would lead to confusion about pronunciation (as in *wo-men*), the word should not be broken.

When a word cannot be included in its entirety or properly divided and hyphenated within the established margin, the entire word should be placed on the next line. No more than two successive lines should end with hyphenated words. Words should not be broken between pages. Also, try to avoid carrying over just one line of a paragraph to the following page. APA does not permit division of words in final copy.

Elements considered as whole and not divided

The following elements should never be divided: letters that are the names of radio or television stations, government agencies, institutions, or companies; the name of the month and the day; years; hours of the day; monetary expressions; and parts of an equation.

KWLZ RFC March 2 $6x + 4y = 27$

$C + O_2 = CO_2$ $1,378.50 525 B.C.E. 4:00 a.m.

In the case of proper names, the given name and surname or initials and surname should be on the same line when possible; very long names are an exception.

Very long formulas or equations may be set on centered lines by themselves, if necessary, to avoid breaking. If an equation is so long and complex that it must be run over to another line, the break should come if possible before the equal sign (in algebraic equations) or after the arrow (in chemical equations).

ALIGNMENT OF NUMERALS When numerals are arranged in vertical lists, both arabic and roman numerals should be aligned on the right side. This alignment makes the left side uneven, but it is the accepted form. When starting a column, make space allowance for the longest number to be listed. Columns of figures should appear as follows:

```
      I.            1
     II.            7
    III.           18
    XIV.          296
 XXXIII.       26,173
XXXVIII.    1,008,957
```

Numbers with decimals are aligned on the decimal points.

```
  7.9

123.657

 54.4

  7.3333
```

PUNCTUATION Periods, colons, commas, question marks, and semicolons follow the previous letter without spacing. One space follows a period, colon, semicolon, and comma. Dashes are indicated by two consecutive hyphens (--), which you can have your program automatically change to a dash. Neither hyphens nor dashes have space on either side of them.

`She needs these materials: one saw, one hammer, and one`

`nail.`
(one space after a colon in text)

`New York: Random House`
(one space after a colon in facts of publication)

<u>`Writing the Research Paper: A Guide and Sourcebook`</u>
(one space after a colon between title and subtitle)

`To err is human; to forgive, divine.`
(one space after semicolon)

`The stock--American Can--sold above par.`
(no space on either side of a dash)

`He won by a two-thirds majority.`
(no space on either side of a hyphen)

LEADERS On pages containing the table of contents and the list of tables and figures, you may use leaders, or spaced periods, to guide the reader's eye. They must be arranged so that the periods are aligned vertically and will end at the same point on the right-hand side, usually about two or three spaces before the end material.

▪ Quotations

SUPERSCRIPTS Within the text, a superscript indicating a footnote or endnote should be placed without any intervening space after the end punctuation, including quotation marks. In notes, the superscript should be indented five spaces and followed by one space.

RUN-IN PROSE QUOTATIONS Run short prose quotations (fewer than four typed lines, or about forty words) into the text and enclose them in double quotation marks. If the original excerpt contains a direct quotation, change the double quotation marks around the internal quotation to single quotation marks.

SET-OFF PROSE QUOTATIONS Set off long quotations (more than four typed lines) in indented, block-style paragraphs. Unlike run-in quotations, quotations that are set off are not enclosed in quotation marks.

The major style manuals call for double-spacing set-off quotations, particularly in materials that will be typeset by a printer. Separate set-off quotations from the text by one line of space both above and below. Indent set-off quotations five spaces from the left and indent an additional three spaces to mark paragraphs in the original.

MLA indention of set-off quotations

MLA indents set-off quotations ten spaces, with an additional three spaces to indicate paragraphing in the original.

Single-spacing of set-off quotations

Single-spacing may be preferred for theses and dissertations to save space and to make the finished paper resemble a book.

POETRY Short excerpts of poetry (less than two lines) should be run into the text and enclosed in double quotation marks. Separate each line of poetry by a slanted line, leaving a space on either side of it. Excerpts of three or more lines should be set off and may be single- or double-spaced in keeping with your policy for other set-off quotations. Leave one line of space between stanzas. Indent poetry ten spaces from the left margin; reduce the indention when the line would otherwise have to be broken. Lines of poetry extending beyond one line should be indented five spaces, broken, and indented ten spaces on the next line. Alignment and spacing within the set-off quotation should follow the original as closely as possible.

EPIGRAPHS Direct quotations that precede an entire text or a chapter should be aligned twenty spaces from the left margin and continue to the right margin. Leave one line of space between the chapter title and the epigraph. Epigraphs may be single- or double-spaced. Indention in the original is indicated with an additional five-space indention. The placement of the quotation normally suffices to indicate that the epigraph is a direct quotation; quotation marks are not needed. Position the attribution of the quotation flush with the right margin. Leave one line of space between the bottom of the attribution of the epigraph and the beginning of the text.

ELLIPSES Indicate the omission of any portion of a quoted excerpt with three ellipsis points (three spaced dots). When an ellipsis is used within a sentence, leave a space before the first dot and after the third. Use four dots (a period plus three ellipsis points) to signify the omission of any of the following: (1) the end of a quoted sentence, (2) the beginning of the following sentence, (3) one or more sentences, and (4) one or more paragraphs. Place the first of the four dots, with no intervening space, immediately after the last quoted word. The omission of the end of a sentence and the omission of one or more subsequent sentences are indicated in the same way. A complete sentence must precede the four dots, and another complete sentence must follow them.

When you retain the original punctuation at the end of a cut or a complete sentence, that mark of punctuation (question mark, exclamation point, semicolon, colon, comma) takes the place of the period. (See examples and explanations on page 75.)

A full line of ellipsis points signals the omission of more than a few paragraphs. When a line of ellipsis points is used to indicate such an omission, the dots run between the margins of the indented material. In set-off quotations of poetry, ellipsis points running the length of the longest line indicate the omission of one or more lines.

BRACKETS Enclose in square brackets ([ ]) corrections, clarifications, and editorial comments inserted in direct quotations. Also, when you need to indicate a parenthesis within a parenthesis, use brackets.

QUOTATIONS IN NOTES Run in all direct quotations in both footnotes and endnotes, regardless of the length of the quotation. Use single- or double-spacing consistent with other notes in your paper. If the quotation consists of more than one paragraph, begin each paragraph at the left margin without indention. Place quotation marks at the beginning of each paragraph and at the beginning and end of the entire quotation. Provide any bibliographical information for the quotation within parentheses directly after the quotation. Poetry in notes should be blocked and indented, as in the text.

▪ Endnotes and Footnotes

PLACEMENT OF THE SUPERSCRIPT IN THE TEXT Leave no space between the superscript (note number) in the text and the word or mark of punctuation that it follows. Place the superscript before a dash but after all other marks of punctuation.

SEQUENCE OF NOTE NUMBERS Number endnotes or footnotes consecutively through each chapter. Some institutions may want notes to run consecutively throughout the entire dissertation. To run notes throughout a multichapter text, you may have to create one large file of all the chapters.

LOCATION OF FOOTNOTES Your software probably will be able to place footnotes at the bottom of the page on which the citation appears. If your computer does not enter a division between text and notes automatically, use the underline key to create a one-and-one-half-inch line starting from the left margin, one double space below the last line of the text. Place the first footnote one double space below the line.

SPACING OF FOOTNOTES Indent the first line of each note five spaces. Subsequent lines start at the left margin. Leave one space between the superscript and the first letter in the note. Single-space within footnotes, and double-space between them.

CONTINUED FOOTNOTES When a footnote cannot be included without running into the bottom margin (one inch) and cannot be omitted without making the page noticeably short, the footnote may be split and carried over to the next page. On the second page of a footnote, continue it without indention, ahead of the next footnote in the series.

LOCATION OF ENDNOTES Endnotes should be placed in a separate section entitled `Notes` (not Endnotes) either at the end of the entire paper immediately preceding the bibliography or at the end of each chapter. Endnotes may be numbered consecutively throughout each chapter or throughout the entire paper.

SPACING OF ENDNOTES Indent the first line of each note five spaces. Subsequent lines start at the left margin. Leave one space between the superscript and the first word of the note. Double-space within and between entries.

▪ Headings within Chapters

The headings you select for your text (see the explanations on pages 47–48 in Chapter 2) should be spaced as follows:

Double-space above and below centered headings. Capitalize the first letter of each word except articles, conjunctions, and prepositions, unless they are the first or last word in the heading. If a heading is more than four inches long (forty spaces), use a double-spaced inverted-pyramid format. The title should not have terminal punctuation, unless it ends with a question mark or an exclamation point.

Leave a double-space above and below freestanding side headings. Align such heads with the left margin; capitalize and punctuate them as you would a centered heading. If a side heading is more than about two and one-half inches long (twenty-five spaces), divide the heading, placing the second line a double space below, with a two-space hanging indention.

Leave one full line of space above run-in paragraph headings and indent them five spaces. Capitalize the first word and proper nouns and adjectives only. End the heading with a period and begin the text on the same line.

Tables and Figures

PLACEMENT The following guidelines apply to the placement of tables and figures within the text:

1. Confine each table or figure to one page. Leave the usual margins.
2. Insert a table or figure that occupies no more than half the page into the running text. The page should begin with text. Leave four lines of space both above and below a table or figure.
3. Place a table or figure between complete paragraphs.
4. A series of small tables or figures discussed together in the text may be grouped together on one page.

PAGINATION Place the assigned page number (and any running head) in the usual position in the upper right-hand corner on all pages containing tables and figures.

MARGINS If a table or figure is less than six inches wide, center it between the margins. Try to leave at least one-inch margins; three-fourths of an inch should be the absolute minimum.

Tables

CAPTIONS Place captions *above* tables. Block-style captions begin flush with the left margin of the table, which might not coincide with the left margin of other pages. Inverted-pyramid captions should be centered between margins. Leave one line of space between the text of the caption and the table. Begin the table with a single horizontal rule or with two closely spaced horizontal rules extending the width of the table.

Figures

Place captions two to four spaces *below* figures. Otherwise, follow the instructions above for table captions.

Footnotes in tables

FOOTNOTES Double-space below the bottom rule of the table. Align footnotes with the left margin of the table. Space them as you space footnotes in the text.

Footnotes in figures

Double-space below the caption. Align footnotes with the left margin of the figure. Space them as you space footnotes in the text. Alternatively, if you have the space, you may place a footnote in an open space within the figure.

SPACING IN TABLES The spacing and proportion of a table should be designed to contribute to clarity and readability.

Column headings

The following guidelines apply to the spacing of column headings.

1. Leave a blank space above and below all column headings; single-space within headings; and leave at least one space on either side of the longest heading.
2. Center headings between the vertical rules that enclose them or, if there are no vertical rules, in the space allowed for each column. Enclose subheadings in parentheses and center them below the main heading.
3. Align the bottom lines of all column headings on the same plane.
4. Place a horizontal rule one single space below the column headings.
5. If you number the columns, place the numerals in parentheses on the line below the lowest order of column headings.

Body of table

Follow these guidelines for spacing items in the body of a table:

1. Leave enough space between columns so that each entry stands out clearly as a separate item.
2. If columns are divided by vertical rules, create columns two spaces wider than the widest label, placing one space on either side of the label.
3. Align columns of words on the left.
4. Align columns of numbers on their decimal points.
5. In columns of numbers mixed with other items, align the numbers on their decimal points and center other items in the column.
6. Single-space within items and insert one line of space between items, unless space restrictions suggest a better arrangement.

▪ Chapter Numbers and Titles

Type the word `CHAPTER` in full caps, followed by the appropriate arabic numeral (`CHAPTER 1; CHAPTER 5`), and center the line one inch from the top of the page. Center the title, in uppercase and lowercase letters, two spaces below the chapter number. For titles of two or more lines, use inverted-pyramid style, with one line of space between lines of text. The title should not have terminal punctuation unless it ends with a question mark or an exclamation point. Leave one line of space between the title and the first line of the text.

▪ Part-Title Pages

If a work is divided into parts, each part may be introduced with a page devoted to the title of the part. This page should be numbered and counted. Type the part number and title slightly above the center of the page with double-spacing as follows:

```
PART 2

From the Renaissance to Hume
```

When a chapter title follows the part title without intervening text, the chapter title should be placed on the following page. Text following the part title should begin after one line of space below the title.

▪ Bibliographies and Lists of Works Cited

TITLE Type `Bibliography`, `Works Cited`, `References`, or another appropriate heading a double space from your name and the page number, centered between margins and without end punctuation. Double-space to the first entry.

SPACING Bibliographies and works cited lists should be double-spaced. Use a hanging indention, with each entry beginning at the left margin and succeeding lines in each entry indented five spaces.

Chicago Manual and MLA

If you have two or more entries by the same author, type five to ten hyphens (*Chicago*) or three hyphens (MLA), followed by a period or a comma, in place of the author's name for the second and subsequent entries.

PUNCTUATION Periods followed by one space mark the end of the author, title, and facts of publication sections of an entry.

ANNOTATIONS Begin annotations either (1) immediately after the end of an entry or (2) on the next line, indented ten spaces. In either case, indent succeeding lines five spaces from the left margin.

▪ Front Matter for a Thesis or Dissertation

ABSTRACT Center the word `Abstract` one inch from the top of the page. Leave one line of space between `Abstract` and the full title of your thesis or dissertation, which should appear precisely as it does on your title page. Leave one line of space between the title and your full legal name, which should be centered in uppercase and lowercase letters. Double-space to the text of the abstract, which should be double-spaced. The abstract page(s) are neither counted nor numbered.

Because requirements for the format and placement of the abstract vary greatly among institutions and disciplines, be certain to consult your graduate office about its requirements.

TITLE PAGE Use an approved title-page format, either selected from the examples on pages 52 and 53 or as specified by local policy. The title may appear entirely in capital letters or in uppercase and lowercase letters. The title page is counted but not numbered.

COPYRIGHT PAGE The copyright notice, if any, appears on a separate page following the title page. Center the notice, and position the last line one inch from the bottom of the page. Circle a lowercase `c` next to the year or select the copyright character from your menu of symbols; type your full legal name a double space below; and center the words `ALL RIGHTS RESERVED` a double space below your name. (See the sample copyright page on page 54.) The copyright page is counted but not numbered.

TABLE OF CONTENTS Words designating elements of the paper, such as the preface and bibliography, should be typed in uppercase and lowercase (`Table of Contents`), following the rules for capitalization of titles.

Type `Table of Contents` one inch from the top of the page, centered between the margins. No terminal punctuation follows the heading of any line of the table of contents. Place the label `Chapter` flush left and `Page` flush right. Leave one full line of space between the heading and `Page` and place `Chapter` after the listing of the preliminaries. See Chapter 4 for the alignment of period leaders (spaced periods leading from the chapter title or heading on the left to the page number on the right).

Indent one-digit chapter numbers five spaces, and position numbers of two digits or more by aligning the numerals in the right-hand column. The wording, capitalization, and punctuation of titles and headings should appear precisely the same as in the text. Headings and subheadings underlined or italicized in the text should not be underlined or italicized in the table of contents. Use a two-space hanging indention (that is, the first line at the margin and subsequent lines indented) within headings and between successive levels. Type the names for the reference materials (`Bibliography`, `Appendix`, etc.) flush with the left margin; place the page number of the first page of each section in the column at the right. With separate appendixes, list each by letter (`A`, `B`, `C`, etc.) and title, if any.

```
5. Graduate Study and the Preparation of
     Scholars in Art Education . . . . . . . . . . 137

     Growth and Status of Graduate Study in
       Art Education . . . . . . . . . . . . . . . 137

     Technological and Theoretical Roles in
       Art Education . . . . . . . . . . . . . . . 142

       Preparation for the Technological Role  . . 144

         Theoretical competency . . . . . . . . .  144

         Clinical competency  . . . . . . . . . .  149

       Preparation for the Theoretical Role . . .  151

       Personnel in Art Education . . . . . . . .  158

         Students . . . . . . . . . . . . . . . .  158

         Faculty . . . . . . . . . . . . . . . . . 159

       Summary . . . . . . . . . . . . . . . . . . 160
```

6. American Education and the Future of Art
Education 163

Appendix 181

For a partially condensed version of the above, single-space between the second- and third-level headings.

Technological and Theoretical Roles in Art
Education 142

Preparation for the Technological Role . . . 144
Theoretical competency 144
Clinical competency 149
Preparation for the Theoretical Role 151

Personnel in Art Education 158

For an even more condensed version, you may run in second- and third-level heads, use period leaders only with chapter titles, and double-space only between chapters.

5. Graduate Study and the Preparation of Scholars
in Art Education 137
Growth and Status of Graduate Study of Art
Education, 137
Technological and Theoretical Roles in Art
Education, 142; Preparation for the
Technological Role, 144; Preparation for the
Theoretical Role, 151
Personnel in Art Education, 158; Students, 158;
Faculty, 159
Summary, 160

LIST OF TABLES Center the heading `Tables` or `List of Tables` one inch from the top of the page, without terminal punctuation. The labels `Table` and `Page` should be placed flush with the left and right margins, respectively. Indent and space captions for tables, following the guidelines for the Table of Contents on page 55.

LIST OF FIGURES Center the heading `Figures` or `List of Figures` one inch from the top of the page, without terminal punctuation. Place column headings, captions, and page numbers as in a list of tables.

ACKNOWLEDGMENTS OR PREFACE Center the words `Acknowl-edgments` or `Preface`, as appropriate, one inch from the top of the page, without terminal punctuation. Leave one full line of space below this title and the first line of text.

▪ Back Matter for a Thesis or Dissertation

APPENDIX Center the word `Appendix`, along with its appropriate number or letter, one inch from the top of the page, without end punctuation. Leave one full line of space between the title and the text of the appendix, which should be double-spaced.

GLOSSARY Center the word `Glossary` one inch from the top of the page, without end punctuation. Double-space any preliminary explanation of the glossary. Arrange words to be defined along the left margin and their definitions along the right margin. The words and definitions should be close enough to allow readers to find them readily.

ENDNOTES AND BIBLIOGRAPHY OR LIST OF WORKS CITED See pages 126–127 in this chapter for information about endnotes and page 130 for information about bibliographies and lists of works cited.

INDEX Most theses and dissertations do not require an index. If you do want to supply an index, perhaps with an eye toward future publication of the material as a book, you may want to use indexing software, which can produce an index automatically, or to hire a professional indexer.

Center the word `Index` one inch from the top of the page, without terminal punctuation. The index in a typescript should be double-spaced, one column to a page. Indent subheadings five spaces. Entries are followed by a comma and the page number(s) on which the reference to the subject appears.

II Systems of Documentation

General Information on Documentation 136

Purposes of Notes and Parenthetical References 136

The List of Sources 138

7 *Chicago Manual* Style 141

8 Modern Language Association Style 214

9 American Psychological Association Style 245

10 *Columbia Guide to Online Style* 278

General Information on Documentation

Documentation, either through notes or through parenthetical references and an accompanying bibliography or list of works cited, serves to acknowledge the sources of ideas and information in your paper. The authority or source for both facts and opinions—whether quoted directly or indirectly or derived from primary or from secondary sources—must be cited to provide your reader with an accurate account of the materials on which you base your conclusions. By neglecting to provide full, precise documentation, you will cast doubt on the acccuracy of your scholarship and on the value of your conclusions.

The two basic types of systems for documenting materials from other sources are the note-bibliography system and the parenthetical-reference system. The note-bibliography format presents bibliographical information in footnotes or endnotes and in a bibliography. This system has been widely used for undergraduate and graduate research papers in the humanities and the social sciences and for papers in many of the professions. The parenthetical-reference system, which may use either author's name and page number (MLA) or author's name and date of the work cited within parentheses (APA), includes documentation in parentheses within the text and in a list of works cited. In the MLA system, this list is entitled "Works Cited"; in the APA system, it is entitled "References."

This book provides instructions for using both of these systems. The note-bibliography system here is based on *The Chicago Manual of Style*, 14th edition (see pages 141–213). The parenthetical reference systems are (1) Modern Language Association style (see pages 214–244) and (2) American Psychological Association style (see pages 245–277). A section on legal citation, which uses notes only, appears in Appendix A.

Your choice among these systems of documentation might be governed by the conventions of your field of study, the suggestions of your adviser, the requirements of your university, or your personal taste. If you plan to enter a field or profession that uses either MLA or APA style in its journals, you probably will want to begin using that style as soon as possible. You should select a format in the beginning stages of research and follow it consistently throughout the process of preparing your paper.

Purposes of Notes and Parenthetical References

Notes and parenthetical references may serve one or more purposes: to identify the source of your information, to establish the validity of your assertions, to call readers' attention to other parts of your paper, to amplify ideas in the text, and to provide bibliographical information beyond the sources you have cited as evidence.

▪ Identifying Sources of Information

All material gathered from sources, whether quoted directly or indirectly, requires documentation in a research paper. Information that qualifies as common knowledge (see pages 58–59) does not need to be documented except when it is quoted directly. When the audience for a paper is very specialized, the amount of material that constitutes common knowledge may be greater than it is for a research paper directed to a general audience. The citation of sources, then, requires making judgments about whether a piece of information is common knowledge and about the degree of your dependence on a source for the information. When you are in doubt about whether to document something, it is wise to do so, particularly in undergraduate papers.

▪ Establishing the Validity of Evidence

Citation of sources of information gives readers a way to establish the accuracy of direct or indirect quotations and to verify the validity of your interpretation and use of sources.

Even if you use a parenthetical-reference system, you may occasionally use notes for some kinds of documentation. These notes should be complete in themselves, and they should read as additional information that can be removed without changing the meaning of the text. The paper should read logically and coherently without the notes. Essential ideas and information should be presented in the text; unimportant and peripheral information should be omitted.

▪ Providing Cross-References within the Paper

Notes referring readers to materials in other parts of the paper or in the appendixes can help readers establish the proper relationships among ideas and concepts.

▪ Amplifying Ideas

Informational notes can provide discussion or amplification of points in the text. They should be used only when such discussion cannot be included in the text without interrupting or complicating the development. Material such as technical discussions or definitions, incidental comments, corollaries, additional information, and reconciliation of conflicting views might be presented in an informational note.

An example of an informational note follows.

Informational note

    1. Sophocles, Antigone, trans. Elizabeth Wyckoff, in The Complete Greek Tragedies: Sophocles I, ed. David Grene and Richmond Lattimore (Chicago: University of Chicago Press, 1954). The authorship of these lines has long been

disputed, and difference of opinion remains though modern critics tend to accept them, as did Aristotle. Bernard Knox explains the scene as a solitary moment of self-discovery for Antigone: "She can at last identify the driving force behind her action, the private, irrational imperative. . . . It is her fanatical devotion to one particular family, her own, the doomed, incestuous, accursed house of Oedipus." Sophocles, The Three Theban Plays, trans. Robert Fagles and ed. Bernard Knox (New York: Viking, 1982), 33.

▪ Providing Additional Bibliography

Bibliographical notes can allow you to mention sources indirectly relevant to your paper that you have not cited yourself but that another researcher might wish to pursue.

An example of a bibliographical note follows.

Bibliographical note

2. For differing explanations of the causes of Mill's breakdown, see William Albert Levi, "The 'Mental Crisis' of John Stuart Mill," Psychoanalytic Review 23 (1945): 86-101; John Durham, "The Influence of John Stuart Mill's Mental Crisis on His Thoughts," American Imago 20 (1963): 369-84.

The List of Sources

The concluding section of a research paper, thesis, or dissertation is usually an alphabetical listing of source materials. This list is entitled "Bibliography" with note-bibliography format, "Works Cited" with MLA format, and "References" with APA parenthetical documentation. This listing serves several functions. It allows the reader to observe the scope of the research behind the paper or to see if a particular work has been used. When parenthetical documentation is the chosen format, the list of works cited permits a reader to locate full bibliographical information for materials referred to in parenthetical notes. The bibliography may also provide the reader with a foundation for further research.

It is wise to prepare a draft of the bibliography or list of works cited before you begin to write. If you have working bibliography cards written out in the correct form and arranged in alphabetical order, you can easily create a bibliography or list of works cited from them. Having a draft of a bibliography will allow you to make notes or parenthetical references quickly and accurately. For note-bibliography format, you will have all the information you need for first references. For parenthetical documentation, you will be able to make sound judgments about ways of introducing direct and indirect quotations to minimize parenthetical documentation in the text. If, after writing the paper, you find that you have not referred to one or more works, you can eliminate them from your list of works cited before typing the final copy.

■ Alphabetization of Entries

Entries in a bibliography and works cited list are alphabetized by the last name of the author or the first word—excluding the articles *A*, *An*, and *The*—of a group or corporate author. An entry without an identified author, such as a newspaper article or unsigned review, is alphabetized by the first word of the title, excluding articles. *Anonymous* is not used as an author entry, even when it appears on the title page, except in APA style. Alphabetize numbers as if they were spelled out, and alphabetize names beginning with Mc or Mc' as they appear rather than as if they were spelled Mac.

Use the system of letter-by-letter alphabetizing in which every letter is considered, except when a comma separates a surname from a first name. That is, alphabetization continues across hyphens, slanted lines, apostrophes, and serial commas; the space following the comma after a surname precedes any other letter, however. The list below demonstrates the principles of letter-by-letter alphabetization applicable for *Chicago Manual*, MLA, and APA style sheets.

```
"Macadamia Nuts"

The Macadam Road
```

(The space after *Macadam* does not interrupt alphabetization by letter; the letter *i* precedes the *r* in *Road*.)

```
MacDonald, Ramsay

Macdonald Observatory

McCullers, Carson

McCullers, Anderson, and Jones: Three Gothic Novelists
```

(The comma after *MacDonald* ends the alphabetization by letter: thus, *MacDonald, Ramsay,* precedes *Macdonald Observatory,* even though *o* precedes *r* in the alphabet. *McCullers* is alphabetized as it appears. The serial comma in *McCullers, Anderson . . .* does not interrupt the alphabetization, but the comma after *McCullers* does.)

```
Mass, Thomas

"The Mass-luminosity Relation"

Mass Media Events
```

(The comma after the surname *Mass* ends the alphabetization. The hyphen in "Mass-luminosity" does not end it: "Mass-luminosity" precedes *Mass Media* because *l* precedes *m*.)

The entry for a work by two or more authors is alphabetized by the surname of the author listed first on the title page, regardless of whether the names on the title page are in alphabetical order.

Cudjoe, Selwyn R., and William E. Cain, eds. C. L. R. James: His Intellectual Legacies. Amherst: University of Massachusetts Press, 1995.

For rules for alphabetizing references to more than one work by the same author, see instructions in the chapter for the style sheet you are using.

▪ Types of Bibliographies

A bibliography may be one of several types, depending on the requirements of the assignment or the nature of the subject. The type most frequently required for both undergraduate and graduate research papers is a list of the works cited in the notes or parenthetical references. *Chicago Manual* suggests entitling such a list "Bibliography" or "Works Cited." MLA entitles the list of sources used in the paper "Works Cited," and APA labels it "Reference List."

Another type of bibliography goes beyond works actually cited in a paper and includes all the works used in preparation for writing the paper, whether you referred to them or not. This bibliography is sometimes labeled "Works Consulted."

A comprehensive compilation of works on a subject may be a useful addition to a research paper. If such a bibliography is lengthy, you may wish to classify the entries according to one of these categories: form of publication, subject or chapters of the paper, or primary and secondary sources. Lists of works cited should not be divided. Short research papers and reports usually do not require classified bibliographies.

Grouping references according to their form of publication can facilitate use of a bibliography; books might be listed in one group, periodicals in a second group, and government publications in still another, for example. Bibliographies consisting of fewer than thirty entries generally should not be divided, unless some particular value inheres in classification. Use a single alphabetical listing for fewer than twenty entries.

A bibliography may also be divided by subject. A history of home schooling in the United States, for example, might have bibliography entries grouped by time periods, such as decades or centuries, or regions of the country.

The distinction between primary sources and secondary sources is often used as a basis of classification, especially in the humanities and social sciences (see page 38 for a sample). The writer of the history of a university, for example, might want to distinguish between primary sources (such as minutes of meetings, university catalogs, financial records, and students' diaries) and secondary sources (such as previous historical accounts or biographies of prominent faculty members).

Finally, an annotated bibliography, in which each entry is accompanied by a brief description or evaluation of the work, can be very useful to readers (see sample on pages 36–37).

When you have decided which of the three systems of documentation you will use, turn to the appropriate chapter.

7 *Chicago Manual* Style

Endnotes and Footnotes 142
Designation of Notes in the Text 142
First Reference and Subsequent Reference 143
Bibliographies 150
Books 151
Multivolume Works and Series 157
Periodicals 158
Works of Literature 162
Reference Works 163
Public Documents 164
Unpublished Sources 167
Dissertations 169
Nonprint Sources 169
Electronic Sources 173
Examples of Footnote and Endnote Forms and Bibliography Forms 177

This section provides note and bibliography forms for a wide range of sources, from books and articles to electronic media, based on *The Chicago Manual of Style*, 14th edition, 1993. Because types of sources are proliferating rapidly, you may use one that is not mentioned here. In this case, you should look at the closest alternative and construct your own entry according to the basic principles of *Chicago Manual* format. Also, you may have to refer to more than one of the examples given below. To create an entry for an article appearing in a book edited by three people, for example, you would use the form for an article and the form for an edited book, following the rules for citing two or more authors. For sample pages of a research paper in *Chicago Manual* style, see pages 30–38 in Chapter 1.

Endnotes and Footnotes

The citation of a source in the note-bibliography system is indicated in the text with a superscript (raised number), which refers to a note providing information about the source. The notes are called footnotes when they appear at the bottom of the page and endnotes when they are collected in a section at the end of each chapter or at the end of the entire paper.

▪ Designation of Notes in the Text

A note is indicated in the text by a raised arabic numeral. The superscript should be raised one-half space (not a full space) above the line and should be placed directly after the material (without a space) to which the note refers. The best placement of the number is at the end of a sentence or, if that would cause confusion or inaccuracy, at the end of a clause. The number goes outside all punctuation except the dash, and it should not be underlined, circled, or followed by a period. The examples given below demonstrate correct and incorrect placement of the superscript.

Incorrect `Robert Heilbroner explains that "the profit motive as we know it is only as old as 'modern man.`[1]`'"`

Correct `Robert Heilbroner explains that "the profit motive as we know it is only as old as 'modern man.'"`[1]

Incorrect `Robert Heilbroner`[1] `explains that "the profit motive . . .`

Correct `"The profit motive as we know it is only as old as 'modern man,'" according to Robert Heilbroner.`[1]

Incorrect `"The profit motive as we know it is only as old as 'modern man'"--`[1]`ancient civilizations did not have that concept.`

Correct `"The profit motive as we know it is only as old as 'modern man'"`[1]`--ancient civilizations . . .`

Correct `"The profit motive as we know it is only as old as 'modern man'":`[1] `ancient civilizations . . .`

Numbering of notes

Both endnotes and footnotes are usually numbered consecutively within a chapter, starting at number one in each new chapter. Some institutions recommend either beginning the numbering afresh on each page when footnotes are used or, with endnotes, numbering throughout the entire thesis.

For guidelines on placement and numbering of notes in figures and tables, see Chapter 5.

---

1. Robert L. Heilbroner, *The Worldly Philosophers: The Lives, Times, and Ideas of the Great Economic Thinkers,* 4th ed. (New York: Simon and Schuster, Touchstone Books, 1972), 22.

First Reference and Subsequent Reference

First reference

The first time you cite a source in the notes, give a complete entry in the correct format for the bibliographical style you are using throughout the paper. For a book, a complete entry includes the following information (if applicable): complete name of the author; title of the book; editor, compiler, or translator; series and number; edition (other than first); number of volumes; city and state of publication; publisher; date of publication; volume number; page number(s). For an article in a periodical, a complete entry usually includes the following: complete name of the author; title of the article; name of the periodical; volume and/or number of the issue; date; page number(s). (See the first-reference forms for numerous types of sources on the "Footnotes and Endnotes" pages, the even-numbered pages from 178–212.)

Subsequent reference

After the first complete reference note, use a shortened format for subsequent references to the same work. In most cases, the last name of the author and the page number serve to identify the work. When you have more than one work by the same author, use the author's name, the title (abbreviated if it is lengthy) of the work, and the page number, as the examples below illustrate. Subsequent reference notes should provide enough information to allow the reader to locate the original note or the bibliography entry, but they should not be longer than necessary.

LAST NAME OF THE AUTHOR Subsequent references in the note-bibliography system usually consist of the last name of the author, the page number(s), and any other information required for identification of the source.

2. Leonard Shatzkin, <u>In Cold Type: Overcoming the Book Crisis</u> (Boston: Houghton Mifflin, 1982), 45.

3. Benjamin Woolley, <u>Virtual Worlds: A Journey in Hype and Hyperreality</u> (Cambridge, England: Blackwell, 1992), 100.

4. Shatzkin, 45-47.

5. Woolley, 81.

6. Shatzkin, 45.

Subsequent references to work without author

When an article or book does not have a named author, the subsequent reference includes the title of the article or book (shortened when the title is long) and the page number(s).

Shortening titles

Shortened titles should include significant identifying words. Abbreviations should not be used, and the original word order should not be changed. *Chicago Manual* does not advise shortening a title of fewer than five words except for the omission of an initial article. Subtitles should always be omitted in subsequent references.

ORIGINAL TITLE	SHORTENED VERSION
Teaching and Learning English as a Foreign Language	Teaching and Learning English
When Literacy Empowers: Navajo Language in Print	When Literacy Empowers

First reference

7. "Student-built Shelter Used in Hurricane Relief," Chronicle of Higher Education, 14 Oct. 1992, A5.

Intervening note

8. Heilbroner, 14.

Subsequent reference

9. "Student-built Shelter," A5.

Subsequent references to more than one work by an author

When more than one work by an author is cited, each subsequent reference must include not only the name of the author, but also the title of the article or book (shortened when the title is long).

First references

10. Václav Havel, Keeping the Faith: Summer Meditations (New York: Knopf, 1990), 15.

11. Václav Havel, Living in Truth (New York: Knopf, 1987), 43.

Subsequent references

12. Havel, Keeping the Faith, 43.

13. Havel, Living in Truth, 72.

Subsequent references to work with more than one author

For a work with multiple authors, give the last names of up to three authors. When a work has four or more authors, give the name of the first author followed by et al. (the abbreviation for *et alii*, "and others").

First reference

14. Cleanth Brooks and Robert Penn Warren, Modern Rhetoric, 4th ed. (New York: Harcourt, 1979), 56.

Subsequent reference

15. Brooks and Warren, 89.

First reference

16. Janice M. Lauer et al., Four Worlds of Writing (New York: Harper and Row, 1981), 77.
(The book has four authors.)

Subsequent reference

17. Lauer et al., 80.

Authors with the same last name

When you have more than one author with the same last name, include first names or initials in subsequent references.

First references

18. Helen C. White, The Mysticism of William Blake (New York: Russell, 1964), 75.

19. E. B. White, Charlotte's Web (New York: Harper, 1952), 67.

Subsequent references

20. Helen C. White, 77.

21. E. B. White, 95.

Works with name of editor, compiler, or translator in place of name of author

Some works have the name of an editor, compiler, or translator in place of the name of an author. In subsequent references, you should list the name or names of an editor, compiler, or translator without the accompanying abbreviation (ed., comp., or trans.), which should appear in the bibliography.

First reference

22. Henry Brandon, ed., In Search of a New World Order: The Future of U.S.-European Relations (Washington, D.C.: Brookings, 1992), 231.

Subsequent reference

23. Brandon, 17.

Text

Many of the articles in Research on Composing advocate further exploration of the motivation for writing.[24]

First reference

24. Charles R. Cooper and Lee Odell, eds., Research on Composing: Points of Departure (Urbana: NCTE, 1978), xi-xviii.

Subsequent reference

25. Cooper and Odell, xi-xviii.

Multivolume works

If a multivolume work has one general title, each subsequent citation must include the volume number.

First reference

26. Gerhard von Rad, Old Testament Theology, trans. D. M. G. Stalker, 2 vols. (New York: Harper and Row, 1962-65).
(This initial citation refers to the complete work rather than to any specific page within a volume.)

Subsequent reference

27. Rad, 1:76.
(This citation refers to material on page 76 of volume 1.)

When each volume in a multivolume work has a separate title, however, the title of the volume serves as identification.

28. James C. Crutchfield, ed., The Fisheries: Problems in Resource Management, vol. 1 of Studies on Public Policy Issues in Resource Management (Seattle: University of Washington Press, 1965), 61.

29. Crutchfield, Fisheries, 62.

Indirect citation

A note should indicate the source to which you are indebted for a piece of information, whether the source is primary (the original work, document, or manuscript) or secondary (a quoted excerpt or paraphrase of one source in another work). Your authority is the work you actually consulted, and that work should be cited in the notes and in the bibliography. Try to work from original sources whenever possible and appropriate, but if the original source is not available and you must quote from another, indicate the secondary nature of the reference. This kind of note provides an honest statement of the nature and scope of your research; should the secondary work have misquoted or misrepresented the original, you account for the sources of your error.

Depending on whether the emphasis in your text is on the cited source or the original source of the material, an indirect citation may take one of two forms, as is illustrated below for a reference to material from Matthew Josephson that the writer located in a work by Ron Chernow.

Emphasis on the cited source

30. Ron Chernow, The House of Morgan (New York: Simon & Schuster, Touchstone, 1990), 47, citing [or quoting] Matthew Josephson, The Robber Barons (New York: Harcourt, Brace, 1934), 338.

Emphasis on the original source

31. Matthew Josephson, The Robber Barons (New York: Harcourt, Brace, 1934), 338, cited [or quoted] in Ron Chernow, The House of Morgan (New York: Simon & Schuster, Touchstone, 1990), 47.

Only the work you actually consulted appears in the bibliography.

MULTIPLE NOTES When you wish to list more than one source for a sentence, you may use a multiple note. Each part of the note should take the appropriate form for either the first or a subsequent reference; the two forms may be used together in one note. Separate each reference in the series with a semicolon.

32. David Bromwich, Politics by Other Means: Higher Education and Group Thinking (New Haven: Yale University Press, 1993), 45; Francis Oakley, Community of Learning: The American College and the Liberal Arts Tradition (London: Oxford University Press, 1993), 57-62; Shatzkin, 52.

LATIN ABBREVIATIONS Latin abbreviations for subsequent references are now rarely used. They should not be used at all with MLA and APA formats.

Ibid.

In consecutive references to the same source, the abbreviation ibid. ("in the same place"), the only Latin abbreviation acceptable for bibliographical information, may be used to avoid repetition. If the second reference is to the same page as the initial reference, ibid. alone is used. It may also be used with a page number, to indicate a different page in the same source.

33. Robert C. Solomon, Ethics and Excellence (Oxford: Oxford University Press, 1992), 179.

34. Ibid.

35. Ibid., 100.

Ibid. may be used to refer to a second article by the same author in the same book or issue of a periodical, but not to a different book by the same author. The following examples illustrate references to two contributions by the same author to a book of readings.

36. John Drury, "Luke," in The Literary Guide to the Bible, ed. Robert Alter and Frank Kermode (Cambridge: Harvard University Press), 418.

37. Drury, "Mark," ibid., 402.

Ibid. should not be used to refer to a work in a multiple note. In footnotes, ibid. should not be used more than two pages after the original citation. Ibid. and other such abbreviations should appear in roman rather than italic type; they should not be underlined in a typescript. Previously, these abbreviations were underlined or italicized.

TITLE ONLY: WORKS OF LITERATURE Although the first reference to a work of literature gives full details on the author, title, and facts of publication, subsequent references may be abbreviated, sometimes leaving out the name of the author and shortening the title of the work when it is well known. Abbreviations should be used to designate the parts of a literary work: volume (vol.), part (pt.), number (no.), numbers (nos.), book (bk.), chapter (chap.). The word line(s) should not be abbreviated because l. and ll. are easily confused with numbers.

38. John Milton, Paradise Lost, ed. Merritt Y. Hughes (New York: Odyssey, 1962), bk. 9, lines 342-75.

Abbreviated references

After you have indicated the kinds of sections to which your numbers refer, as is done in note 38 with bk. and lines, you may omit the designations in following citations. Subsequent references to well-known works do not include the author's name, and they have no comma between the title and the designation of book(s), chapter(s), or line(s).

39. Paradise Lost 3.1-55.

Citations for a play should include the numbers of acts, scenes, and lines in arabic numerals. These numerals should be separated by periods without spacing:

40. Othello 3.2.1-5.

For a well-known work, you may shorten the title even further. See the *MLA Handbook* for acceptable abbreviations of the works of Shakespeare and Chaucer.

41. Oth. 3.2.1-5.

Subsequent references

Subsequent references to less well-known works of literature may include the last name of the author (particularly for audiences outside the field of literature or in the case of obscure works). If the reader will understand the reference, subsequent citations may be reduced to a shortened version of the title and designation of the sections:

42. Robert Browning, "Soliloquy of the Spanish Cloister," in The Norton Anthology of English Literature, ed. M. H. Abrams et al., 4th ed. (New York: Norton, 1986), stanza 4, lines 25-32.

43. Browning, "Soliloquy" 7.49-52.

or

44. "Soliloquy" 7.49-52.

When a work has other types of divisions or when the meaning of a sequence of numbers might not be obvious, use an explanatory note identifying each element of a citation and abbreviate the note accordingly in subsequent references.

45. George Eliot, Middlemarch, ed. W. J. Harvey (Harmondsworth, England: Penguin, 1965). Subsequent references to this edition will be abbreviated as M. The first number of each citation refers to the volume, the second to the book, and the third to the chapter. The page numbers refer to the Viking edition.

46. M 1.2.13.

or

47. M 1.2.13, p. 155.

Even when a page number would suffice to identify a passage, designate passages in works of literature by names and numbers of sections because, particularly in the case of widely reprinted works, readers often use many different editions.

Sacred writings

References to the Bible and other sacred writings begin with the particular chapter or book you wish to cite. Titles of the books of the Bible should be abbreviated but not underlined; chapters and verses are expressed in arabic numerals separated by a colon without spacing. The citation may appear only in the text or in the notes with an abbreviation for the particular translation or edition used. A bibliography entry is optional; if used, it should give only the name of the edition, not the chapter and verse. For accepted abbreviations of books of the Bible, consult a standard dictionary or *The Chicago Manual of Style*.

48. 1 Sam. 14:6-9 NRSV.

(bibliography entry optional)

49. 2 Cor. 15:10.
(with edition specified in the bibliography)

Classical works

Refer to classical works by title and main divisions—volume, book, chapter, pages, sections, or lines, as appropriate—in subsequent references. Numerals should be separated by periods without spacing. The initial citation names the translator and editor. This is important information about any work, but it is essential for classical works, where the translator's task can involve making decisions about the text or applying new theories about the meaning of words.

First reference

50. Aristotle, Nicomachean Ethics, trans. Terence Irwin (Indianapolis: Hackett, 1988), 1097b3.

Subsequent references to the classics omit the name of the author, and they have no comma between the title and the designation of sections or parts. Use the traditionally accepted enumeration of sections, not page numbers.

51. Nicomachean Ethics 1123a34.

PARENTHETICAL REFERENCES IN THE TEXT Even when you use the note-bibliography format, you may use some parenthetical references, particularly when, as in a paper on literature, you have multiple references to the same work. Parenthetical references should consist of short entries giving the last name of the author (or an abbreviated title), followed by a comma when the author's name rather than the title is used, and the page number(s). Final punctuation follows the parentheses.

First reference

In The Creators Daniel C. Boorstin argues that the Japanese myths of creation fostered an attitude toward nature that differs markedly from the Western.[52]

----

52. Daniel C. Boorstin, The Creators: A History of the Heroes of the Imagination (New York: Random House, Vintage, 1992), 136.

Subsequent reference

The subsequent reference to the same work by Daniel Boorstin may appear in the text.

While Europeans did not climb their highest mountain, Mont Blanc, until 1786, the Japanese have climbed Mt. Fuji throughout recorded history (Boorstin, 137).

Literature

After the first reference, information such as act, scene, and line; part, verse, and line; and book, chapter, and page number may be included in parentheses after the quotation, whether it is run in or set off. When such a parenthetical reference follows a direct quotation that is run into your own prose, the punctuation for the sentence follows the parentheses. Particularly in a paper involving several works by one author, abbreviations may be substituted for the title.

```
Indeed, the truth about Jim's affair is so elusive that even

after innumerable evenings spent spinning out the story on

verandahs all over the Pacific, Marlow knows that "the last

word is not said--probably shall never be said" (LJ 137).
```

(After the edition is cited in the first reference, the novel *Lord Jim* is indicated in subsequent parenthetical references with the abbreviation *LJ*.)

When the quotation is set off, the parenthetical reference appears after the period marking the end of the quotation, without a subsequent period.

```
Marlow mocks Jim's self-assurance.

    The tumult and the menace of wind and sea now appeared
    very contemptible to Jim, increasing the regret of his
    awe at their inefficient menace.  Now he knew what to
    think of it.  It seemed to him he cared nothing for the
    gale.  He could affront greater perils.  (LJ 6)
```

Bibliographies

Three categories of information are needed for each bibliography entry: author, title, and facts of publication. Each of these categories may contain more than one piece of information. A book may have more than one author, and the facts of publication for some materials may be complicated. A period follows each category of information in a bibliography entry—that is, a period follows the author's name, the title, and the facts of publication. Because an entry in a bibliography (unlike an entry in a note) refers to the complete work rather than to a specific passage, a bibliography entry does not include page numbers. A bibliography entry for an article lists the inclusive pages of the entire article rather than the specific pages from which material was selected for citation.

Arrangement of entries

Entries appear in alphabetical order according to the last name of the author or, if there is no author given, by the first word in the title, excluding articles. For the principles of alphabetization in a reference list or bibliography, see pages 139–140.

Reference to more than one work

When you have two or more works by the same author, alphabetize entries by the first word in the title. Entries after the first begin with three hyphens positioned at the left margin, followed by a period and one space.

```
Churchland, Paul M. Matter and Consciousness. Boston: MIT
    Press, Bradford Books, 1984.
```

---. A Neurocomputational Perspective: The Nature of Mind. Boston: MIT Press, Bradford Books, 1989.

The hyphens stand for the same author or authors named in the preceding entry. If the person named served as editor, translator, or compiler, place a comma and the appropriate abbreviation after the hyphens. When an author listed alone is listed later as a coauthor, you must spell out the full author entry.

An author entry precedes an entry for the same person as an editor, which precedes an entry for the same person as a coeditor or coauthor.

Edelman, Gerald. Brilliant Air, Brilliant Fire. New York: HarperCollins, 1992.

---. Topobiology. New York: Basic Books, 1966.

---, ed. Signal and Sense. New York: Wiley, Liss, 1990.

Edelman, Gerald, and V. B. Mountcastle. The Mindful Brain. Cambridge: MIT Press, 1978.

Books

The author category for a book may include one or more authors, editors, compilers, and translators, or a corporate author or institution. The title category includes the title and subtitle. The facts of publication category identifies the series in which the work appears, the number of volumes in a multivolume work or the particular number of a volume, the edition if it is other than the first, the city of publication (the state is generally omitted), the name of the publisher, and the year of publication.

The basic form of a bibliography entry for a book reads as follows:

Basic bibliography form

Henderson, Hazel. Paradigms in Progress: Life beyond Economics. Indianapolis: Knowledge Systems, 1992.

Periods mark the end of the author, title, and facts of publication sections. One space follows each period, comma, and colon. (See pages 124 and 130.)

NAME OF AUTHOR In a bibliography entry, the name of the author appears with the last name first for purposes of alphabetization.

When there are two or more authors, the names are listed in the order in which they appear on the title page, whether or not that order is alphabetical. Only the name of the first author appears in inverted order. A comma separates the first name of the first author from succeeding names.

Two (or three) authors

Simonds, Wendy, and Barbara Katz Rothman. Centuries of Solace: Grief in Popular Literature. Philadelphia: Temple University Press, 1992.

More than three authors

If a book has more than three authors, list each of their names in the bibliography.

McPherson, William, Stephen Lehmann, Craig Likness, and Marcia Pankake. English and American Literature: Sources and Strategies for Collection Development. Chicago: American Library Association, 1987.

In the note form, use only the name of the author listed first on the title page, followed by et al.

Two authors with same last name

When two authors have the same last name, the name should be repeated.

Price, Richard, and Sally Price. Equatoria. New York: Routledge, 1992.

Pseudonyms

When an author's name as given on the title page is a pseudonym (pen name), the bibliography entry begins with the pseudonym and continues with the author's real name in brackets.

Green, Hannah [Joanne Greenberg]. I Never Promised You a Rose Garden. New York: Holt, Rinehart and Winston, 1964.

If the pseudonym is better known than the real name, you may use the pseudonym alone. If you wish to designate the name given on the title page as a pseudonym but do not know the author's real name, place the abbreviation pseud. within brackets. For an author who first published a work under a pseudonym, but is now known by the real name, you may omit the pseudonym or, if you have some reason for doing so, place it within brackets.

Brontë, Emily. Wuthering Heights. Ed. David Daiches. Harmondsworth, England: Penguin, 1967.

or

Brontë, Emily [Ellis Bell, pseud.]. Wuthering Heights. London, 1850.

Anonymous works

When no author's name appears on a work or when the title page names *Anonymous* as the author, list the work by title alone. If you know the author's name, you may place it in brackets and list the work in the bibliography under that name. *Anonymous* should not be used as an author entry.

[Adams, Henry]. Democracy: An American Novel. New York: Holt, 1880.

or

Democracy: An American Novel. New York: Holt, 1880.

Names with a suffix

When inverted for bibliographical form, any suffix attached to a name, such as Jr. or III, follows the first name.

Christian, William A., Jr. Apparitions in Late Medieval and Renaissance Spain. Princeton: Princeton University Press, 1981.

In the first name-last name order of the note, no comma separates the name from the suffix: William A. Christian Jr., John J. Jones III. (Previously *Chicago Manual* did use the comma between name and suffix, as MLA and APA continue to do.)

Group or corporation as author

When the author is a group or corporation, list the publication under the name of the organization.

Bicycling Magazine. Reconditioning the Bicycle. New York: Rodale, 1989.

When the corporate author is also the publisher, give the full name for both functions.

American Museum of Natural History. Annual Report, 1993-1994. New York: American Museum of Natural History, 1995.

Editor or compiler as author

A compilation, a book consisting of discrete selections by one or more authors, may be listed either by the editor or compiler or by the author of an individual article. In references to the book as a whole, place the name of the compiler(s) or editor(s) first, with the abbreviation comp., comps., ed., or eds., as appropriate. Although the terms *compiler* and *editor* are sometimes used interchangeably, an editor usually has a more active role in shaping the materials presented than a compiler, whose role is something like that of collector.

Baum, Robert, ed. Reform and Reaction in Post-Mao China: The Road through Tiananmen. New York: Routledge, 1992.

Perkins, George, Bradley Scully, Richmond Croom Beatty, and E. Hudson Long, comps. The American Tradition in Literature. 6th ed. 2 vols. New York: Random House, 1985.

When you want to emphasize an article or chapter in the collection, place the name of the author of the article or chapter first and indicate the title of the volume, the editor, and the inclusive page numbers of the article. You may indicate the function of the editor with the phrase edited by or its abbreviation, ed., and that of the compiler with compiled by or comp. While *Chicago Manual* prefers the longer versions, *Form and Style* uses the abbreviated forms, which are more in keeping with current trends toward concision.

Burghardt, Gordon M. "On the Origins of Play." In Play in Animals and Humans, ed. Peter K. Smith, 5-42. Oxford: Basil Blackwell, 1984.

Compilation of material previously published elsewhere

A complete entry for a compilation consisting of material previously published elsewhere gives the original facts of publication as well as the information about the compilation.

Greenblatt, Stephen. "Towards a Poetics of Culture." In The New Historicism, ed. H. Aram Veeser, 1-14. New York: Routledge, 1989. First published in Southern Review (Australia) 20 (1987): 3-15.

When a compilation reprints an article under a title different from the original title, indicate that the title has been changed in the later collection.

Matthews, Gareth. "Ritual and the Religious Feelings." In Explaining Emotions, ed. Amélie Oksenberg Rorty, 339-53. Berkeley: University of California Press, 1980. First published as "Bodily Motions and Religious Feelings," Canadian Journal of Philosophy 1 (1971): 75-86.

In the note form, cite only the edition you actually used.

Emphasis on writer of introduction or foreword

To cite the introduction or foreword to a book in your bibliography, place the name of the author of this section first.

Conquest, Robert. Introduction to The World I Left Behind, by Luba Brezhneva. New York: Random House, 1995.

or

Brezhneva, Luba. The World I Left Behind. Introd. Robert Conquest. New York: Random House, 1995.

Edition or translation of work

When a work has been edited or translated by a person other than the author, you need to decide under which name to alphabetize the work. If the emphasis of your investigation or analysis is on the author, the author's name precedes the title and a period follows the title. The appropriate abbreviation and one or more names to indicate compiler(s), editor(s), or translator(s) follow the title. Use `comp.` (compiled by), `ed.` (edited by), `trans.` (translated by), or the plural forms `comps.`, `eds.`, and `trans.`, as appropriate.

Emphasis on author

Shakespeare, William. King Lear. Ed. Kenneth Muir. The Arden Shakespeare. London: Methuen, 1972.

To emphasize the work of a particular editor, place that name, followed by a comma, the appropriate abbreviation, and a period, in the author position of the entry. The names of the author and the title form a unit: the author's name follows the title in the first name-last name order preceded by a comma, one space, and the word `by`.

Emphasis on editor

Muir, Kenneth, ed. King Lear, by William Shakespeare. The Arden Shakespeare. London: Methuen, 1972.

Emphasis on author of translated work

Appelfeld, Aharon. Katerina. Trans. Jeffrey Green. New York: Random House, 1992.

Emphasis on translator

Green, Jeffrey, trans. Katerina, by Aharon Appelfeld. New York: Random House, 1992.

TITLE The title of a book should appear in the bibliography exactly as it is on the title page, with the exception that capitalization and punctuation may be changed to conform to the principles outlined in Chapter 4, pages 90–93. Separate a subtitle from the main title with a colon followed by one space. A subtitle must appear in the bibliography entry, but it is optional in notes. The full title should be underlined.

McCannell, Dean. Empty Meeting Grounds: The Tourist Papers. New York: Routledge, 1992.

Chicago Manual places titles within book titles in quotation marks, even for long poems and novels: A Study of James Joyce's "Ulysses."

Edition other than the first

For an edition other than the first, provide the number of the edition, as well as its date of publication. Unless you have a particular reason for using an earlier edition, refer to the latest edition of a work. Additional editions may have a variety of designations, such as 2nd rev. ed. (second revised edition), or 3rd enl. and rev. ed. (third enlarged and revised edition), and these should be recorded as they appear on the title page. Ordinal numbers are used to designate editions: 2nd, 3rd, 4th, and so on.

Trimmer, Joseph F. Writing with a Purpose. 11th ed. Boston: Houghton Mifflin, 1995.

FACTS OF PUBLICATION The facts of publication are the place of publication, the name of the publishing house, and the date of publication. The city name alone (without the state name) serves as the place of publication except when it might be confused with another city of the same name. When a publisher lists several cities, select the first as the place of publication. When a book is published simultaneously by two companies, name either the first publisher mentioned on the title page or both publishers, separating the names with a semicolon.

Shortening the name of the publisher

The name of the publisher may be shortened as long as its identity remains clear. Abbreviations such as *Inc.*, *Co.*, and *Ltd.* and an initial *The* should be omitted. *Chicago Manual* preserves the rest of the name, as in Holt, Rinehart and Winston and University (or Univ.) of Chicago Press. Decide on a policy for shortening names of publishers and use it consistently throughout your paper. When you cannot find an unambiguous or widely accepted way to shorten a name, write out the full name.

Date of publication

The date of publication for any work other than an article in a periodical is the year alone, without the month or day. This date generally appears on the title page or on the copyright page. When various printings are listed, the date of the first printing is used in the bibliography or list of works cited.

The most recent edition of a book should be cited unless there is some reason to cite a previous edition. An edition is a new version of a text. A printing, which does not usually need to be designated, is a press run of a book.

When the publisher is a division of a publishing company, that information should appear in the entry. In the following entry, Basic Books is a division of HarperCollins.

```
Bell, Derrick. Faces at the Bottom of the Well: The
     Permanence of Racism. New York: HarperCollins, Basic
     Books, 1992.
```

Below is a list of *Chicago Manual* style for some well-known imprints.

```
Dell, Laurel Editions
Dell, Laurel Leaf Classics
Doubleday, Anchor Books
Doubleday, Dial Press
Doubleday, Image Books
Doubleday, Quantum Press
Harcourt Brace, Harbinger Books
Harcourt Brace, Harvest Books
HarperCollins, Colophon Books
HarperCollins, Perennial Library
HarperCollins, Torchbooks
Holt, Rinehart and Winston, Owl Books
Houghton Mifflin, Clarion Books
Houghton Mifflin, Riverside Editions
Alfred A. Knopf, Dragonfly Books
William Morris, Reynal
New American Library, Mentor Books
new American Library, Plume Books
New American Library, Signet Books
Pocket Books, Poseidon Press
Simon and Schuster, Touchstone Books
```

Work out of print, republished

An entry for a work that was out of print but has been republished should indicate the original date of publication and the fact that the work is a reprint.

```
Cather, Willa. One of Ours. New York: Knopf, 1922.
     Reprint, New York: Vintage Books, 1971.
```

Paperbound editions

When a paperbound book is an original edition, as many now are, it is listed just as any other book would be.

```
Van Ness, Peter H. Spirituality, Diversion, and Decadence:
     The Contemporary Predicament. Binghamton: State
     University of New York Press, 1992.
```

When the hard cover and paperbound editions are not published simultaneously, the paperbound is considered a reprint. In this case, the entry indicates the date of publication of the hardcover edition, identification as a reprint, and facts of publication for both. You can usually locate the date of the hard cover edition on the copyright page.

Davies, Paul. God and the New Physics. London: Dent, 1983. Reprint, New York: Simon and Schuster, Touchstone, 1984.

Missing information

When you cannot locate one or more pieces of information concerning publication, you should use one of the following abbreviations in the appropriate place in the entry:

No place: n.p. ***or*** N.p.
No publisher: n.p.
No date: n.d.
No page: n.pag. ***or*** unpaginated

Capitalize the abbreviation only when it begins a section of the entry.

Eliot, George. Felix Holt. Edinburgh: William Blackwood, n.d.

Eliot, George. Felix Holt. N.p.: William Blackwood, n.d.

▪ Multivolume Works and Series

A multivolume work consists of two or more volumes under one general title. Each separate volume may either have its own title or be identified by volume number only.

Reference to complete multivolume work

To refer to a complete multivolume work rather than to any specific volume, include the total number of volumes and the inclusive dates of publication, if applicable, in the bibliography entry.

Bowsky, William M., ed. Studies in Medieval and Renaissance History. 4 vols. Lincoln: University of Nebraska Press, 1963-67.

The entry for the date indicates that the first volume was published in 1963 and the fourth volume in 1967. It is not necessary to specify intermediate dates. Your note or parenthetical reference will specify the particular volume cited in each instance.

Reference to volume with individual title

When each volume in a multivolume work has an individual title, the entry takes the following form:

Freehling, William W. The Road to Disunion. Vol. 1 of Secessionists at Bay, 1776-1854. New York: Oxford University Press, 1992.

Multivolume work with different editors for each volume

When each volume in a multivolume work has a different author or editor, include the name of the author or editor of the entire series after that title.

Duby, Georges, ed. Revelations of the Medieval World. Vol. 2 of A History of Private Life, ed. Philippe Ariès and Georges Duby. Trans. Arthur Goldhammer. Cambridge: Harvard University Press, Belknap Press, 1988.

Independent work in a series

A series consists of works that are independent of one another but numbered as belonging to a group. The name of the series follows the title and is not underlined.

```
Eiser, J. Richard, ed. Attitudinal Judgment. Springer
     Series in Social Psychology, no. 11. New York:
     Springer-Verlag, 1990.
```

Work in series with editor of series named

To name the editor(s) of the entire series, insert the name(s) between the name of the series and the number of the particular volume.

```
Propp, Vladimir. Theory and History of Folklore. Trans.
     Ariadna Y. Martin and Richard P. Martin. Theory and
     History of Literature, ed. Wlad Godzich and Jochen
     Schülte-Sasse, no. 5. Minneapolis: University
     of Minnesota Press, 1984.
```

▪ Periodicals

Any publication that comes out at regular intervals is a periodical. Periodicals for an academic or professional audience are usually called journals; periodicals intended for the general public are often called magazines. The bibliography entry for a periodical includes the author's complete name, the title of the article, and the facts of publication, which include the name of the periodical, the number of the volume, the date of the volume or the issue number, and the inclusive page numbers for the entire article. (For instructions regarding inclusive page numbers, see Chapter 4).

Article in a scholarly journal, continuously paginated

JOURNALS Most journals paginate continuously through each volume; that is, each issue continues the numbering of the previous issue rather than beginning anew with page 1. One space follows the author and title entries; one space separates the elements of the facts of publication section. The basic format for an entry referring to such a continuously paginated journal is the following:

```
Gaunt, Simon. "The Significance of Silence." Paragraph 13
     (1990): 202-16.
```

When the season or month of the issue is necessary for identification, as in a journal that does not use issue numbers and begins new pagination with each issue, or when you wish to indicate the month or the season, that information should precede the date within the parentheses. Months should be abbreviated as follows: `Jan.`, `Feb.`, `Mar.`, `Apr.`, `Aug.`, `Sept.`, `Oct.`, `Nov.`, and `Dec.` The months May, June, and July are not abbreviated. Some journals use seasons to identify the volume. Seasons (fall or autumn, winter, spring, summer) should not be abbreviated or capitalized. (Previously *Chicago Manual* did capitalize the seasons in documentation.)

Article in a journal paginating each issue separately

When a journal begins each issue in a volume with page 1, include either the number of the issue (preferred) or the season.

Daly, Robert. "Engines of Discourse: God and the Odds in Postmodern Literature." Denver Quarterly 27, no. 4 (1993): 6-16.

or

Daly, Robert. "Engines of Discourse: God and the Odds in Postmodern Literature." Denver Quarterly 27 (spring 1993): 6-16.

Article in journal with more than one series

Include a series number or designation in citing periodicals that have been published in more than one series. An old series or original series is indicated by `o.s.`; a new series is identified by `n.s.` Numbered series are indicated by ordinal numbers preceding the volume number.

Klein, Milton M. "The Pleasures of Teaching and Writing History." William and Mary Quarterly, 3rd ser., 52 (July 1995): 483-87.

Erickson, Peter. "Singing America: From Walt Whitman to Adrienne Rich." Kenyon Review, n.s., 12 (winter 1995): 103-19.

Journals with issue numbers rather than volumes

For a journal that numbers issues rather than volumes, designate the issue with the abbreviation `no.`, preceded by a comma and followed by the number.

Nwezeh, C. E. "The Comparative Approach to Modern African Literature." Yearbook of General and Comparative Literature, no. 28 (1979): 22.

Abbreviations of journal titles

In some fields, abbreviations for titles of periodicals are used. If you want to use such abbreviations, follow an authoritative source as a guide to acceptable forms. Many indexes, such as the *Applied Science and Technology Index*, the *Cumulated Index Medicus*, the *Education Index*, the *MLA International Bibliography*, and the *Music Index*, contain glossaries of journal abbreviations used in their compilations. Use an abbreviation only when you supply the reader with a key. The following entry abbreviates the title of the journal *Yearbook of General and Comparative Literature*.

Abbreviated journal title

Nwezeh, C. E. "The Comparative Approach to Modern African Literature." YGCL, no. 28 (1979): 22.

Quotations within titles

When double quotation marks appear within the title of an article, they should be changed to single quotation marks.

Sanders, Charles. "'The Waste Land': The Last Minstrel Show?" Journal of Modern Literature 8 (1980): 23-28.

When another mark of punctuation, such as the question mark in the example above, comes at the end of the title, it takes the place of the period.

Chicago Style

MAGAZINES Issues of magazines are most often identified by date only, even when they have volume numbers. Page numbers are separated from the date by a comma (rather than a colon, as in journal entries). When magazine articles run on discontinuous pages, either leave the bibliography entry without any pages or enter the page numbers on which the article actually appears: `38-45, 50, 53-57` for an article that begins on page 38 and ends on page 57 but is interrupted by other material. A comma between page numbers indicates discontinuous pagination. In the note, cite only the pages to which you actually refer.

Basic form, monthly magazine

Kleppner, Daniel. "About Benjamin Thompson." Physics Today, Sept. 1992, 9-10.

Basic form, weekly magazine

"The Bard of Betrayal." Observer Magazine, 27 Sept. 1992, 44-46.

Discontinuous pagination, page numbers omitted

Seibert, Charles. "The DNA We've Been Dealt." New York Times Magazine, 17 Sept. 1995.

or

Page numbers specified

Seibert, Charles. "The DNA We've Been Dealt." New York Times Magazine, 17 Sept. 1995, 50-57, 64, 74, 93-94, 104.

For a magazine article that is included in a section with a title, include that title after the name of the article.

"The Devastated Fisheries." Canada Notes. Macleans's, 21 Aug. 1995, 17.

NEWSPAPERS The bibliography entry for a newspaper should include the name of the author (if available), the title of the article (headline) in quotation marks, and the name of the newspaper, underlined, omitting any initial article such as `The`.

Basic entry

Mercer, Pamela. "U.S. Venture Bets on Colombian Coal." New York Times, 27 July 1995, D7.

Section numbers

When a newspaper has more than one section, enter the number or the letter of the section along with the page number. When the section is designated by a number, use the abbreviation `sec.` When a page number follows a section number, insert the abbreviation `p.` or `pp.` for page or pages to avoid confusion. (See examples below.)

Interpolation of city and state

If the name of the newspaper does not indicate its place of publication, interpolate the name of the city, state, or nation in parentheses before or after the title. Nationally circulated newspapers, such as the *Christian Science Monitor* and the *Wall Street Journal*, do not require the addition of the place of publication.

"Unknown Author of Wind Answers Crane Criticism." Sweetwater (Texas) Daily Reporter, 15 Dec. 1925, 6.

Observer (London), 17 Oct. 1990, sec. 2, pp. 5, 8.
(Names of foreign cities are placed after the title and are not italicized.)

More than one edition

If a newspaper prints more than one edition (for example, the late city edition, the international edition, the final sports edition), designate the edition cited after the date.

Green, Wayne E. "Cold-Fusion Development Spurs Hot Race for Patents." Wall Street Journal, 9 June 1989, eastern ed., B1.

Special types of articles

Designate editorials and other special classes of articles.

"Potomac Yard Decision." Editorial. Washington Post, 16 Oct. 1992, A24.

Lightfoot, Frederick S. Letter. New York Times, 21 Oct. 1992, Long Island ed., A22.

REVIEWS An entry for a review of a book, film, or performance begins with the name of the reviewer, includes the title (if any) of the review, gives the name of the author and the work being reviewed, and ends with the name of the periodical in which the review appeared, together with the volume number (if applicable), date, and page(s). If the review is unsigned and untitled, the entry begins with `Review of` or `Rev. of`. Alphabetize the review in the bibliography by the first word in the entry.

Book review, signed

Moore, Walter. "Great Physicist, Great Guy." Review of Genius: The Life and Science of Richard Feynman, by James Gleick. New York Times Book Review, 11 Oct. 1992, 3.

Untitled book review

Kienitz, Gail M. Review of Tennyson and the Doom of Romanticism, by Herbert F. Tucker. Religion and Literature 24 (spring 1992): 87-90.

Unsigned book review

Review of Married to Genius, by Jeffrey Meyers. Journal of Modern Literature 7 (1979): 579-80.

Drama review

Hassell, Graham. "Sometimes Excess Isn't Enough." Review of The Grand Ceremonial, by Fernando Arrabal. Lyric Studio, Hammersmith, England. Times Literary Supplement (London), 14 July 1995, 20.

Movie review

Rickey, Carrie. "Disney's Pocahontas: Is It Fact or Fiction?" Review of Pocahontas (Miramax movie). Philadelphia Inquirer, 18 June 1995, H1, H9.

Review of television program

Bohlen, Celestine. "Wine and Women in Tuscany: Bertolucci Lightens Up." Review of Stealing Beauty (movie). New York Times, Arts and Leisure Section, 27 Aug. 1995, H10.

Review of musical performance

Oestreich, James R. "In a Choral Requiem, a Climax and Last Hurrah." Review of concert performance of Requiem, by Giuseppe Verdi, Tanglewood Festival Chorus, Lenox, Mass. New York Times, 29 Aug. 1995, C13.

▪ Works of Literature

The bibliography entry for a book-length work of literature should follow the principles for creating an entry for a book. For a short work included in a book or periodical, the entry follows the form for an article in a collection.

Basic form

When the entry refers to the work in an edition without editing or commentary, the basic form for a book is used.

Tan, Amy. The Joy Luck Club. New York: Ballantine, Ivy, 1989.

When the entry refers to a particular edition or translation of a work, the name of the editor or translator should be supplied. When the emphasis is on the work rather than the editor, the note begins with the name of the author.

Conrad, Joseph. Lord Jim. Ed. Thomas C. Moser. New York: Norton, 1968.

Emphasis on translator

When the editor or translator has most importance, that name begins the entry.

Bergin, Thomas G., trans. and ed. The Divine Comedy, by Dante Alighieri. New York: Appleton-Century-Crofts, 1955.

Emphasis on writer of introduction

When the emphasis is on the author of the introduction to a particular edition, the entry may begin with that name.

Daiches, David. Introduction to Pride and Prejudice, by Jane Austen. New York: Random House, Modern Library, 1950.

Titles of full-length works, including novels, plays, and long poems, are underlined in bibliography and note entries. Titles of parts of books, such as chapters, short poems, short stories, and essays, are placed within quotation marks. (See Chapter 4 for further information on capitalization of titles.)

SACRED WORKS If you wish to include a sacred work in a bibliography (this is optional), enter the title of the version or translation, but not the citation of chapter and verse, which appears in the notes only. The titles of sacred works should not be underlined. If the translation or version is well known, the name alone suffices without additional facts of publication. To provide more information, follow the standard entry for a book.

The Bible. New Revised Standard Version.

The Book of Mormon.

The Koran.

Sandmell, Samuel, et al., eds. The New English Bible with the Apocrypha. Oxford Study Edition. New York: Oxford University Press, 1976.

CLASSICAL WORKS Give full information concerning the edition in the bibliography.

Aristotle. Nicomachean Ethics. Trans. Terence Irwin. Indianapolis: Hackett, 1988.

▪ Reference Works

Entries for widely known reference works, such as dictionaries, encyclopedias, atlases, and yearbooks, need not include the facts of publication. The edition number or the year suffices for identification of the work. In the note, the title of the reference work is underlined, and the abbreviation s.v., meaning *sub verbo* or *under the word*, precedes the article or entry, which appears within quotation marks. The bibliography entry, which is optional, gives only the name of the reference work.

Encyclopedia entry
Note form

53. Encyclopaedia Britannica, 15th ed., s.v. "logic."

Bibliography form

Encyclopaedia Britannica, 15th ed.

Dictionary entry
Note form

54. Webster's Third New International Dictionary, s.v. "rhetoric."

Bibliography form

Webster's Third New International Dictionary.
(Because the number of the edition appears in the title, the date is not necessary.)

Atlas entry
Note form

55. Times Atlas of the World, 1990 ed., s.v. "World Air Routes."

Bibliography form

Times Atlas of the World, 1990 ed.

Signed entry

When an article or entry is signed, the name of the author may be included. If only the initials of the author are given, the full name, if you can locate it in a list of contributors for the work, should be supplied in brackets.

Note form

56. Collier's Encyclopedia, 1987 ed., s.v. "Page, Thomas Nelson," by Harriet R. Holman.

Bibliography form

Collier's Encyclopedia, 1987 ed.

Note form

57. Encyclopaedia Britannica, 1973 ed., s.v. "amphitheatre," by J[ames] H[armon] B[utler].

Bibliography form

Encyclopaedia Britannica, 1973 ed.

Little-known reference work

Entries for little-known or specialized reference works should include the full facts of publication.

Ealwell, John, Murray Millgate, and Peter Newman. The New Palgrave: A Dictionary of Economics. London: Macmillan, 1987.

If you wish to identify the author of an article in a specialized or little-known reference work, do so in the note but not in the bibliography entry.

Bibliography form

Corsini, Raymond J., ed. Encyclopedia of Psychology. New York: Wiley, 1984.

Note form

58. Raymond J. Corsini, ed., Encyclopedia of Psychology (New York: Wiley, 1984), s.v. "Birth Order," by C. Reginald Brasingly.

▪ Public Documents

A publication authorized or printed by a government entity, such as a nation, state, or city, is called a *public document*. Public documents take a wide variety of forms: records of meetings and proceedings, regulations, reports of research, guidelines for industries, and statistics on current and future trends. The *Monthly Catalog of U.S. Government Publications*, 1930–, provides a full listing of the publications by various branches of government in the United States. Many states and cities also publish such listings. In addition, the federal government regularly publishes a *Checklist of United States Public Documents*.

Bibliographical entries for public documents, like those for other kinds of works, consist of three parts—author, title, and facts of publication—each of which may contain several elements. Each part ends with a period, followed by one space.

Because there are many types and sources of documents, it may be difficult to know where to place all the information. When you cannot follow the rules given below, use your judgment about presenting the information in a way that allows your reader to locate the document.

Author entry

The author entry may include several elements, presented in this order:

1. The governing body—such as nation, state, county, or city—in order of size and importance
2. The identity of the division of government—such as Congress, Senate, or Department of State
3. The name of any particular committee and subcommittee within the division

The author entry for a document prepared by a subcommittee of the United States Senate Committee on Agriculture would read as follows:

U.S. Senate. Committee on Agriculture. Subcommittee on
    Loans.

Even when the name of an individual author appears on the title page, in most cases the author of a document is still considered to be the governing body that commissioned and published the work. The personal names of individual authors usually follow the title.

Title entry

The title entry for a public document includes the following:

1. The name of the publication, underlined
2. The name of any individual authors (or editors or compilers)
3. A designation of the document's identity—such as *Hearing*, *Proclamation*, *Executive Order*, *Report*, or *Document*—when applicable
4. Information about the date or origin, such as the session of Congress or the number of the document

Within the title entry, you may use abbreviations: S. for Senate, H. for House, Cong. for Congress, res. for resolution, doc. for document, sess. for session. The title entry for a document that has an individual author would read as follows:

Precedents, Decisions on Points of Order, with Phraseology, in the United States Senate. Report prepared by Henry Gilfry. 62nd Cong., 2nd sess., 1938. S. Doc. 1123.

Alternatively, if the name of the author seems to be more important than the name of the government body, either for the purposes of your research or for accurate attribution of the work, you may begin the entry with the name of the individual author.

Gates, Jane Potter. Educational and Training Opportunities in Sustainable Agriculture. Report prepared for U.S. Department of Agriculture. Beltsville, Md.: National Agricultural Library, 1991.

Facts of publication

The facts of publication include the following:

1. The city of publication
2. The publisher
3. The date of publication, as distinct from the date of the session of Congress that produced the information

The publisher of most United States government documents is the Government Printing Office, abbreviated GPO, located in Washington, D.C. The usual facts of publication for a U.S. government document read as follows: Washington, D.C.: GPO, 19XX. These facts of publication may be omitted in citations to congressional and other documents that already contain detailed identifying information. When a document has another publisher, follow the general rules for the facts of publication.

Chicago Style

Enter the page number, following the rules for a book or article, as appropriate. When a page number follows the number for a part or section, introduce it with the abbreviation p. or pp. to avoid confusion.

A bibliography entry for a document with author, title, and facts of publication, then, reads as follows:

U.S. Congress. House. Committee on Agriculture. Subcommittee on Dairy and Poultry. Federal Loan for Poultry Processing Plant in New Castle, Pa. Hearing. 89th Cong., 1st sess., 19 Oct. 1965. Washington, D.C.: GPO, 1966.

Congressional Record

Because the *Congressional Record* is widely known and often cited, it may be entered without the author entry or the facts of publication.

Congressional Record. 89th Cong., 2nd sess., 1966. Vol. 72, pt. 5, pp. 12161-214.

Although you may encounter numerous kinds of documents, the most frequently used belong in one of the following categories:

Constitution of the United States

The Constitution of the United States need not appear in the bibliography. The note or parenthetical reference should include the article or amendment and section, as well as the clause, if appropriate (see page 198).

Congressional documents

An entry for a hearing, a transcript of the testimony of witnesses before congressional committees, should include the name of the committee to which testimony was presented.

U.S. Congress. Senate. Committee on Environment and Public Works. Construction and Repair Programs to Alleviate Unemployment. Hearing. 97th Cong., 2nd sess., 1 Dec. 1982. Washington, D.C.: GPO, 1983.

Individual acts of Congress are published separately after passage. These separate publications should be cited as documents.

U.S. Congress. Senate. Committee on Commerce, Science, and Transportation. Subcommittee on Surface Transportation. Household Goods Transportation Act of 1980. Washington, D.C.: GPO, 1983.

After the laws have been compiled in the *Statutes at Large,* they should be cited as laws (see the discussion of legal citation in Appendix B).

Entries for reports prepared by Congress should follow the basic form for a document.

U.S. Congress. House. Committee on Post Office and Civil Service. Background on the Civil Service Retirement System. Report prepared by the Congressional Research Service. Washington, D.C.: GPO, 1983.

Executive documents

The executive branch issues presidential proclamations, executive orders, and reports of executive departments and bureaus.

U.S. President. Proclamation. "Martin Luther King Day." 15 Jan. 1988.

U.S. Department of Commerce. Bureau of the Census. Aircraft Propellers. Washington, D.C.: Bureau, 1979.

Treaties made by the United States since 1950 have been published in *United States Treaties and Other International Agreements*. Entries for treaties, as well as for other kinds of documents published in books, include the title of the collection.

U.S. Department of State. "General Agreement on Tariffs and Trade," 10 Mar. 1955. TIAS no. 3437. United States Treaties and Other International Agreements, vol. 6, pt. 5.

City and state documents

Note and bibliography entries for documents published by states and cities, as well as by other nations, follow the same principles as those for Federal documents.

Georgia. Department of Human Resources. Division of Physical Health. Georgia Vital and Health Statistics, 1978. Atlanta, 1980.

Allentown, Pa. Urban Observatory. An Analysis of Tire Service Delivery for Master Planning in Allentown, Pa. 1977.

Unpublished documents

Unpublished documents, or those published for a small audience, often do not include all of the information necessary for a complete bibliography entry. When that is the case, you will fill in the entry with descriptions of the material sufficient to enable the reader to locate it. Titles of unpublished materials are placed within quotation marks rather than underlined, as in the following examples:

"Automobile, Aerospace and Agricultural Implement Workers of America: International Union, United, AFL-CIO, and the Ford Motor Company, Agreement between." 20 Oct. 1961.

Stone Cutters Association of North America. Journeymen. "Constitution and By-Laws." 1926.

▪ Unpublished Sources

In citing unpublished sources, improvisation is occasionally necessary. You may encounter sources that do not provide all of the usual information. When that is the case, include any other piece of information according to the principles of other *Chicago Manual* entries.

If the source has an individual or corporate author, list the name as in any author entry. Titles of unpublished works are not underlined but are enclosed in double quotation marks. If you have to supply a title for the source, that title is neither underlined nor quoted. The facts of publication include the origin or location of the source and the date.

Manuscript materials

A citation to manuscript materials—such as letters, scrapbooks, diaries, sermons, financial records, minutes of meetings, and legal transactions—includes the name of the author, the name of the collection and the library, the location of the library, the nature of the materials, and any other relevant information.

An entry for a letter gives the names of the sender and addressee, the date, and the location.

```
Cockburn, Robert. Letter to Lord Melville. 17 May 1819.
     Group 125, Manuscript Collection. Rutgers University,
     New Brunswick, N.J.
```

For a letter cited from a published volume, the entry follows the format for citation of a book or a collection, as appropriate.

The nature of the manuscript materials should be indicated in the entry.

```
Towne, Zaccheus. Diary. July 1776-Feb. 1777. Group 615,
     Manuscript Collection. Rutgers University, New
     Brunswick, N.J.
```

Supplied titles

When a manuscript does not have an author or a title, the writer supplies a description of the materials so that they can be identified and located. Supplied titles and descriptions are neither underlined nor enclosed in quotation marks.

```
Papers on Industrial Espionage. Report of Agent 106. 17
     July 1919. University of Washington, Seattle.
```

Manuscript: MS

A manuscript—a handwritten copy—is indicated by the abbreviation MS.

```
Scarborough, Dorothy. "The Wind." MS. Dorothy Scarborough
     Papers. The Texas Collection. Baylor University,
     Waco, Tex.
```

Typescript: TS

A typescript—a typewritten copy of a work or a transcription of an oral source such as an interview—is designated with the abbreviation TS.

```
The Oral Memoirs of J. R. Smith. TS. Oral History
     Division. Butler College, Butler, N.Y.
```

Photocopied material

The form of a work duplicated by photocopying machine, mimeograph, or ditto should be indicated in the citation.

```
Yaffe, James. "A Report on the [University of Nebraska]
     Summer Writing Institute: 1979." Lincoln: Department
     of English, n.d. Photocopy.
```

■ Dissertations

When dissertations and theses are cited as unpublished sources, their titles appear within quotation marks.

Virgili, Carmen. "Literature of the Spanish Civil War." Ph.D. diss., New York University, 1990.

A dissertation published by a microfilm service should be entered in a bibliography according to the guidelines for a book, with the title appearing in italics.

Moskop, William W. The Prudent Politician: An Extension of Aristotle's Ethical Theory. Ph.D. diss., George Washington University, 1984. Ann Arbor, Mich.: UMI, 1985. 85-13289.

When you cite the abstract for a dissertation, follow the above format, but include also a reference to *Dissertation Abstracts International (DAI)*, published until 1969 as *Dissertation Abstracts (DA)*.

Stone, James Clement. The Evolution of Civil War Novels for Children. Ph.D. diss., University of Cincinnati, 1991. Abstract in Dissertation Abstracts International 51 (1991): 2299A.

■ Nonprint Sources

For nonprint sources, provide some equivalent of author, title, and facts of publication. Because such sources usually have many persons identifiable as author in the broadest sense of the word, you will have to select those you consider necessary for locating the source and those important for your purpose in citing it. Include any significant information about writers or performers before or after the title with these abbreviations: `Prod.` for *Producer* or *Produced by*, `Writ.` for *Writer* or *Written by*, `Dir.` for *Director* or *Directed by*, `Perf.` for *Performer* or *Performed by*, `Narr.` for *Narrator* or *Narrated by*, `Adapt.` for *Adapter* or *Adapted by*, and `Cond.` for *Conductor* or *Conducted by*. Entries for the same source in two papers with different emphases, one on writers and the other on directors, would be constructed differently and would most likely provide different information. In either case, the reader should be able to identify and locate the material.

Films

In an entry for a film, the writer, producer, or director may take the position of author, depending on the relative importance of each. The title of the film is underlined, and the entry should include the company and the year of release.

Country Life. Writ. and dir. Michael Blakemore. Perf. Sam Neill, Greta Scacchi, John Hargreaves, and Kerry Fox. Miramax, 1995.

Costner, Kevin, perf. Waterworld. Writ. Peter Rader and David Twohy. Prod. Charles Gordon and John Davis. Universal, 1995.

If your readers might not readily identify the entry as a film, or if the format requires an explanation, place a description of the medium after the entry: filmstrip, slides, made for television movie, as appropriate.

Fields, Lawrence C. Sea Anemones and Corals of the Atlantic Ocean. Woods Hole, Mass.: Marine Biology Laboratory, 1951. Filmstrip.

Television or radio program

An entry for a television or radio program includes the following information, if available and appropriate in a particular instance: title of episode, in quotation marks; title of the program, underlined; title of the series; name of the network; call letters and city of local station; date of broadcast.

"Some Can Sing." The Language of Life. Writ. and narr. Bill Moyers. With Robert Hass, Claribel Alegría, and Carolyn Forché. PBS, WNET, Newark, N.J., 9 July 1995.

"Hiroshima: Why the Bomb Was Dropped." Peter Jennings Reporting. Prod. David Gelber and Martin Smith. ABC, WLOV, Columbus, Miss., 27 July 1995.

Performances

Performances of music, ballet, or drama should be identified by the author, director, conductor, choreographer, and/or principal participants, depending on your emphasis. The entry should also include the name of the theater, the city, and the date.

The entry for a performance, such as a concert or play, usually begins with the title of the work. If you wish to emphasize any of the persons involved, place that name in the author position.

Molnar, Frederic. The Play's the Thing. Adapt. P. G. Wodehouse and dir. Gloria Muzio. Roundabout Theatre Company, New York, 15 July 1995.

Close, Glenn, perf. Sunset Boulevard, by Andrew Lloyd Webber. Minskoff Theatre, New York, 1 Apr. 1995.

Robbins, Jerome, dir. and chor. Jerome Robbins' Broadway. Imperial Theatre, New York, 14 June 1989.

Schwarz, Gerard, cond. Piano Concerto in F major, by Wolfgang Amadeus Mozart. Perf. Cecile Licad. Mostly Mozart Festival Orchestra. Avery Fisher Hall, New York, 28 July 1994.

Beatty, Talley, chor. Come and Get the Beauty of It Hot. Perf. Marilyn Banks. Symphony Space Theater, New York, 12 Sept. 1995.

Musical compositions

An entry for a musical composition begins with the name of the composer, followed by the title of the piece. When identified by the type or key of the work, these titles are not underlined. If the composition goes by another title, that title is underlined.

Beethoven, Ludwig von. Sonata no. 19 in G minor, op. 49, no. 1.

Schubert, Franz. Symphony No. 8 (Unfinished).

Musical scores

Cite a score in published form like a book, underlining and capitalizing principal words, even those for number and form, and providing the city of publication, publisher, and date.

Sound recordings

For a recording of music or voice, underline the title of the complete work and place any segment of it within quotation marks. After the title, identify the medium (CD-ROM, diskette, etc.), the producer or publisher, and the year of release. The entry may begin with any of the composers, authors, or performers you wish to emphasize, identifying the function if it is not obvious for your readers. You may include identifying numbers or letters at the end of the entry.

Handel, George Frideric. Water Music/Wassermusik. Cond. Neville Marriner. Academy of St. Martin-in-the-Fields. EMI, 1989. Compact disk 549810.

As a title of a recording, the identification of a musical composition by key and number is underlined.

Karajan, Herbert von, cond. Brahms's Symphony No. 1 in C minor, op. 68. Vienna Philharmonic Orchestra. London Records, STS 15194, 1960. Recording.

Enclose a selection within quotation marks.

Dave Brubeck Quartet. "Far More Blue." Time Further Out. New York: CBS, n.d. Audiocassette.

If you know the writer of the song, include the name(s) after the title.

The Beatles. "The Long and Winding Road," by John Lennon and Paul McCartney. Let It Be. New York: Apple, n.d. Recording.

Treat a spoken recording like a musical recording.

Thomas, Dylan. "Fern Hill." Dylan Thomas Reading. Vol. 1. Caedmon, n.d. Recording.

Tapes and cassettes

Citations for tape recordings, audiocassettes, or videocassettes should follow the format for recordings. Specify the nature of the material.

Dalton, Dennis. Aristotle's "Politics": The Golden Mean and Just Rule. Dubuque, Iowa: The Teaching Company. Videocassette No. BM-G001.

Family Counseling. Narr. K. Hunter. Washington, D.C.: American Psychological Association, 1989. Audiocassette.

Works of art

Titles of works of art are underlined and identified by their location, either in a museum or other collection or institution or in a book with reproductions.

Gainsborough, Thomas. The Morning Walk. National Gallery, London.

Vallayer-Coster, Anne. The White Soup Bowl. Private Collection, Paris. Plate 52 in Women Artists, 1550-1950, by Ann Sutherland Harris and Linda Nochlin. New York: Knopf, 1977.

Personal contact with sources

Personal contact between the writer and another scholar or an expert in the field might include interviews, telephone conversations, and letters. These are treated in notes and bibliography as unpublished sources. When you quote such a source, you must obtain permission, unless, as in the case of a public speech, general permission is implicitly granted.

Mazzeo, Joseph A. Letters to author, 8 Aug. to 31 Dec. 1996.

Holwitz, Stanley. Telephone conversation with author, 25 Oct. 1998.

Wenig, Judith C. E-mail to author, 15 May 1999.

Speeches and addresses

References to a speech or paper delivered at a meeting include the name of the speaker, the title of the speech or paper, the name of the group, and the date and location of the meeting.

Jochens, Jenny. "Gender Equality in Law?: The Case of Medieval Iceland." Paper presented at the Center for Medieval and Early Renaissance Studies, 26th Annual Conference, Binghamton, N.Y., 15 Oct. 1992.

Treat a speech included in a published conference proceedings like an article in a collection (see pages 153 and 207).

Classroom lectures and comments or speeches made at meetings should provide the name of the speaker, a descriptive title, the location, and the date.

Rittner, Robert. "The Great Awakening." Lecture to History 101. State University of New York, Buffalo, N.Y. 25 Apr. 1995.

Randall, Emily. Speech at student council meeting. Ventura County Community College, Ventura, Calif. 15 Sept. 1996.

■ Electronic Sources

The citation for an electronic source should provide sufficient information to permit your reader to locate material identical to the material you used. Because electronic sources can be easily altered or erased, meeting this criterion requires more information than you normally need for print sources.

Electronic sources can be divided into two types, depending on whether or not they utilize the Internet.

SOURCES ON THE INTERNET Entries for materials from the Internet, accessed via the World Wide Web, should present first the same facts of publication that are applicable for print sources: the full name of the author, editor, or compiler, followed by the appropriate abbreviation; the title of the section you used, in quotation marks (for articles or the equivalent); the title of the entire source, underlined (for books or the equivalent); when the entry does not begin with it, the name of the editor, compiler, or translator (followed by the appropriate abbreviation); and if a print version exists, the facts of publication for it.

In addition to the above information, entries for sources on the Web require the following information: the title of the database, project, or site, underlined, or for those without a title, a description, such as `Home page`; name of the editor of the database or site; the version number of the source (if it is not part of the title); the date of electronic publication of the latest update; the number of pages, paragraphs, or sections, if marked; the date you accessed the site; and the electronic address (Uniform Resource Locator). To locate some of this information, you may have to explore the entire site carefully. Also, some of the copyright information may be on the Home page from which the site branches: to find this page, remove the final segments of the address one by one or click the appropriate link on the site itself.

If you cannot locate some of the required information, cite whatever you do have. Be certain to include the date you accessed the site. Recording each different time you visit a site and take notes requires particular attention, but it is essential because electronic sources can easily be altered or erased. You might want to make a habit of printing out any site you think you may want to use in your paper. If you think the site may not be available any longer on the Web, you might include some or all of it in an appendix.

Book online Calahan, Margaret, et al. Fall Staff in Postsecondary Institutions, 1993. [book online] (Washington, D.C.: GPO, 1996, accessed 30 Nov. 1998); available from http://nces.ed.gov/pubsearch/pubsinfo.asp?pubid=96323XXXXX.

Poem online Pinsky, Robert. "Ginza Samba." Internet Poetry Archive. [online] (U of North Carolina P and North Carolina Arts Council, 16 Sept. 1997, accessed 25 Nov. 1998); available from http://www.sunsite.unc.edu/ipa/pinsky/ginza/html.

Reference work online

Americana Online, 2001 ed.; accessed 13 Nov. 2001; available from http://go.grolier.com/gol.

Article in an online journal

Readings, Bill. "Notes from the Electronic Underground." Surfaces 4 (1994), 53 pars. [journal online]; accessed 14 Nov. 1998; available from http://tornade.ere.umontreal.ca/~boudreaj/vol4/readings.htm.

Article in an online magazine

Church, Sue. "Irish Expatriate Keeps in Touch via the Web." Computer Mediated Communication Magazine, Aug. 1996 [magazine online]; accessed 20 Nov. 1998; available from http://www.december.com/cmc/mag/1996/aug/church.html.

Newspaper article, online version

Schiff, David. "Leonard Bernstein: The Man Who Mainstreamed Mahler." New York Times 4 Nov. 2001 [newspaper online]; accessed 6 Nov. 2001; available from http://www.nytimes.org/2001/11/04/arts/music/04SCHI.html.

Review online

Cupples, Douglas W. Review of The Lost Colony of the Confederacy, by Eugene C. Harter. [online]; accessed 30 Nov. 1998; available from http://www.h-net.msu.edu/reviews/index.cgi.

Scholarly project

American Verse Project. University of Michigan Humanities Text Initiative and University of Michigan Press (16 Oct. 1996) [poetry anthology online]; accessed 30 Nov. 1998; available from http://www.hti.umich.edu/english/amverse.

Posting on an electronic discussion list

Franklin, Phyllis. "Climbing Mt. Everest," E-GRAD 10 June 1977 [online posting]; accessed 15 Sept. 1998; available from http://www.reg.unci.edu/UCI/HUMANITIES/ENGLISH/egrad.html.

ELECTRONIC MATERIALS NOT ON THE WORLD WIDE WEB
Certain materials, such as computer software and CD-ROM, are accessed electronically, but in themselves they may not be electronic. In addition to the information you would normally provide for any source, such as author and title, you need to provide a description of the medium (CD-ROM, diskette, etc.); the name of the database or vendor, underlined, and if it is not well known, an address preceded by the word `Available`; the date of electronic publication; if necessary for your purpose, the equipment required to run it; and the date you accessed the source. If you cannot locate some of the required information, cite whatever you do have.

Computer program or software

Microsoft Windows 95. Computer software. Ver. 4. CD-ROM. Redmond, Wash.: Microsoft, 1995. MS-DOS 3.1, 386DX, 4MB.

Availability specified

Quotation Reference Collection. Computer software. Reno: AAPEX, 1995. IBM, Windows. Available from AAPEX Software, 955 South Virginia, Suite 116, Reno, Nev. 89502.

Material from electronic database

Identify the medium of the database you used: CD-ROM, diskette, videodisc, magnetic tape, and so on. When you cite only part of a database, identify it within quotation marks.

Guerrini, Anita. "The Ethics of Animal Experimentation in Seventeenth-Century England." Historical Abstracts on Disc, 1982-1995. Spring 1995 update. CD-ROM. Retrieval Software, 1992.

"Pomona College." Peterson's College Database. Magnetic tape. Princeton: Peterson's, 1992.

Underline or quote the title as *Chicago Manual* format would require in any other context.

Gainsborough, Thomas. The Morning Walk. On Microsoft Art Gallery: The Collection of the National Gallery, London. CD-ROM. Redmond, Wash.: Microsoft, 1994.

If the material has an equivalent version in print, cite the print version first, then the information about your electronic source.

Laroche, Jacques M. "Typology of Instructional Theories." International Review of Applied Linguistics in Language Teaching, 22 (Feb. 1984): 41-52. DIALOG, PsycINFO file 11, 72-03548.

For material requiring or including more than one electronic medium, name all of them.

Perseus 1.0: Interactive Sources and Studies on Ancient Greece. CD-ROM, videodisc. New Haven: Yale University Press, 1992.

Examples of Footnote and Endnote Forms and Bibliography Forms

The following pages show examples of note forms and bibliography forms in *Chicago Manual* style. The form for notes is on the left-hand page; the corresponding form for the bibliography (or the list of works cited) is on the right.

Books 178
Multivolume Works and Series 184
Journals 186
Magazines 188
Newspapers 188
Reviews 190
Works of Literature 192
Reference Works 194
Public Documents 196
Unpublished Sources 200
Dissertations 202
Nonprint Sources 202
Microform Materials 208
Electronic Sources 208

FOOTNOTES AND ENDNOTES

Books

Basic form

1. Hazel Henderson, Paradigms in Progress: Life beyond Economics (Indianapolis: Knowledge Systems, 1992), 62. (The subtitle is optional in the note.)

Two authors

2. Wendy Simonds and Barbara Katz Rothman, Centuries of Solace: Grief in Popular Literature (Philadelphia: Temple University Press, 1992), 35.

Four or more authors

3. William McPherson et al., English and American Literature: Sources and Strategies for Collection Development (Chicago: American Library Association, 1987), 67.

Two authors with same last name

4. Richard Price and Sally Price, Equatoria (New York: Routledge, 1992), 75-77.

Pseudonym (real name supplied)

5. Hannah Green [Joanne Greenberg], I Never Promised You a Rose Garden (New York: Holt, Rinehart and Winston, 1964), 15

Pseudonym supplied

6. Emily Brontë [Ellis Bell, pseud.], Wuthering Heights (London, 1850).

Author's name missing, supplied

7. [Henry Adams], Democracy: An American Novel. (New York Holt, 1880), 27.

Author's name missing, omitted

8. Democracy: An American Novel. (New York: Holt, 1880).

Name with suffix

9. William A. Christian Jr., Apparitions in Late Medieval and Renaissance Spain (Princeton: Princeton University Press, 1981), 125.

Indirect citation, emphasis on the cited source

10. Ron Chernow, The House of Morgan (New York: Simon & Schuster, Touchstone, 1990), 47, citing [or quoting] Matthew Josephson, The Robber Barons (New York: Harcourt, Brace, 1934) 338.

BIBLIOGRAPHY

Books

Henderson, Hazel. Paradigms in Progress: Life beyond Economics. Indianapolis: Knowledge Systems, 1992.

Simonds, Wendy, and Barbara Katz Rothman. Centuries of Solace: Grief in Popular Literature. Philadelphia: Temple University Press, 1992.

McPherson, William, Stephen Lehmann, Craig Likness, and Marcia Pankake. English and American Literature: Sources and Strategies for Collection Development. Chicago: American Library Association, 1987.

Price, Richard, and Sally Price. Equatoria. New York: Routledge, 1992.

Green, Hannah [Joanne Greenberg]. I Never Promised You a Rose Garden. New York: Holt, Rinehart and Winston, 1964.

Brontë, Emily [Ellis Bell, pseud.]. Wuthering Heights. London, 1850.

[Adams, Henry]. Democracy: An American Novel. New York: Holt, 1880.

Democracy: An American Novel. New York: Holt, 1880.

Christian, William A., Jr. Apparitions in Late Medieval and Renaissance Spain. Princeton: Princeton University Press, 1981.

Chernow, Ron. The House of Morgan, 47. New York: Simon & Schuster, Touchstone, 1990. Citing [or Quoting] Matthew Josephson, The Robber Barons (New York: Harcourt, Brace, 1934), 338.

FOOTNOTES AND ENDNOTES

Books *continued*

Indirect citation, emphasis on the original source

11. Matthew Josephson, The Robber Barons (New York: Harcourt, Brace, 1934), 338, cited [or quoted] in Ron Chernow, The House of Morgan (New York: Simon & Schuster, Touchstone, 1990), 47.

Group or corporation as author

12. Bicycling Magazine, Reconditioning the Bicycle (New York: Rodale, 1989), 25.

Group or corporation as author and publisher

13. American Museum of Natural History, Annual Report, 1993-1994 (New York: American Museum of Natural History, 1995), 12.

Edited work or compilation

14. Robert Baum, ed., Reform and Reaction in Post-Mao China: The Road through Tiananmen (New York: Routledge, 1992), 25-34.

Two editors

15. Evelyn Fox Keller and Elizabeth A. Lloyd, eds., Keywords in Evolutionary Biology (Cambridge: Harvard University Press, 1992), 15.

Four compilers

16. George Perkins et al., comps., The American Tradition in Literature, 6th ed., 2 vols. (New York: Random House, 1985), 1:275.

Edited volume, emphasis on author of one article

17. Gordon H. Burghardt, "On the Origins of Play," in Play in Animals and Humans, ed. Peter K. Smith (Oxford: Basil Blackwell, 1984), 40.

Article reprinted in an edited volume

18. Stephen Greenblatt, "Towards a Poetics of Culture," in The New Historicism, ed. H. Aram Veeser (New York: Routledge, 1989), 12.

BIBLIOGRAPHY

Books *continued*

Josephson, Matthew. The Robber Barons, 338. New York: Harcourt, Brace, 1934. Cited [or Quoted] in Ron Chernow, The House of Morgan (New York: Simon & Schuster, Touchstone, 1990), 47.

Bicycling Magazine. Reconditioning the Bicycle. New York: Rodale, 1989.

American Museum of Natural History. Annual Report, 1993-1994. New York: American Museum of Natural History, 1995.

Baum, Robert, ed. Reform and Reaction in Post-Mao China: The Road through Tiananmen. New York: Routledge, 1992.

Keller, Evelyn Fox, and Elizabeth A. Lloyd, eds. Keywords in Evolutionary Biology. Cambridge: Harvard University Press, 1992.

Perkins, George, Bradley Sculley, Richmond Croom Beatty, and E. Hudson Long, comps. The American Tradition in Literature. 6th ed. 2 vols. New York: Random House, 1985.

Burghardt, Gordon M. "On the Origins of Play." In Play in Animals and Humans, ed. Peter K. Smith, 5-42. Oxford: Basil Blackwell, 1984.

Greenblatt, Stephen. "Towards a Poetics of Culture." In The New Historicism, ed. H. Aram Veeser, 1-14. New York: Routledge, 1989. First published in Southern Review (Australia) 20 (1987): 3-15.

FOOTNOTES AND ENDNOTES

Books *continued*

Article reprinted under a different title

19. Gareth Matthews, "Ritual and the Religious Feelings," in Explaining Emotions, ed. Amélie Oksenberg Rorty (Berkeley: University of California Press, 1980), 340.

Article in collection of conference proceedings

20. Connie C. Eble, "Etiquette Books as Linguistic Authority," in The Second LACUS Forum, 1975, ed. Peter A. Reich (Columbia, S.C.: Hornbeam, 1976), 473.

Book with introduction by another writer

21. Luba Brezhneva, The World I Left Behind, introd. Rober Conquest (New York: Random House, 1995), 100.

Emphasis on writer of introduction

22. Robert Conquest, introduction to The World I Left Behind, by Luba Brezhneva (New York: Random House, 1955), xii.

Edited work, emphasis on author

23. William Shakespeare, King Lear, ed. Kenneth Muir, The Arden Shakespeare (London: Methuen, 1972), act 4, sc. 7, lines 19-20.

Edited work, emphasis on editor

24. Kenneth Muir, ed., King Lear, by William Shakespeare, The Arden Shakespeare (London: Methuen, 1972), act 3, sc. 4, lines 6-21.

Translation, emphasis on author

25. Aharon Appelfeld, Katerina, trans. Jeffrey Green (New York: Random House, 1992), 67.

Translation, emphasis on translator

26. Jeffrey Green, trans., Katerina, by Aharon Appelfeld (New York: Random House, 1992).

Book, edition other than the first

27. Joseph F. Trimmer, Writing with a Purpose, 11th ed. (Boston: Houghton Mifflin, 1996), 167.

Book, publication by division of a publisher

28. Derrick Bell, Faces at the Bottom of the Well: The Permanence of Racism (New York: HarperCollins, Basic Books, 1992), 124.

BIBLIOGRAPHY

Books *continued*

Matthews, Gareth. "Ritual and the Religious Feelings." In Explaining Emotions, ed. Amélie Oksenberg Rorty, 339-53. Berkeley: University of California Press, 1980. First published as "Bodily Motions and Religious Feelings," Canadian Journal of Philosophy 1 (1971): 75-86.

Eble, Connie C. "Etiquette Books as Linguistic Authority." In The Second LACUS Forum, 1975, ed. Peter A. Reich, 468-75. Columbia, S.C.: Hornbeam, 1976.

Brezhneva, Luba. The World I Left Behind. Introd. Robert Conquest. New York: Random House, 1995.

Conquest, Robert. Introduction to The World I Left Behind, by Luba Brezhneva. New York: Random House, 1955.

Shakespeare, William. King Lear. Ed. Kenneth Muir. The Arden Shakespeare. London: Methuen, 1972.

Muir, Kenneth, ed. King Lear, by William Shakespeare. The Arden Shakespeare. London: Methuen, 1972.

Appelfeld, Aharon. Katerina. Trans. Jeffrey Green. New York: Random House, 1992.

Green, Jeffrey, trans. Katerina, by Aharon Appelfeld. New York: Random House, 1992.

Trimmer, Joseph F. Writing with a Purpose. 11th ed. Boston: Houghton Mifflin, 1996.

Bell, Derrick. Faces at the Bottom of the Well: The Permanence of Racism. New York: HarperCollins, Basic Books, 1992.

Chicago Style

FOOTNOTES AND ENDNOTES

Books *continued*

Republished work

29. Willa Cather, One of Ours (New York: Knopf, 1922; reprint, New York: Vintage Books, 1971), 72.

Book originally published as paperbound

30. Peter H. Van Ness, Spirituality, Diversion, and Decadence: The Contemporary Predicament (Binghamton: State University of New York Press, 1992), 333.

Paperbound book, reprinted edition

31. Paul Davies, God and the New Physics (London: Dent, 1983; reprint, New York: Simon and Schuster, Touchstone, 1984), 25.

Facts of publication missing

32. George Eliot, Felix Holt (Edinburgh: William Blackwoo n.d.), 17.

33. George Eliot, Felix Holt (n.p.: William Blackwood, n.d.), 17.

34. George Eliot, Felix Holt (Edinburgh: n.p., n.d.), 17.

35. George Eliot, Felix Holt (Edinburgh: William Blackwoo n.d.), n. pag. (or unpaginated).

Multivolume Works and Series

Multivolume work, general title, reference to a particular volume

36. William M. Bowsky, ed., Studies in Medieval and Renaissance History, 4 vols. (Lincoln: University of Nebraska Press, 1963-67), 2:273-96.

Multivolume work, individual titles

37. William W. Freehling, The Road to Disunion, vol. 1 of Secessionists at Bay, 1776-1854 (New York: Oxford University Press, 1992), 23.

Multivolume work with different editor(s) for each volume

38. Georges Duby, ed., Revelations of the Medieval World, vol. 2 of A History of Private Life, ed. Philippe Ariès and Georges Duby, trans. Arthur Goldhammer (Cambridge: Harvard University Press, Belknap Press, 1988), 234.

BIBLIOGRAPHY

Books *continued*

Cather, Willa. One of Ours. New York: Knopf, 1922. Reprint, New York: Vintage Books, 1971.

Van Ness, Peter H. Spirituality, Diversion, and Decadence: The Contemporary Predicament. Binghamton: State University of New York Press, 1992.

Davies, Paul. God and the New Physics. London: Dent, 1983. Reprint, New York: Simon and Schuster, Touchstone, 1984.

Eliot, George. Felix Holt. Edinburgh: William Blackwood, n.d.

Eliot, George. Felix Holt. N.p.: William Blackwood, n.d.

Eliot, George. Felix Holt. Edinburgh: n.p., n.d.

Eliot, George. Felix Holt. Edinburgh: William Blackwood, n.d.

Multivolume Works and Series

Bowsky, William M., ed. Studies in Medieval and Renaissance History. 4 vols. Lincoln: University of Nebraska Press, 1963-67.

Freehling, William W. The Road to Disunion. Vol. 1 of Secessionists at Bay, 1776-1854. New York: Oxford University Press, 1992.

Duby, Georges, ed. Revelations of the Medieval World. Vol. 2 of A History of Private Life, ed. Philippe Ariès and Georges Duby. Trans. Arthur Goldhammer. Cambridge: Harvard University Press, Belknap Press, 1988.

FOOTNOTES AND ENDNOTES

Multivolume Works and Series *continued*

Work in a series

39. J. Richard Eiser, ed., Attitudinal Judgment, Springer Series in Social Psychology, no. 11 (New York and Berlin: Springer-Verlag, 1990), 45.

Work in a series with editor of series named

40. Vladimir Propp, Theory and History of Folklore, trans Ariadna Y. Martin and Richard P. Martin, Theory and History of Literature, ed. Wlad Godzich and Jochen Schülte-Sasse, no. 5 (Minneapolis: University of Minnesota Press, 1984), 46.

Work in a series, proceedings

41. Walter L. Smith and William E. Wilkinson, eds., Proceedings of the Symposium on Congestion Theory, Probability and Statistics Monograph Series, no. 2 (Chapel Hill: University of North Carolina Press, 1965), 401.

Journals

Article in a scholarly journal

42. Simon Gaunt, "The Significance of Silence," Paragraph 13 (1990): 204.

Article in a journal paginating each issue separately

43. Robert Daly, "Engines of Discourse: God and the Odds in Postmodern Literature," Denver Quarterly 27, no. 4 (1993): 15.

Article in a journal with more than one series

44. Milton M. Klein, "The Pleasures of Teaching and Writing History," William and Mary Quarterly, 3rd ser., 52 (July 1995): 485.

Article in a journal with new series, season identified

45. Peter Erickson, "Singing America: From Walt Whitman to Adrienne Rich," Kenyon Review, n.s., 12 (winter 1995): 112.

Journal with issue numbers rather than volumes

46. C. E. Nwezeh, "The Comparative Approach to Modern African Literature," Yearbook of General and Comparative Literature, no. 28 (1979): 22.

BIBLIOGRAPHY

Multivolume Works and Series *continued*

Eiser, J. Richard, ed. Attitudinal Judgment. Springer Series in Social Psychology, no. 11. New York: Springer-Verlag, 1990.

Propp, Vladimir. Theory and History of Folklore. Trans. Ariadna Y. Martin and Richard P. Martin. Theory and History of Literature, ed. Wlad Godzich and Jochen Schülte-Sasse, no. 5. Minneapolis: University of Minnesota Press, 1984.

Smith, Walter L., and William E. Wilkinson, eds. Proceedings of the Symposium on Congestion Theory. Probability and Statistics Monograph Series, no. 2. Chapel Hill: University of North Carolina Press, 1965.

Journals

Gaunt, Simon. "The Significance of Silence." Paragraph 13 (1990): 202-16.

Daly, Robert. "Engines of Discourse: God and the Odds in Postmodern Literature." Denver Quarterly 27, no. 4 (1993): 6-16.

Klein, Milton M. "The Pleasures of Teaching and Writing History." William and Mary Quarterly, 3rd ser., 52 (July 1995): 483-87.

Erickson, Peter. "Singing America: From Walt Whitman to Adrienne Rich." Kenyon Review, n.s., 12 (winter 1995): 103-19.

Nwezeh, C. E. "The Comparative Approach to Modern African Literature." Yearbook of General and Comparative Literature, no. 28 (1979): 22.

Chicago Style

FOOTNOTES AND ENDNOTES

Magazines

Journal title abbreviated

47. C. E. Nwezeh, "The Comparative Approach to Modern African Literature," <u>YGCL</u>, no. 28 (1979): 22.

Basic form, signed article, monthly magazine

48. Daniel Kleppner, "About Benjamin Thompson," <u>Physics Today</u>, Sept. 1992, 9.

Basic form, unsigned article, weekly magazine

49. "The Bard of Betrayal," <u>Observer Magazine</u>, 27 Sept. 1992, 44-46.

Magazine article with discontinuous pagination

50. Charles Siebert, "The DNA We've Been Dealt," <u>New York Times Magazine</u>, 17 Sept. 1995, 56.

Magazine article with discontinuous pagination, all pages specified in bibliography entry

51. Charles Siebert, "The DNA We've Been Dealt," <u>New York Times Magazine</u>, 17 Sept. 1995, 56.

Item in named weekly column

52. "The Devastated Fisheries," Canada Notes, <u>Macleans's</u>, 21 Aug. 1995, 17.

Newspapers

Basic form

53. Pamela Mercer, "U.S. Venture Bets on Colombian Coal," <u>New York Times</u>, 27 July 1995, D7.

State interpolated

54. "Unknown Author of <u>Wind</u> Answers Crane Criticism," <u>Sweetwater (Texas) Daily Reporter</u>, 15 Dec. 1925, 6.

Foreign city interpolated, with section number

55. <u>Observer</u> (London), 17 Oct. 1990, sec. 2, p. 5.

Edition specified

56. Wayne E. Green, "Cold-Fusion Development Spurs Hot Race for Patents," <u>Wall Street Journal</u>, 9 June 1989, eastern ed., B1.

Editorial

57. "Potomac Yard Decision," editorial, <u>Washington Post</u>, 16 Oct. 1992, A24.

BIBLIOGRAPHY

Magazines

Nweze h, C. E. "The Comparative Approach to Modern African Literature." YGCL, no. 28 (1979): 22.

Kleppner, Daniel. "About Benjamin Thompson." Physics Today, Sept. 1992, 9-10.

"The Bard of Betrayal." Observer Magazine, 27 Sept. 1992, 44-46.

Siebert, Charles. "The DNA We've Been Dealt." New York Times Magazine, 17 Sept. 1995.

Siebert, Charles. "The DNA We've Been Dealt." New York Times Magazine, 17 Sept. 1995, 50-57, 64, 74, 93-94, 104.

"The Devastated Fisheries." Canada Notes. Macleans's, 21 Aug. 1995, 17.

Newspapers

Mercer, Pamela. "U.S. Venture Bets on Colombian Coal." New York Times, 27 July 1995, D7.

"Unknown Author of Wind Answers Crane Criticism." Sweetwater (Texas) Daily Reporter, 15 Dec. 1925, 6.

Observer (London), 17 Oct. 1990, sec. 2, pp. 5, 8.

Green, Wayne E. "Cold-Fusion Development Spurs Hot Race for Patents." Wall Street Journal, 9 June 1989, eastern ed., B1.

"Potomac Yard Decision." Editorial. Washington Post, 16 Oct. 1992, A24.

FOOTNOTES AND ENDNOTES

Newspapers *continued*

Letter to editor

58. Frederick S. Lightfoot, letter, New York Times, 21 Oc 1992, Long Island ed., A22.

Cartoon

59. Bill Watterson, Calvin and Hobbes, cartoon, Miami Herald, 22 July 1995, internat'l ed., 9A.

Advertisement

60. Tiffany and Co., advertisement, New York Times, 27 July 1995, late city ed., A3.

Material identified by column, numbered section

61. San Francisco Sunday Examiner & Chronicle, 26 June 1990, sec. 2, p. 4, col. 1.

Reviews

Signed, with title, in magazine

62. Walter Moore, "Great Physicist, Great Guy," review of Genius: The Life and Science of Richard Feynman, by James Gleick, New York Times Book Review, 11 Oct. 1992, 3.

Signed, untitled, in journal

63. Gail M. Kienitz, review of Tennyson and the Doom of Romanticism, by Herbert F. Tucker, Religion and Literature 24 (spring 1992): 87-90.

Unsigned, untitled, in journal

64. Review of Married to Genius, by Jeffrey Meyers, Journ of Modern Literature 7 (1979): 579.

Drama review

65. Graham Hassell, "Sometimes Excess Isn't Enough," revi of The Grand Ceremonial, by Fernando Arrabal, as performed by Lyric Studio, Hammersmith, England, Times Literary Supplement (London), 14 July 1995, 20.

Movie review

66. Carrie Rickey, "Disney's Pocahontas: Is It Fact or Fiction?" review of Pocahontas (Miramax movie), Philadelphia Inquirer, 18 June 1995, H1.

BIBLIOGRAPHY

Newspapers *continued*

Lightfoot, Frederick S. Letter. New York Times, 21 Oct. 1992, Long Island ed., A22.

Watterson, Bill. Calvin and Hobbes. Cartoon. Miami Herald, 22 July 1995, internat'l ed., 9A.

Tiffany and Co. Advertisement. New York Times, 27 July 1995, late city ed., A3.

San Francisco Sunday Examiner & Chronicle, 26 June 1990, sec. 2, p. 4, cols. 1-3.

Reviews

Moore, Walter. "Great Physicist, Great Guy." Review of Genius: The Life and Science of Richard Feynman, by James Gleick. New York Times Book Review, 11 Oct. 1992, 3.

Kienitz, Gail M. Review of Tennyson and the Doom of Romanticism, by Herbert F. Tucker. Religion and Literature 24 (spring 1992): 87-90.

Review of Married to Genius, by Jeffrey Meyers. Journal of Modern Literature 7 (1979): 579-80.

Hassell, Graham. "Sometimes Excess Isn't Enough." Review of The Grand Ceremonial, by Fernando Arrabal. Lyric Studio, Hammersmith, England. Times Literary Supplement (London), 14 July 1995, 20.

Rickey, Carrie. "Disney's Pocahontas: Is It Fact or Fiction?" Review of Pocahontas (Miramax movie). Philadelphia Inquirer, 18 June 1995, H1, H9.

Chicago Style

FOOTNOTES AND ENDNOTES

Reviews *continued*

Review of television program

67. Celestine Bohlen, "Wine and Women in Tuscany: Bertolucci Lightens Up," review of Stealing Beauty (movie), New York Times, Arts and Leisure Section, 27 Aug. 1995, H10.

Review of musical peformance

68. James R. Oestreich, "In a Choral Requiem, a Climax and Last Hurrah," review of concert performance of Requiem, by Guiseppe Verdi, Tanglewood Festival Chorus, Lenox, Mass., New York Times, 29 Aug. 1995, C13.

Works of Literature

Without editing or commentary

69. Amy Tan, The Joy Luck Club (New York: Ballantine, Ivy, 1989), 125.

Edited, emphasis on author

70. Joseph Conrad, Lord Jim, ed. Thomas C. Moser (New York Norton, 1968), 65.

Edited, emphasis on editor or translator

71. Thomas G. Bergin, trans. and ed., The Divine Comedy, by Dante Alighieri (New York: Appleton-Century-Crofts, 1955), 1

Edited, emphasis on writer of introduction

72. David Daiches, introduction to Pride and Prejudice, by Jane Austen (New York: Modern Library, 1950), vii.

Play: act, scene, line

73. William Shakespeare, Othello, in The Riverside Shakespeare, ed. G. Blakemore Evans (Boston: Houghton Mifflin, 1974), act 3, sc. 2, lines 1-5.

(first reference)

74. Othello 3.2.1-5.

75. Oth. 4.1.5-17.

(subsequent reference, either in notes or within parentheses in the text)

BIBLIOGRAPHY

Reviews *continued*

Bohlen, Celestine. "Wine and Women in Tuscany: Bertolucci Lightens Up." Review of Stealing Beauty (movie). New York Times, Arts and Leisure Section, 27 Aug. 1995, H10.

Oestreich, James R. "In a Choral Requiem, a Climax and Last Hurrah." Review of concert performance of Requiem, by Guiseppe Verdi, Tanglewood Festival Chorus, Lenox, Mass. New York Times, 29 Aug. 1995, C13.

Works of Literature

Tan, Amy. The Joy Luck Club. New York: Ballantine, Ivy, 1989.

Conrad, Joseph. Lord Jim. Ed. Thomas C. Moser. Norton Critical Edition. New York: Norton, 1968.

Bergin, Thomas G., trans. and ed. The Divine Comedy, by Dante Alighieri. New York: Appleton-Century-Crofts, 1955.

Daiches, David. Introduction to Pride and Prejudice, by Jane Austen. New York: Modern Library, 1950.

Shakespeare, William. Othello. In The Riverside Shakespeare, ed. G. Blakemore Evans. Boston: Houghton Mifflin, 1974.

Chicago Style

FOOTNOTES AND ENDNOTES

Works of Literature *continued*

Long poem: book or canto, line

76. John Milton, Paradise Lost, ed. Merritt Y. Hughes (New York: Odyssey, 1962), bk. 9, lines 342-75.
(first reference)

77. Paradise Lost 3.1-55.

or

78. PL 3.1-55.
(subsequent reference, either in notes or parenthetically in text)

Short poem: stanza, line

79. Walt Whitman, "Song of Myself," in The American Tradition in Literature, comp. George Perkins et al., 6th ed., vol. 2 (New York: Norton, 1985), sec. 6, lines 131-35.
(first reference)

80. "Song of Myself" 7.145-48.
(subsequent reference)

Biblical citation, chapter, verse; identified by translation

81. 1 Cor. 14:6-9 NRSV.

Biblical citation; identified by edition in bibliography

82. Gen. 15:1-10.

Classical translation; book, chapter

83. Aristotle, Nicomachean Ethics, trans. Terence Irwin (Indianapolis: Hackett, 1988), 1095b6.
(first reference)

84. Nicomachean Ethics 1113b-1114a10.
(subsequent reference)

Reference Works

Encyclopedia entry, unsigned

85. Encyclopaedia Britannica, 15th ed., s.v. "logic."

BIBLIOGRAPHY

Works of Literature *continued*

Milton, John. Paradise Lost. Ed. Merritt Y. Hughes. New York: Odyssey, 1962.

Perkins, George, Sculley Bradley, Richmond Croom Beatty, and E. Hudson Long, comps. The American Tradition in Literature. 6th ed. 2 vols. New York: Norton, 1985.

The Bible. New Revised Standard Version.

Sandmell, Samuel, et al., eds. The New English Bible with the Apocrypha. Oxford Study Edition. New York: Oxford University Press, 1976.

Aristotle. Nicomachean Ethics. Trans. Terence Irwin. Indianapolis: Hackett, 1988.

Reference Works

Encyclopaedia Britannica. 15th ed.

FOOTNOTES AND ENDNOTES

Reference Works *continued*

Dictionary entry, edition identified in title

86. Webster's Third New International Dictionary, s.v. "rhetoric."

Atlas entry

87. Times Atlas of the World, 1990 ed., s.v. "World Air Routes."

General encyclopedia, signed entry

88. Collier's Encyclopedia, 1987 ed. s.v. "Page, Thomas Nelson," by Harriet R. Holman.

General encyclopedia, initialed article, name supplied

89. Encyclopaedia Britannica, 1973 ed., s.v. "amphitheate by J[ames] H[armon] B[utler].

Dictionary not widely known

90. John Ealwell, Murray Millgate, and Peter Newman, The New Palgrave: A Dictionary of Economics (London: Macmillan, 1987), s.v. "inflation."

Reference work not widely known, emphasis on writer of entry

91. Raymond J. Corsini, ed., Encyclopedia of Psychology (New York: Wiley, 1984), s.v. "Birth Order," by C. Reginald Brasingly.

Public Documents

Document with author and title

92. Jane Potter Gates, Educational and Training Opportunities in Sustainable Agriculture, report prepared for U.S. Department of Agriculture (Beltsville, Md.: National Agricultural Library, 1991), 23.

Congressional hearing, House

93. Congress, House, Committee on Agriculture, Subcommitt on Dairy and Poultry, Federal Loan for Poultry Processing Plan in New Castle, Pa., hearing, 89th Cong., 1st sess., 19 Oct. 19 (Washington, D.C.: GPO, 1966), 47.

Congressional Record

94. Congressional Record, 89th Cong., 2nd sess., 1966, vol. 72, pt. 5, p. 12161.

BIBLIOGRAPHY

Reference Works *continued*

Webster's Third New International Dictionary.

Times Atlas of the World. 1990 ed.

Collier's Encyclopedia. 1987 ed.

Encyclopaedia Britannica. 1973 ed.

Ealwell, John, Murray Millgate, and Peter Newman. The New Palgrave: A Dictionary of Economics. London: Macmillan, 1987.

Corsini, Raymond J., ed. Encyclopedia of Psychology. New York: Wiley, 1984.

Public Documents

Gates, Jane Potter. Educational and Training Opportunities in Sustainable Agriculture. Report prepared for U.S. Department of Agriculture. Beltsville, Md.: National Agricultural Library, 1991.

U.S. Congress. House. Committee on Agriculture. Subcommittee on Dairy and Poultry. Federal Loan for Poultry Processing Plant in New Castle, Pa. Hearing. 89th Cong., 1st sess., 19 Oct. 1965. Washington, D.C.: GPO, 1966.

Congressional Record, 89th Cong., 2nd sess., 1966. Vol. 72, pt. 5, pp. 12161-214.

Chicago Style

FOOTNOTES AND ENDNOTES

Public Documents *continued*

Constitution

95. U.S. Constitution, art. 3, sec. 1.

Congressional hearing

96. Congress, Senate, Committee on Environment and Public Works, Construction and Repair Programs to Alleviate Unemployment, hearing, 97th Cong., 2nd sess., 1 Dec. 1982 (Washington, D.C.: GPO, 1983), 8.

Act of Congress

97. Congress, Senate, Committee on Commerce, Science, and Transportation, Subcommittee on Surface Transportation, Household Goods Transportation Act of 1980 (Washington, D.C.: GPO, 1983), 2.

Congressional report prepared by another agency

98. Congress, House, Committee on Post Office and Civil Service, Background on the Civil Service Retirement System, report prepared by the Congressional Research Service (Washington, D.C.: GPO, 1983), 17.

Executive document

99. President, proclamation, "Martin Luther King Day," 15 Jan. 1988.

Cabinet report

100. Department of Commerce, Bureau of the Census, Aircraft Propellers (Washington, D.C.: Bureau, 1979), 13.

Treaties

101. Department of State, "General Agreement on Tariffs and Trade," 10 Mar. 1955, TIAS no. 3437, United States Treaties and Other International Agreements, vol. 6, pt. 5, p. 5815.

State documents

102. Georgia, Department of Human Resources, Division of Physical Health, Georgia Vital and Health Statistics, 1978 (Atlanta, 1980), 120.

City documents

103. Allentown, Pa., Urban Observatory, An Analysis of Tire Service Delivery for Master Planning in Allentown, Pa. (1977), 5.

BIBLIOGRAPHY

Public Documents *continued*

U.S. Congress. Senate. Committee on Environment and Public Works. Construction and Repair Programs to Alleviate Unemployment. Hearing, 97th Cong., 2nd sess., 1 Dec. 1982. Washington, D.C.: GPO, 1983.

U.S. Congress. Senate. Committee on Commerce, Science, and Transportation. Subcommittee on Surface Transportation. Household Goods Transportation Act of 1980. Washington, D.C.: GPO, 1983.

U.S. Congress. House. Committee on Post Office and Civil Service. Background on the Civil Service Retirement System. Report prepared by the Congressional Research Service. Washington, D.C.: GPO, 1983.

U.S. President. Proclamation. "Martin Luther King Day." 15 Jan. 1988.

U.S. Department of Commerce. Bureau of the Census. Aircraft Propellers. Washington, D.C.: Bureau, 1979.

U.S. Department of State. "General Agreement on Tariffs and Trade," 10 Mar. 1955. TIAS no. 3437. United States Treaties and Other International Agreements, vol. 6, pt. 5.

Georgia. Department of Human Resources. Division of Physical Health. Georgia Vital and Health Statistics, 1978. Atlanta, 1980.

Allentown, Pa. Urban Observatory. An Analysis of Tire Service Delivery for Master Planning in Allentown, Pa. 1977.

FOOTNOTES AND ENDNOTES

Public Documents *continued*

State statutes

104. California, Education Code, Sec. 13444 (1990).

Unpublished document

105. "Automobile, Aerospace and Agricultural Implement Workers of America: International Union, United, AFL-CIO, and the Ford Motor Company, Agreement between," 20 Oct. 1961, 184-85.

Untitled, unpublished document

106. Stone Cutters Association of North America, Journeyme "Constitution and By-Laws," 1926, 4.

Convention proceedings

107. Longshoremen's and Warehousemen's Union, Internationa CIO, Proceedings of the Seventh Biennial Convention of San Francisco, 7 Apr. to 11 Apr. 1947 (San Francisco: Trade Pressroom, n.d.), 83.

Unpublished Sources

Manuscript, letter

108. Robert Cockburn, letter to Lord Melville, 17 May 181 Manuscript Collection, Rutgers University, New Brunswick, N.J. group 125.

Manuscript, nature identified

109. Zaccheus Towne, diary, July 1776-Feb. 1777, Manuscri Collection, Rutgers University, New Brunswick, N.J., group 615

Manuscript, title supplied

110. Papers on Industrial Espionage, report of Agent 106, 17 July 1919, University of Washington, Seattle.

Manuscript, handwritten

111. Dorothy Scarborough, "The Wind," MS, Dorothy Scarbor Papers, The Texas Collection, Baylor University, Waco, Tex., 2

Typescript

112. The Oral Memoirs of J. R. Smith, TS, Oral History Division, Butler College, Butler, N.Y., 75.

BIBLIOGRAPHY

Public Documents *continued*

California. Education Code. 1990.

"Automobile, Aerospace and Agricultural Implement Workers of America: International Union, United, AFL-CIO, and the Ford Motor Company, Agreement between." 20 Oct. 1961.

Stone Cutters Association of North America. Journeymen. "Constitution and By-Laws." 1926.

Longshoremen's and Warehousemen's Union, International, CIO. Proceedings of the Seventh Biennial Convention of San Francisco, 7 Apr. to 11 Apr. 1947. San Francisco: Trade Pressroom, n.d.

Unpublished Sources

Cockburn, Robert. Letter to Lord Melville. 17 May 1819. Group 125, Manuscript Collection. Rutgers University, New Brunswick, N.J.

Towne, Zaccheus. Diary. July 1776-Feb. 1777. Group 615, Manuscript Collection. Rutgers University, New Brunswick, N.J.

Papers on Industrial Espionage. Report of Agent 106. 17 July 1919. University of Washington, Seattle.

Scarborough, Dorothy. "The Wind." MS. Dorothy Scarborough Papers. The Texas Collection. Baylor University, Waco, Tex.

The Oral Memoirs of J. R. Smith. TS. Oral History Division. Butler College, Butler, N.Y.

Chicago Style

FOOTNOTES AND ENDNOTES

Unpublished Sources *continued*

Photocopied work

113. James Yaffe, "A Report on the [University of Nebrask Summer Writing Institute: 1979," photocopy (Lincoln: Departmen of English, n.d.), 4.

Dissertations

Dissertation, typescript

114. Carmen Virgili, "Literature of the Spanish Civil War (Ph.D. diss., New York University, 1990), 22.

Dissertation published by microfilm service

115. William W. Moskop, <u>The Prudent Politician: An Extens of Aristotle's Ethical Theory</u>, Ph.D. diss., George Washington University, 1984 (Ann Arbor, Mich.: UMI, 1985), 79.

Abstract of dissertation

116. James Clement Stone, <u>The Evolution of Civil War Nove for Children</u>, Ph.D. diss., University of Cincinnati, 1991, abstract in <u>Dissertation Abstracts International</u> 51 (1991): 22

Nonprint Sources

Film, basic entry

117. <u>Country Life</u>, writ. and dir. Michael Blakemore, perf. Sam Neill, Greta Scacchi, John Hargreaves, and Kerry Fox, Miramax, 1995.

Film, emphasis on actor

118. Kevin Costner, perf., <u>Waterworld</u>, writ. Peter Rader a David Twohy, prod. Charles Gordon and John Davis, Universal, 1

Film, emphasis on director

119. Phil Alden Robinson, dir., <u>Field of Dreams</u>, with Kevi Costner, Amy Madigan, and James Earl Jones, Universal, 1989.

Filmstrip

120. Lawrence C. Fields, <u>Sea Anemones and Corals of the Atlantic Ocean</u> (Woods Hole, Mass.: Marine Biology Laboratory, 1951), filmstrip.

BIBLIOGRAPHY

Unpublished Sources *continued*

Yaffe, James. "A Report on the [University of Nebraska] Summer Writing Institute: 1979." Lincoln: Department of English, n.d. Photocopy.

Dissertations

Virgili, Carmen. "Literature of the Spanish Civil War." Ph.D. diss., New York University, 1990.

Moskop, William W. The Prudent Politician: An Extension of Aristotle's Ethical Theory. Ph.D. diss., George Washington University, 1984. Ann Arbor, Mich.: UMI, 1985. 85-13289.

Stone, James Clement. The Evolution of Civil War Novels for Children. Ph.D. diss., University of Cincinnati, 1991. Abstract in Dissertation Abstracts International 51 (1991): 2299A.

Nonprint Sources

Country Life. Writ. and dir. Michael Blakemore. Perf. Sam Neill, Greta Scacchi, John Hargreaves, and Kerry Fox. Miramax, 1995.

Costner, Kevin, perf. Waterworld. Writ. Peter Rader and David Twohy. Prod. Charles Gordon and John Davis. Universal, 1995.

Robinson, Phil Alden, dir. Field of Dreams. With Kevin Costner, Amy Madigan, and James Earl Jones. Universal, 1989.

Fields, Lawrence C. Sea Anemones and Corals of the Atlantic Ocean. Woods Hole, Mass.: Marine Biology Laboratory, 1951. Filmstrip.

FOOTNOTES AND ENDNOTES

Nonprint Sources *continued*

Television or radio broadcast, writer named

121. "Some Can Sing," The Language of Life, writ. and nar Bill Moyers, with Robert Hass, Claribel Alegría, and Carolyn Forché, PBS, WNET, Newark, N.J., 9 July 1995.

Television or radio broadcast, producer named

122. "Hiroshima: Why the Bomb Was Dropped," Peter Jenning Reporting, prod. David Gelber and Martin Smith, ABC, WLOV, Columbus, Miss., 27 July 1995.

Performance, drama; emphasis on playwright

123. Frederic Molnar, The Play's the Thing, adapt. P. G. Wodehouse and dir. Gloria Muzio, Roundabout Theatre Company, N York, 15 July 1995.

Performance, drama; emphasis on actor

124. Glenn Close, perf., Sunset Boulevard, by Andrew Lloy Webber, Minskoff Theatre, New York, 1 Apr. 1995.

Performance, musical theater

125. Jerome Robbins, dir. and chor., Jerome Robbins' Broadway, Imperial Theatre, New York, 14 June 1989.

Orchestral performance

126. Gerard Schwarz, cond., Piano Concerto in F major, by Wolfgang Amadeus Mozart, perf. Cecile Licad, Mostly Mozart Festival Orchestra, Avery Fisher Hall, New York, 28 July 1994.

Performance, dance

127. Talley Beatty, chor., Come and Get the Beauty of It Hot, perf. Marilyn Banks, Symphony Space Theater, New York, 12 Sept. 1995.

Musical composition, identified by key

128. Ludwig von Beethoven, Sonata no. 19 in G minor, op. 49, no. 1.

Musical composition, identified by title

129. Franz Schubert, Symphony No. 8 (Unfinished).

Sound recording

130. George Frideric Handel, Water Music/Wassermusik, con Neville Marriner, Academy of St. Martin-in-the-Fields (EMI, 1989), compact disk 549810.

BIBLIOGRAPHY

Nonprint Sources *continued*

"Some Can Sing." The Language of Life. Writ. and narr. Bill Moyers. With Robert Hass, Claribel Alegría, and Carolyn Forché. PBS, WNET, Newark, N.J., 9 July 1995.

"Hiroshima: Why the Bomb Was Dropped." Peter Jennings Reporting. Prod. David Gelber and Martin Smith. ABC, WLOV, Columbus, Miss., 27 July 1995.

Molnar, Frederic. The Play's the Thing. Adapt. P. G. Wodehouse and dir. Gloria Muzio. Roundabout Theatre Company, New York, 15 July 1995.

Close, Glenn, perf. Sunset Boulevard, by Andrew Lloyd Webber. Minskoff Theatre, New York, 1 Apr. 1995.

Robbins, Jerome, dir. and chor. Jerome Robbins' Broadway. Imperial Theatre, New York, 14 June 1989.

Schwarz, Gerard, cond. Piano Concerto in F major, by Wolfgang Amadeus Mozart. Perf. Cecile Licad. Mostly Mozart Festival Orchestra. Avery Fisher Hall, New York, 28 July 1994.

Beatty, Talley, chor. Come and Get the Beauty of It Hot. Perf. Marilyn Banks. Symphony Space Theater, New York, 12 Sept. 1995.

Beethoven, Ludwig von. Sonata no. 19 in G minor, op. 49, no. 1.

Schubert, Franz. Symphony No. 8 (Unfinished).

Handel, George Frideric. Water Music/Wassermusik. Cond. Neville Marriner. Academy of St. Martin-in-the-Fields. EMI, 1989. Compact disk 549810.

Chicago Style

FOOTNOTES AND ENDNOTES

Nonprint Sources *continued*

Selection on sound recording

131. Dave Brubeck Quartet, "Far More Blue," Time Further Out (New York: CBS, n.d.), audiocassette.

Selection on sound recording, author identified

132. The Beatles, "The Long and Winding Road," by John Lennon and Paul McCartney, Let It Be (New York: Apple, n.d.), recording.

Spoken recording

133. Dylan Thomas, "Fern Hill," Dylan Thomas Reading, vol. 1 (Caedmon, n.d.), recording.

Videocassette

134. Dennis Dalton, Aristotle's "Politics": The Golden Mean and Just Rule (Dubuque, Iowa: The Teaching Company), videocassette no. BM-G001.

Audiocassette

135. Family Counseling, narr. K. Hunter (Washington, D.C. American Psychological Association, 1989), audiocassette.

Work of art, in museum

136. Thomas Gainsborough, The Morning Walk, National Gallery, London.

Work of art, reproduced in book

137. Anne Vallayer-Coster, The White Soup Bowl, private collection, Paris; plate 52 in Women Artists, 1550-1950, by An Sutherland Harris and Linda Nochlin (New York: Knopf, 1977), 8

Personal letter

138. Joseph A. Mazzeo, letter to author, 8 Aug. 1996.

Telephone conversation

139. Stanley Holwitz, telephone conversation with author, 25 Oct. 1998.

Electronic mail

140. Judith C. Wenig, E-mail to author, 15 May 1999.

Speech at conference or meeting

141. Jenny Jochens, "Gender Equality in Law?: The Case of Medieval Iceland," paper presented at the Center for Medieval and Early Renaissance Studies, 26th Annual Conference, Binghamton, N.Y., 15 Oct. 1992.

BIBLIOGRAPHY

Nonprint Sources *continued*

Dave Brubeck Quartet. "Far More Blue." Time Further Out. New York: CBS, n.d. Audiocassette.

The Beatles. "The Long and Winding Road," by John Lennon and Paul McCartney. Let It Be. New York: Apple, n.d. Recording.

Thomas, Dylan. "Fern Hill." Dylan Thomas Reading. Vol. 1. Caedmon, n.d. Recording.

Dalton, Dennis. Aristotle's "Politics": The Golden Mean and Just Rule. Dubuque, Iowa: The Teaching Company. Videocassette No. BM-G001.

Family Counseling. Narr. K. Hunter. Washington, D.C.: American Psychological Association, 1989. Audiocassette.

Gainsborough, Thomas. The Morning Walk. National Gallery, London.

Vallayer-Coster, Anne. The White Soup Bowl. Private Collection, Paris. Plate 52 in Women Artists, 1550-1950, by Ann Sutherland Harris and Linda Nochlin. New York: Knopf, 1977.

Mazzeo, Joseph A. Letters to author, 8 Aug. to 31 Dec. 1996.

Holwitz, Stanley. Telephone conversation with author, 25 Oct. 1998.

Wenig, Judith C. E-mail to author, 15 May 1999.

Jochens, Jenny. "Gender Equality in Law?: The Case of Medieval Iceland." Paper presented at the Center for Medieval and Early Renaissance Studies, 26th Annual Conference, Binghamton, N.Y., 15 Oct. 1992.

Chicago Style

FOOTNOTES AND ENDNOTES

Nonprint Sources *continued*

Class lecture

142. Robert Rittner, "The Great Awakening," lecture to History 101, State University of New York, Buffalo, N.Y., 25 Apr. 1995.

Speech or comment at informal meeting

143. Emily Randall, speech at student council meeting, Ventura County Community College, Ventura, Calif., 15 Sept. 1996.

Microform Materials

Well-known microform service

144. James J. Groark, <u>Utilization of Library Resources b</u> <u>Students in Non-residential Degree Programs</u> (ERIC, ED 121 236 1974), 7.

Microfiche

145. "The Miracullous [sic] Power of Clothes, and the Dignity of Taylors [sic]" (Philadelphia: Mentz, 1772), in <u>Ear</u> <u>American Imprints, 1639-1900</u> (Worcester, Mass.: American Antiquarian Society, n.d.), microfiche 12464-12467, no. 2, ro 3, col. 11.

Electronic Sources

Computer program or software

146. <u>Adobe Acrobat</u>, computer software, ver. 5.0.5, CD-RO (San Jose, Calif.: Adobe, 2001), Windows, Macintosh.

Computer software with information on availability

147. <u>Quotation Reference Collection</u>, computer software (Reno: AAPEX, 1995), IBM, Windows.

Material from electronic database, CD-ROM

148. Anita Guerrini, "The Ethics of Animal Experimentati in Seventeenth-Century England," <u>Historical Abstracts on Disc</u> <u>1982-1995</u>, spring 1995 update, CD-ROM, Retrieval Software, 19

Magnetic tape

149. "Pomona College," <u>Peterson's College Database</u>.

BIBLIOGRAPHY

Nonprint Sources *continued*

Rittner, Robert. "The Great Awakening." Lecture to History 101. State University of New York, Buffalo, N.Y. 25 Apr. 1995.

Randall, Emily. Speech at student council meeting. Ventura County Community College, Ventura, Calif. 15 Sept. 1996.

Microform Materials

Groark, James J. Utilization of Library Resources by Students in Non-residential Degree Programs. ERIC, 1974. ED 121 236.

"The Miracullous [sic] Power of Clothes, and the Dignity of Taylors [sic]." Philadelphia: Mentz, 1772. In Early American Imprints, 1639-1900. Worcester, Mass.: American Antiquarian Society, n.d. Microfiche 12464-12467, no. 2, rows 3-4, cols. 11-14, 1-7.

Electronic Sources

Adobe Acrobat. Computer software. Ver. 5.0.5. CD-ROM. San Jose, Calif.: Adobe, 2001. Windows, Macintosh.

Quotation Reference Collection. Computer software. Reno: AAPEX, 1995. IBM, Windows. Available from AAPEX Software, 955 South Virginia, Suite 116, Reno, Nev. 89502.

Guerrini, Anita. "The Ethics of Animal Experimentation in Seventeenth-Century England." Historical Abstracts on Disc, 1982-1995. Spring 1995 update. CD-ROM. Retrieval Software, 1992.

"Pomona College." Peterson's College Database. Magnetic tape. Princeton: Peterson's, 1992.

Chicago Style

FOOTNOTES AND ENDNOTES

Electronic Sources *continued*

Electronic database with print equivalent

150. Jacques M. Laroche, "Typology of Instructional Theories," International Review of Applied Linguistics in Language Teaching 22 (Feb. 1984): 41, DIALOG, PsycINFO file 1 72-03548.

Electronic material requiring more than one medium

151. Perseus 1.0: Interactive Sources and Studies on Ancient Greece, CD-ROM, videodisc (New Haven: Yale University Press, 1992).

Material from an online source

152. U.S., Congress, Senate, Line Item Veto Act, 104th Cong., 1st sess., 10 Jan. 1995, online, available from Netscape@ftp://ftp.loc.gov/pub/thomas/C104/S206.ris.FTP.

Online book or text

153. Margaret Calahan, et al., Fall Staff in Postseconda[ry] Institutions, 1993 [book online] (Washington, D.C.: GPO, 1996[;] accessed 30 Nov. 1998); available from http://nces.ed.gov/pubsearch/pubsinfo.asp?pubid=96323XXXXX.

Online poem

154. Robert Pinsky, "Ginza Samba," Internet Poetry Archi[ve] [online] (U of North Carolina P and North Carolina Arts Counc[il,] 16 Sept. 1997, accessed 25 Nov. 1998); available from http://www.sunsite.unc.edu/ipa/pinsky/ginza.html.

Reference work online

155. Americana Online, s.v. "Acupuncture," by C. Richard Chapman and John J. Bonica; 2001 ed.; accessed 13 Nov. 2001; available from http://go.grolier.com/gol.

Article in an online journal

156. Bill Readings, "Notes from the Electronic Underground." Surfaces, 4 (1994): 53 pars. [journal online]; accessed 14 Nov. 1998; available from http://tornade.ere.umontreal.ca/~boudreaj/vol4/readings.htm.

Article in an online magazine

157. Sue Church, "Irish Expatriate Keeps in Touch via the Web," Computer Mediated Communication Magazine, Aug. 1996 [magazine online]; accessed 20 Nov. 1998; available from http://www.december.com/cmc/mag/1996/aug/church/html.

BIBLIOGRAPHY

Electronic Sources *continued*

Laroche, Jacques M. "Typology of Instructional Theories." International Review of Applied Linguistics in Language Teaching 22 (Feb. 1984): 41-52. DIALOG, PsycINFO file 11, 72-03548.

Perseus 1.0: Interactive Sources and Studies on Ancient Greece. CD-ROM, videodisc. New Haven: Yale University Press, 1992.

U.S. Congress. Senate. Line Item Veto Act. 104th Congress, 1st sess., 10 Jan. 1995. Online. Available from Netscape@ftp://ftp.loc.gov/pub/thomas/C104/S206.ris.FTP.

Calahan, Margaret, et al. Fall Staff in Postsecondary Institutions, 1993. [book online] (Washington, D.C.: GPO, 1996, accessed 30 Nov. 1998); available from http://nces.ed.gov/pubsearch/pubsinfo.asp?pubid=96323XXXXX.

Pinsky, Robert. "Ginza Samba." Internet Poetry Archive. [online] (U of North Carolina P and North Carolina Arts Council, 16 Sept. 1997, accessed 25 Nov. 1998); available from http://www.sunsite.unc.edu/ipa/pinsky/ginza.html.

Americana Online, 2001 ed.; accessed 13 Nov. 2001; available from http://go.grolier.com/gol.

Readings, Bill. "Notes from the Electronic Underground." Surfaces 4 (1994), 53 pars. [journal online]; accessed 14 Nov. 1998; available from http://tornade.ere.umontreal.ca/~boudreaj/vol4/readings.htm.

Church, Sue. "Irish Expatriate Keeps in Touch via the Web." Computer Mediated Communication Magazine, Aug. 1996 [magazine online]; accessed 20 Nov. 1998; available from http://www.december.com/cmc/mag/1996/church/html.

FOOTNOTES AND ENDNOTES

Electronic Sources *continued*

Newspaper article, electronic version

158. David Schiff, "Leonard Bernstein: The Man Who Mainstreamed Mahler," New York Times 4 Nov. 2001 [online newspaper]; accessed 6 Nov. 2001; available from http://www.nytimes.org/2001/11/04/arts/music/04SCHI.html

Online review editorial, abstract, or letter

159. Douglas W. Cupples, review of The Lost Colony of the Confederacy, by Eugene C. Harter [online]; accessed 30 Nov. 1998; available from http://www.h-net.msu.edu/reviews/index.cgi.

Scholarly project

160. American Verse Project, ed. University of Michigan Humanities Text Initiative and University of Michigan Press (16 Oct. 1996) [poetry anthology online]; accessed 30 Nov. 1998; available from http://www.hti.umich.edu/english/amverse.

Posting on an electronic discussion list

161. Phyllis Franklin, "Climbing Mt. Everest," E-GRAD, 10 June 1977 [online posting]; accessed 15 Sept. 1998; available from http://www.reg.unci.edu/UCI/HUMANITIES/ENGLISH/egrad.html.

BIBLIOGRAPHY

Electronic Sources *continued*

Schiff, David. "Leonard Bernstein: The Man Who Mainstreamed Mahler." New York Times 4 Nov. 2001 [online newspaper]; accessed 6 Nov. 2001; available from http://www.nytimes.org/2001/11/04/arts/music/04SCHI.html.

Cupples, Douglas W. Review of The Lost Colony of the Confederacy, by Eugene C. Harter [online]; accessed 30 Nov. 1998; available from http://www.h-net.msu.edu/reviews/index.cgi.

American Verse Project, ed. University of Michigan Humanities Text Initiative and University of Michigan Press (16 Oct. 1996) [poetry anthology online]; accessed 30 Nov. 1998; available from http://www.hti.umich.edu/english/amverse.

Franklin, Phyllis. "Climbing Mt. Everest," E-GRAD, 10 June 1977 [online posting]; accessed 15 Sept. 1998; available from http://www.reg.unci.edu/UCI/HUMANITIES/ENGLISH/egrad.html.

8 Modern Language Association Style

Content of Parenthetical Citations 214
Placement and Punctuation of Parenthetical Documentation 219
The List of Works Cited 220
Works Cited Forms 223
- Books 223
- Articles in Periodicals 229
- Electronic Sources 232
- Other Sources 235

MLA-Style Shortened Forms of Publishers' Names and Imprints 239
Sample Pages 243

MLA Style

Modern Language Association (MLA) format requires parenthetical citation within the text rather than endnotes or footnotes. Citation within the text provides information, usually the name of the author and the page number(s), to lead the reader to the accompanying bibliographical entry. Complete information about each source cited in the text is supplied in a list of works cited, located at the end of the research paper. For an example of such a list, see the list of works cited on pages 221–222, which provides bibliographical information for the works used in this chapter to illustrate the nature of parenthetical citation. For information about when to use documentation, see Chapter 3 and "General Information on Documentation," page 131. For information about MLA style and occasional changes and updates, see the MLA Web site at www.mla.org.

Content of Parenthetical Citations

When you cite a source, whether in the form of direct quotation, paraphrase, or summary, include within the text enough information to identify the source, but no more than is necessary. Documentation should be entered in a way that makes the identity of the source entirely clear while avoiding duplication and unnecessary clutter. As you write, keep in mind the need for parenthetical documentation; occasionally you may want to revise a sentence to accommodate or reduce parenthetical material.

Most parenthetical citations include the name of the author and the page number, without an intervening comma. When the author's name appears in the introduction to the material, you need not repeat the name within parentheses, as the following examples indicate.

Author named in text

Graff defines his recent book, Professing Literature, as "a history of academic literary studies in the United States" (1).

Author not named in text

Several scholars have studied recent developments in academia in the context of the history of university teaching (e.g., Graff).

Modern literary studies have their origin in classical studies (Graff 19-35).

Reference to entire book

When you cite an entire work by the name of the author alone or by author and title, you do not need a parenthetical reference. A reader will be able to find bibliographical information by looking up the author's name in your list of works cited:

Slade's revision of Form and Style incorporates changes made in the 1999 edition of the MLA Handbook and the 1998 edition of the MLA Style Manual.

Work with four authors

When a work has four or more authors, you may list all four authors or give only the last name of the first author followed by `et al.` (the abbreviation for *et alii*, "and others"):

The authors of Women's Ways of Knowing make a distinction between "separate knowing" and "connected knowing" (Belenky et al. 100-30).

or

(Belenky, Clinchy, Goldberger, and Tarule 100-30).

Use the same form of reference you choose for the text in the list of works cited.

MLA Style

More than one author with the same last name

When you have more than one author with the same last name, include the first initial in subsequent references. Subsequent references to Helen C. White's *The Mysticism of William Blake* and E. B. White's *Charlotte's Web* would read as follows: `(H. White 75)` and `(E. White 67)`. If the first initials are identical, spell out the first names.

When the two authors are father and son, with the son designated as Jr., include the designation `Jr.` in the reference, preceded by a comma.

```
That book chronicles visionary experiences in early modern
Spain (Christian, Jr.).
```

Reference to a hypothetical author with the designation III or IV after his name would also include the number in Roman numerals, preceded by a comma, if one or more of his predecessors were also represented in the list of works cited. In the list of works cited these suffixes are included whether or not works by the namesakes also appear.

Editor or compiler

List the names of editors, compilers, or translators without the accompanying abbreviation that appears in the list of works cited:

```
Many of the articles in Research on Composing advocate
further exploration of the motivation for writing (Cooper
and Odell).
```

Work listed by title only

For a work listed only by title in your list of works cited, use the title in parentheses, shortening it to two or three words. Your abbreviated title must include the word by which the title is alphabetized in your list. You would not want to abbreviate the title in the example below to "Pharaoh," for example, because the entry should be alphabetized by "Ancient."

```
Due to air pollution, Egypt plans to move the statue of
Ramses II from the main railroad station in Cairo to the
west bank of the Nile ("Ancient Pharaoh Statue").
```

Corporate author

For a corporate author, use the name of the organization (abbreviated if it is lengthy, after the first citation) in place of the name of the author.

```
The annual report revealed substantial progress in
fundraising (American Museum of Natural History 12,
hereafter AMNH). . . . (AMNH 15).
```

Multivolume work

To cite an entire volume of a multivolume work, use the author's name and the abbreviation `vol.`

```
This valuable reference work surveys the major operas of
Mozart and Puccini (Newman, vol. 2).
```

MLA Style

To cite a portion of a volume of a multivolume work, use an arabic numeral to indicate the volume followed by a colon and the page number(s).

Newman discusses the controversy about the quality of Mozart's The Magic Flute (2: 104-05).

If the author's name were not in the sentence, the parenthetical reference would read (Newman 2: 104-05).

Two or more works by same author

When you have two works or more by the same author, use a shortened version of the title in each reference.

Shaughnessy points out that "the beginning writer does not know how writers behave" (Errors 79).

Teachers applauded Shaughnessy's assertion that "teaching them [beginning writers] to write well is not only suitable but challenging work for those who would be teachers and scholars in a democracy" ("Diving In" 68).

Material cited in another source

When you quote material from a source other than the original, introduce the name of the source with qtd. in. The author and title of the source you actually consulted appear in the list of works cited.

Goethe wrote that "it takes more culture to perceive the virtues of The Magic Flute than to point out its defects" (qtd. in Newman 2: 104).

Multiple citations

When you need to include more than one work in a parenthetical citation, separate entries with a semicolon.

(Errors 79; "Diving In" 68; Brooks and Warren 5)

Literary works

Because works of literature, particularly pre-twentieth-century works, usually can be found in numerous editions, provide a section or chapter number, introduced with a semicolon and the appropriate abbreviation, after the page number so that your reader can locate the passage in another edition.

Margery Kempe relates the details of her journey to Constance with pilgrims headed for Jerusalem (96-98; bk. 1, chap. 26).

For drama and poetry, omit the page number and cite the work by act, scene, line, or section, as appropriate. MLA prefers arabic numerals in such citations.

In an aside, Claudius informs the audience that the queen has drunk from the poisoned cup he intended for Hamlet (5.2.274).

Electronic and Internet sources

Material accessed electronically, or by computer, may not have any page numbers or it may appear in differing page configurations on different terminals. To give your reader the best possible opportunity to locate the material, you need to compensate for the variability of appearance. It is also advisable to provide more information about the author, particularly when he or she may not be known to your readers, than you would for a printed source.

If the electronic source provides paragraph numbers, use them in place of page numbers.

Mike Sosteric, editor of an online journal of sociology, estimates that publishing a 60-page paper electronically costs less than a penny more than publishing a paper half that length (par. 17).

or

The editor of EJS (Electronic Journal of Sociology) boasts that he can publish a refereed scholarly article within two days (Sosteric, par. 22).

If the source does not designate either page or paragraph, cite the name of the author only and provide some additional identification, such as the title or the qualifications of the author in your text. In the following example the forum in which the talk was given serves to identify the otherwise unidentified speaker as a person thought, by at least the organizers of the meeting, to have relevant knowledge about electronic publication.

In after-dinner remarks at the 1994 American Psychological Society, Paul Ginsparg estimated the cost of electronic storage at $700 per gigabyte.

(Because this source is not paginated, all identifying information appears within the text.)

Placement and Punctuation of Parenthetical Documentation

Parenthetical references should generally be placed at the end of a sentence. Quotation marks, if any, precede the reference; end punctuation, commas, colons, and semicolons follow it.

```
Tannen argues that "men and women have different assumptions
about the place of talk in relationships" (85).
```

```
"Men and women have different assumptions about the place of
talk in relationships," according to Tannen (85).
```

```
What changes in behavior could result from the assumption
that, as Tannen puts it, "men and women have different
assumptions about the place of talk in relationships" (85)?
```

If confusion might result about the distinction between your own conclusions and an idea from a source, place the parenthetical reference within a sentence, generally at the end of a clause or phrase.

```
Understanding that "men and women have different assumptions
about the place of talk in relationships" (Tannen 85) might
help teachers understand their students' comments.
```

(The sentence itself represents the writer's conclusion, which is stated in part with a quotation from Tannen.)

For an ellipsis at the end of a sentence, the parenthetical reference follows three points indicating the omission and precedes the period.

```
Schele and Freidel explain that for the Mayas "the
Underworld was sometimes called Xibalba . . ." (66).
```

A parenthetical reference at the end of a set-off quotation follows the period. One space separates the period from the reference, which is not followed by a period.

```
According to Schele and Freidel, the Maya represented each
point of the compass with a different color.
```

> East was red and the most important direction since it was where the sun was born. North, sometimes called the "side of heaven," was white and the direction from which the cooling rains of winter came. . . . West, the leaving or dying place of the sun, was black. South was yellow. (66)

(The original passage appears on page 78 of this book.)

The List of Works Cited

With MLA-style parenthetical documentation, a works cited section at the end of your paper is the key to references cited in your text. Follow the guidelines for alphabetizing entries and other instructions given below and on pages 139–140.

The first word of each entry in a works cited list is of particular importance, since that word, whether the last name of an author or the first word of a title, identifies the entry in the parenthetical references within the text. In deciding whether to place a translator's or editor's name first rather than the author's name, for example, you need to know the purpose for which you will cite the work in your paper. If your text will refer primarily to the decisions made by a translator, the translator's name should appear first in the entry. If, on the other hand, you plan to discuss only the original work, the author's name should appear first and the name of the translator should follow the title (see page 224).

A works cited list should not be divided into categories. Your reader needs to be able to locate bibliographical information by looking up the reference in one alphabetized list.

When you use an edited volume or compilation and refer to more than one of the articles in it, you must list each article by author in the works cited section, along with the editor of the volume.

Entry for the entire edited volume

Battaglia, Debbora, ed. Rhetorics of Self-Making. U of California P, 1995.

Entry for article in the edited volume, more than one article cited

Marcus, George E. "On Eccentricity." Battaglia 43-58.

Wagner, Roy. "If You Have the Advertisement You Don't Need the Product." Battaglia 59-76.

When you use only one article in an edited volume or compilation, your entry begins with the author of the article.

Entry for article in edited volume, one article cited

Shaughnessy, Mina P. "Diving In: An Introduction to Basic Writing." The Writing Teacher's Sourcebook. Ed. Gary Tate and Edward P. J. Corbett. New York: Oxford UP, 1981. 62-68.

MLA Style

More than one work by same editor(s)

When you cite more than one work by the same editor(s) or compiler(s), use a shortened form of the title to identify the compilation when listing individual articles within it.

Lloyd-Jones, Richard. "Primary Trait Scoring." Cooper and Odell, Evaluating 77-99.

Petty, Walter T. "The Writing of Young Children." Cooper and Odell, Research 73-84.

Names of publishers

MLA style shortens the names of publishers to one word whenever possible, as in Holt. *University* and *Press* are abbreviated, as in U of Chicago P. MLA also puts the name of the imprint, or division, of a publisher before the name of the publisher, citing a book published in Harper and Row's Colophon series as Colophon-Harper. See pages 239–241 for a listing of numerous publishers and imprints in MLA format.

The following list provides bibliographical information for the works used in the above illustrations of MLA reference citations.

Works Cited

American Museum of Natural History. Annual Report, 1993-1994. New York: 1995.

"Ancient Pharaoh Statue Will Be Moved in Cairo." New York Times 3 Sept. 1995, late city ed.: A4.

Battaglia, Debbora, ed. Rhetorics of Self-Making. U of California P, 1995.

Belenky, Mary Field, Blythe McVicker Clinchy, Nancy Rule Goldberger, and Jill Mattuck Tarule. Women's Ways of Knowing: The Development of Self, Voice, and Mind. New York: Basic, 1986.

or

Belenky, Mary Field, et al. Women's Ways of Knowing: The Development of Self, Voice, and Mind. New York: Basic, 1986.

Brooks, Cleanth, and Robert Penn Warren. Modern Rhetoric. 4th ed. New York: Harcourt, 1979.

Christian, William A. An Interpretation of Whitehead's Metaphysics. New Haven: Yale UP, 1959.

Christian, William A., Jr. Apparitions in Late Medieval and Renaissance Spain. Princeton: Princeton UP, 1981.

Cooper, Charles R., and Lee Odell, eds. Evaluating Writing: Describing, Measuring, Judging. Urbana: NCTE, 1977.

---. Research on Composing: Points of Departure. Urbana: NCTE, 1978.

Ginsparg, Paul. After-dinner remarks. APS Meeting at LANL. 1994. 30 Nov. 1998 <http://www.lan.gov/blurb/pg14Oct94.html>.

Graff, Gerald. Professing Literature: An Institutional History. Chicago: U of Chicago P, 1987.

Kempe, Margery. The Book of Margery Kempe. Trans. Barry Windeatt. Harmondsworth, Eng.: Penguin, 1985.

Lloyd-Jones, Richard. "Primary Trait Scoring." Cooper and Odell, Evaluating 77-99.

Marcus, George E. "On Eccentricity." Battaglia 43-58.

Newman, Ernest. Great Operas: The Definitive Treatment of Their History, Stories, and Music. 2 vols. New York: Vintage, 1958.

Schele, Linda, and David Freidel. A Forest of Kings: The Untold Story of the Ancient Maya. New York: William Morrow, 1990.

Shakespeare, William. Hamlet. Ed. Susanne Wofford. Case Studies in Contemporary Criticism. Boston: Bedford-St. Martin's, 1994.

Shaughnessy, Mina P. "Diving In: An Introduction to Basic Writing." The Writing Teacher's Sourcebook. Ed. Gary Tate and Edward P. J. Corbett. New York: Oxford UP, 1981. 62-68.

---. Errors and Expectations: A Guide for the Teacher of Basic Writing. New York: Oxford UP, 1977.

Slade, Carole. Form and Style: Research Papers, Reports, Theses. 12th ed. Boston: Houghton, 2003.

Sosteric, Mike. "Electronic Journals and Scholarly Communication: Notes and Issues." Electronic Journal of Sociology 2.1 (1996): 73 pars. Apr. 28, 1998 <http://www.sociology.org/vol002.001/Sosteric-Article.html>.

Tannen, Deborah. You Just Don't Understand: Women and Men in Conversation. New York: Ballantine-Random, 1990.

Wagner, Roy. "If You Have the Advertisement You Don't Need the Product." Battaglia 59-76.

White, E. B. Charlotte's Web. New York: Harper, 1952.

White, Helen C. The Mysticism of William Blake. New York: Russell, 1964.

Works Cited Forms

This section provides reference forms for a wide range of sources, from books and articles to new types of electronic media. Because types of sources are proliferating rapidly, you may use one not illustrated here. If so, look at the closest alternative and construct your own entry according to the basic principles of MLA format. Also, you may have to refer to more than one of the examples given below. To create an entry for an article appearing in a book edited by two authors, for example, you would use the form for an article and the form for an edited book, following the rules for citing two authors.

If you have previously used MLA format, you will notice numerous changes, most notably the reduction of spaces after the periods from two to one. These changes reflect the modifications made in the fifth edition of the *MLA Handbook for Writers of Research Papers* (1999).

▪ Books

Basic form

The bibliographical listing for a book includes the name(s) of the author(s) or of the editor(s), compiler(s), or translator(s), as appropriate for the particular book; the title of the book with any subtitle; and the facts of publication, which include the city of publication (and, if needed for clarification, the state), the publisher, and the date of publication. Each portion ends with a period followed by one space. Invert the first author's name, placing a comma after the surname and a period after the first name(s), which should be spelled out in their entirety unless the title page displays initials; the names of any additional authors are not inverted. Underline the complete title and subtitle, but not the final period. Take the facts of publication from the title page or the copyright page. Abbreviate the publisher's name (see pages 239–241). If several cities are listed, cite only the first. If the state is needed for clarification, use U. S. Postal Service abbreviations (see Appendix B), and if the country or province is needed, include a standard abbreviation, available in most dictionaries.

Book by a single author

Winfield, Richard Dien. Law in Civil Society. Madison: U of Wisconsin P, 1995.

Book by two or three authors

Simonds, Wendy, and Barbara Katz Rothman. Centuries of Solace: Grief in Popular Literature. Philadelphia: Temple UP, 1992.

Book by four or more authors

You may include the names of all authors if you have some reason to do so, but the abbreviation et al., meaning "and others," is preferred.

McPherson, William, et al. English and American Literature: Sources and Strategies for Collection Development. Chicago: ALA, 1987.

or

McPherson, William, Stephen Lehmann, Craig Likness, and Marcia Pankake. English and American Literature: Sources and Strategies for Collection Development. Chicago: ALA, 1987.

An edited, compiled, or translated volume

The name of the person(s) responsible for the book go(es) in the author's position, followed by an abbreviation for the function—ed. for *editor,* eds. for *editors,* comp. for *compiler,* comps. for *compilers,* or trans. for *translator(s).*

Baum, Robert, ed. Reform and Reaction in Post-Mao China: The Road through Tiananmen. New York: Routledge, 1992.

When the person(s) have more than one function, include all of them.

Vaughan, James H., and Daryl M. Hafter, eds. and trans. The Diary of Hamman Yaji: Chronicle of a West African Muslim Ruler. Bloomington: Indiana UP, 1995.

Group or corporate author

Bicycling Magazine. Reconditioning the Bicycle. New York: Rodale, 1989.

When the corporate author is also the publisher, the name is not repeated.

American Museum of Natural History. Annual Report, 1993-1994. New York, 1995.

Anonymous work

Times Atlas of the World. 8th ed. London: Times, 1990.

If you know the name of the author, provide it within brackets, but do not use *Anonymous*, even if it appears on the title page.

[Scarborough, Dorothy]. The Wind. New York: Harper, 1925.

Work in an anthology, particular selection singled out

The title of the anthology or collection follows the title of the particular work you used, and its inclusive page numbers follow the entire entry. The name(s) of the editor(s) are not inverted. Underline or quote the title of the individual work as MLA format would require in any other situation.

Burghardt, Gordon M. "On the Origins of Play." Play in Animals and Humans. Ed. Peter K. Smith. Oxford: Basil Blackwell, 1984. 5-42.

Wilson, August. Ma Rainey's Black Bottom. Modern and Contemporary Drama. Ed. Miriam Gilbert, Carl H. Klaus, and Bradford S. Field, Jr. New York: St. Martin's, 1994.

Previously published article in a collection

Begin with the original publication information and introduce the collection with `Rpt. in` for *Reprinted in.*

Ten, C. L. "Mill on Self-Regarding Actions." Philosophy 43 (1968): 29-37. Rpt. in John Stuart Mill, On Liberty. Ed. David Spitz. Norton Critical Edition. New York: Norton, 1972. 238-46.

Reprinted work assigned new title

Begin with the publication information for the edition you used and introduce the initial version with `Rpt. of` for *Reprint of.*

Matthews, Gareth. "Ritual and the Religious Feelings." In Explaining Emotions. Ed. Amélie Oksenberg Rorty. Berkeley: U of California P, 1980. 339-53. Rpt. of "Bodily Motions and Religious Feelings," Canadian Journal of Philosophy 1 (1971): 75-86.

Entry in a reference book

Treat entries in a reference book like articles in a collection.

"Vicksburg Campaign." Encyclopaedia Britannica. 1973 ed.

"World Climatology." Times Atlas of the World. 1990 ed.

For less well-known reference works, provide full publication information.

Brasingly, C. Reginald. "Birth Order." Encyclopedia of Psychology. Ed. Raymond J. Corsini. New York: Wiley, 1984.

Introduction, preface, foreword, afterword emphasize

Howard, Maureen. Foreword. Mrs. Dalloway. By Virgina Woolf. New York: Harvest-Harcourt, 1981. vii-xiv.

Multivolume work, inclusive reference to all volumes

If you use more than one volume in a multivolume work, cite the entire work. If the volumes were published over a period of years, give the first and last years.

Wellek, René. A History of Modern Criticism, 1750-1950. New Haven: Yale UP, 1955-92. 8 vols.

Multivolume work, reference to one volume

To cite one volume of a multivolume work with all volumes bearing the same title, provide the number of the one you used.

Wellek, René. A History of Modern Criticism, 1750-1950. Vol. 8. New Haven: Yale UP, 1992.

You may also choose to include publication information for the entire multivolume work.

Wellek, René. A History of Modern Criticism, 1750-1950. Vol. 8. New Haven: Yale UP, 1992. 8 vols. 1955-92.

When each volume has a separate title, you may cite the work without referring to the other volumes or you may include the title of the particular volume along with that of the complete volumes.

Freehling, William W. The Road to Disunion. New York: Oxford UP, 1991.

or

Freehling, William W. The Road to Disunion. New York: Oxford UP, 1991. Vol. 1 of Secessionists at Bay, 1776-1854. 2 vols. 1991-92.

Book in a series

When the title page indicates that a book is part of a series, give the series title and number before the city of publication.

Eiser, J. Richard, ed. Attitudinal Judgment. Springer Series in Social Psychology 11. New York: Springer-Verlag, 1990.

Publisher's imprint

If the book is part of an imprint, a name given to a group of books within a company's publications, the name of the imprint comes first, followed by a hyphen and the name of the publishing company. See pages 239–241 for a selected listing of publishers and their imprints in MLA format.

Bell, Derrick. Faces at the Bottom of the Well: The Permanence of Racism. New York: Basic-Harper 1992.

Reprinted work

Cite the original date of publication if it differs from the date of any particular edition, as with a paperbound edition of a hardcover book or a work brought back into print after a number of years.

Jamieson, Neil L. Understanding Vietnam. 1993. Berkeley: U of California P, 1995.

Markham, Beryl. West with the Night. 1942. Berkeley: North Point, 1983.

Edited work

When an editor has prepared a version of a text by another author, supply the editor's name preceded by the abbreviation Ed. for *Editor.*

Conrad, Joseph. Lord Jim. Ed. Thomas C. Moser. Norton Critical Edition. New York: Norton, 1968.

Translated work

Appelfeld, Aharon. Katerina. Trans. Jeffrey Green. New York: Random House, 1992.

To emphasize the name of the translator, place that name in the author position of the entry.

MLA Style

Green, Jeffrey, trans. Katerina. By Aharon Appelfeld. New York: Random House, 1992.

Work with multiple publishers

Shelley, Percy Bysshe. Selected Poems. Ed. Timothy Webb. London: Dent; Totowa: Rowman, 1977.

Published conference proceedings

Treat the proceedings like a book, but supply information about the conference if it is not included in the title.

Eble, Connie C. "Etiquette Books as Linguistic Authority." The Second LACUS Forum, 1975. Ed. Peter A. Reich. Columbia, SC: Hornbeam, 1976. 468-75.

Glasscoe, Marion, ed. The Medieval Mystical Tradition in England. Papers read at Dartington Hall, July 1984. Cambridge, Eng.: Brewer, 1984.

Article in collection of proceedings

Treat a paper within the proceedings like an article in a collection.

Bradley, Ritamary. "The Speculum Image in Medieval Mystical Writers." The Medieval Mystical Tradition in England. Papers read at Dartington Hall, July 1984. Ed. Marion Glasscoe. Cambridge, Eng.: Brewer, 1984. 9-27.

Book in a foreign language

If you wish to clarify any portion of the entry with an English translation, place it in brackets immediately following the original language version, which should be punctuated and capitalized according to rules for the particular language.

Buendía, Felicidad. Libros de caballerías españoles [Spanish Novels of Chivalry]. Madrid: Aguilar, 1960.

Pamphlet

The entry for a pamphlet follows the rules for a book.

Government publications

When the author of a government publication is identified, list it like a book.

Gates, Jane Potter. Educational and Training Opportunities in Sustainable Agriculture. U.S. Department of Agriculture. Beltsville, MD: National Agricultural Library, 1991.

Otherwise, list the document by the government agency that produced or sponsored it, using the following abbreviations:

Cong. for Congress
Dept. for Department
sess. for session
Cong. Rec. for *Congressional Record*
S. Rept. for Senate Report
H. Rept. for House Report
S. Res. for Senate Resolution
H. Res. for House Resolution
GPO for Government Printing Office

When used as an author entry, as in the entry below, United States is spelled out; otherwise it is abbreviated as U.S., as in the entry immediately above.

United States. Cong. Senate. Committee on Environment and Public Works. Construction and Repair Programs to Alleviate Unemployment. Hearing. 97th Cong., 2nd sess., 1 Dec. 1982. Washington: GPO, 1983.

United States. President. Proclamation. Martin Luther King Day. 15 Jan. 1988.

Cong. Rec. 17 Nov. 1980: 3852.

Titles within titles

When the interior title would normally be underlined, leave it without underlining, but underline punctuation that is part of the longer title.

Doris Lessing's The Four-Gated City: The Summer before the Dark

The Plays of Samuel Beckett: Waiting for Godot and Endgame

When the interior title would normally be in quotation marks, underline the entire title.

Coleridge's "Kubla Khan" and "Rime of the Ancient Mariner"

Book with unspecified publisher, place, date, or pagination

Use the following abbreviations for missing information at the appropriate place in the entry: n.d. for no date, n.p. for no place, n.p. for no publisher, n. pag. for no pagination.

Eliot, George. Felix Holt. Edinburgh: William Blackwood, n.d.

Eliot, George. Felix Holt. N.p.: William Blackwood, n.d.

Eliot, George. Felix Holt. Edinburgh: n.p., n.d.

Eliot, George. Felix Holt. Edinburgh: William Blackwood, n.d. N. pag.

Unpublished dissertation

The title of an unpublished dissertation should be placed in quotation marks (not underlined), and should be identified with the abbreviation Diss., the name of the institution, and the year.

Virgili, Carmen. "Literature of the Spanish Civil War." Diss. New York U, 1990.

Published dissertation

Underline the title of a dissertation published on microfilm, identify the institution and date, and supply publication information for University Microfilms International, abbreviated as UMI.

Moskop, William W. The Prudent Politician: An Extension of Aristotle's Ethical Theory. Diss. George Washington U, 1984. Ann Arbor: UMI, 1985. 85-13289.

■ Articles in Periodicals

Basic form

Citations for articles include (1) the name(s) of the author(s) or editor(s); (2) the full title of the article within quotation marks; and (3) the facts of publication, which usually include the name of the periodical (underlined), the series name and number if any, the volume number (for a scholarly journal only), the date of publication followed by a colon, and the inclusive page numbers on which the article appears. Omit any introductory article in the periodical title (Los Angeles Times, not The Los Angeles Times). When an article does not appear on consecutive pages, but rather is dispersed throughout a publication, MLA uses only the first page number followed by the symbol +, as in 67+ for an article appearing on pages 67–79 and 84, 85, and 89.

Article in a scholarly journal

Gaunt, Simon. "The Significance of Silence." Paragraph 13 (1990): 202-16.

Article in a journal paginating each issue separately

Gardner, Thomas. "An Interview with Jorie Graham." Denver Quarterly 26.4 (1992): 79-104.

Journal using only issue numbers

When a journal numbers by issue rather than by volume, treat the issue number like a volume number.

Nwezeh, C. E. "The Comparative Approach to Modern African Literature." Yearbook of General and Comparative Literature 28 (1979): 22.

Article in journal with more than one series

Identify the series immediately after the title by ordinal number (2nd, 3rd) or ns for new series and os for old series.

Klein, Milton M. "The Pleasures of Teaching and Writing History." William and Mary Quarterly 3rd ser. 52 (July 1995): 483-87.

Erickson, Peter. "Singing America: From Walt Whitman to Adrienne Rich." Kenyon Review ns 12.1 (1995): 103-19.

Article in a newspaper

For an article in a newspaper, use the name of the newspaper as it appears on the masthead, excluding any introductory article, such as *The*.

Mercer, Pamela. "U.S. Venture Bets on Colombian Coal." New York Times 27 July 1995, late city ed.: D7.

When the location of the publication is neither included in the title nor widely known, include it within brackets after the title without underlining.

MLA Style

"Unknown Author of Wind Answers Crane Criticism." Sweetwater Daily Reporter [Texas] 15 Dec. 1925: 6.

Observer [London] 17 Oct. 1990, sec. 2: 5+.

When a particular edition of a newspaper is specified, include its designation, abbreviated, after the date (natl. for national, intl. for international, and so on).

Donnelly, John. "Unrest in Iraq May Be a Mirage." Miami Herald 22 July 1995, intl. ed.: 1A+.

Article in a magazine

For a weekly magazine, give day, month, and year; for a monthly, give the month and year only. Abbreviate all months except May, June, and July.

Kinoshita, June. "The Mapping of the Mind." New York Times Magazine 18 Oct. 1992: 44+.

Brody, Howard. "How Would a Physicist Design a Tennis Racket?" Physics Today Mar. 1995: 26-31.

Anonymous magazine article

"Weather Satellite Finally Fit for Work." Science News 18 Mar. 1995: 171.

Editorial

"Potomac Yard Decision." Editorial. Washington Post 16 Oct. 1992: A24.

Letter to editor

Lightfoot, Frederick S. Letter. New York Times 21 Oct. 1992: A22.

A response to a letter to the editor should be so designated.

Fleishman, Avrom. Reply to letter of David E. Johnson. College English 57 (1995): 224-26.

Review of a book

Give the reviewer's name, if any, followed by the title of the book introduced with Rev. of, the name of the author, and the facts of publication.

Moore, Walter. "Great Physicist, Great Guy." Rev. of Genius: The Life and Science of Richard Feynman, by James Gleick. New York Times Book Review 11 Oct. 1992: 3.

Kienitz, Gail M. Rev. of Tennyson and the Doom of Romanticism, by Herbert F. Tucker. Religion and Literature 24 (Spring 1992): 87-90.

Review of a performance

Include information identifying the performance after the title of the review.

Hassell, Graham. "Sometimes Excess Isn't Enough." Rev. of The Grand Ceremonial, by Fernando Arrabal. Lyric Studio, Hammersmith, Eng. Times Literary Supplement [London] 14 July 1995: 20.

Review of a film or video

Rickey, Carrie. "Disney's Pocahontas: Is It Fact or Fiction?" Rev. of Pocahontas, dir. Michael Gabriel and Eric Goldberg. Philadelphia Inquirer 18 June 1995: H1+.

Titles within titles

Change double quotation marks to single quotation marks when they appear within another quoted title.

"A Reading of Coleridge's 'Kubla Khan'"

An underlined title appearing within a title in quotation marks remains underlined.

"A Principle of Unity in Between the Acts"

Serialized article

Cite a series of articles published in more than one issue of a periodical under the same title in one entry.

McPhee, John. "Annals of the Former World." New Yorker 7 Sept. 1992: 36+; 14 Sept. 1992: 44+; 21 Sept. 1992: 39+.

If the articles have different titles, enter each one separately with a brief descripton of the series. Alphabetize the entries by the names of the authors, or, if the authors are the same, by title.

Kolbert, Elizabeth, and Adam Clymer. "The Politics of Layoffs: In Search of a Message." New York Times 8 March 1996: A1+. Pt. 6 of a series, The Downsizing of America, begun 3 March 1996.

---. "The Price of Jobs Lost: A National Heartache." New York Times 3 March 1996: A1+. Pt. 1 of a series, The Downsizing of America.

Abstract in an abstracts journal

Moskop, William W. The Prudent Politician: An Extension of Aristotle's Ethical Theory. Diss. George Washington U, 1984. DAI 45 (1984): 4445B.

Dyson, Anne Haas. "Writing Children: Reinventing the Development of Childhood Literacy." Written Communication 12 (1995): 527-47. Current Index to Journals in Education 28 (1996): item EJ251057.

Microform collection

Nicoll, Allardyce, and George Freeley, eds. American Drama of the Nineteenth Century. New York: Readex Microprint, 1965-. Micro-opaque.

MLA Style

▪ Electronic Sources

Electronic sources can be divided into two types, depending on whether or not they utilize the Internet.

ELECTRONIC SOURCES ON THE INTERNET The citation for an electronic source on the Internet should provide information sufficient to permit your reader to locate the exact same material you used. Because sources on the Internet can be easily altered or erased, meeting this criterion often requires more information than is normally needed for print sources.

The minimum information for an electronic source includes

1. the author, editor, or translator of the source (as available and relevant), reversed for alphabetizing and, in the case of an editor or translator, followed by the appropriate abbreviation;
2. the title of the section you used, in quotation marks or underlined, as MLA style would require in any other context;
3. the title of the entire source, underlined, whether it is a book, a Web site, or a scholarly project;
4. a description of the source (if it has no title) not underlined, as in `Home page`;
5. the name of the editor or translator (if not cited at the beginning of the citation) preceded by the appropriate abbreviation, such as `Ed.` or `Trans.`;
6. publication information for a print version of the source (if one exists);
7. the date of electronic publication or the latest update;
8. the number of pages, paragraphs, or other sections, if they are numbered (but not the number of pages in your printed copy of the source);
9. the date you accessed the source (*not* followed by a period);
10. the electronic address of the source, surrounded by angle brackets and followed by a period. If the URL is long or complicated, provide enough detail to enable your reader to get to the search page.

If you need to break an electronic address, split it only after a slash mark.

Book

Johnstone, Catherine Laura. Winter and Summer Excursions in Canada. London: Digby, Long, 1894. Early Canadiana Online. 2 Nov. 2001 <http://www.canadiana.org/cgi-bin/ECO/>.

Book, published simultaneously in print form

Audi, Robert. Moral Knowledge and Ethical Character. New York: Oxford UP, 1997. Electronic Text Service. Columbia University. 1 Nov. 2001 <https://www1.columbia.edu/sec/dlc/oup/audi/>.

Book with author, editor, and translator

Merriam, Brian. The Midnight Court [Cúirt an Mheádhon Oídhche]. Trans. and ed. Noel Fahey. 1998. Noel Fahey. 26 Oct. 2001 <http://www.homesteader.com/merriman/welcome.html>.

Book with editors emphasized

Kerst, Friedrich, and Henry Edward Krehbiel, eds. Mozart, the Man and the Artist, As Revealed in His Own Words. By Wolfgang Amadeus Mozart. Project Gutenberg Release #4042. 1 Nov. 2001 <ftp://ftp.ibiblio.org/pub/docs/books/gutenberg/etext99/swnsg10.txt>.

Article accessed electronically, with print equivalent

Campbell, James. "Alfred Nobel and His Prizes." Boston Review 26:5 (2001): 27-30. 29 Oct. 2001 <http://bostonreview.mit.edu/BR26.5/Campbell.htm>.

Article in an online journal

Readings, Bill. "Notes from the Electronic Underground." Surfaces 4 (1994): 53 pars. 14 Nov. 1998 <http://tornade.ere.umontreal.ca/~boudreaj/vol4/readings.htm>.

Article in an online magazine

Church, Sue. "Irish Expatriate Keeps in Touch via the Web." Computer Mediated Communication Magazine August 1996. 30 Nov. 1998 <http://www.december.com/cmc/mag/1996/aug/church.html>.

Newspaper article, electronic version

Schiff, David. "Leonard Bernstein: The Man Who Mainstreamed Mahler." New York Times 4 Nov. 2001. 6 Nov. 2001 <http://www.nytimes.org/2001/11/04/arts/music/04SCHI.html>.

Document online

Calahan, Margaret, et al. Fall Staff in Postsecondary Institutions, 1993. Washington: GPO, 1996. NCES 96-323. Natl. Center for Educ. Statistics, 30 Nov. 1998 <http://nces.ed.gov/pubsearch/pubsinfo.asp?pubid=96323XXXXX>.

Poem online

Pinsky, Robert. "Ginza Samba." Internet Poetry Archive. 16 Sept. 1997. U of North Carolina P and North Carolina Arts Council. Internet, RealAudio. 25 Nov. 1998 <http://www.sunsite.unc.edu/ipa/pinsky/ginza/html>.

(without print equivalent)

Pinsky, Robert. "The Tuning." Atlantic Monthly. Apr. 1995. Atlantic Unbound. 30 Dec. 1998 <http://www.theatlantic.com/unbound/poetry/antholog/tuning.htm>.

(with print equivalent)

Play online

Chekhov, Anton. The Swan Song. Trans. Marian Fell. Project Gutenberg Release #1753. 5 Nov. 2001 <ftp://ftp.ibiblio.org/pub/docs/books/gutenberg/etext99/swnsg10.txt>.

Scholarly project

Internet Medieval Sourcebook. Ed. Paul Halsall. 8 Jan. 2000. Fordham U. 1 Nov. 2001 <http://www.fordham.edu/halsall/sbook.html>.

Professional site

Center for Creative Photography. 11 Oct. 2001. U of Arizona and U of Arizona Main Library. 1 Nov. 2001 <http://dizzy.library.arizona.edu/branches/ccp/home/main.html>.

Personal site

Smith, Michael W. Home Page. 15 Oct. 2001 <http://www.gse.rutgers.edu/people/mws.htm>.

Document created by a private organization, no date

Oxfam International. Towards Global Equity: Strategic Plan Summary 2001-2004. 20 Oct. 2001 <http://www.oxfam.org/strategic_plan/equity.htm>.

Online review, editorial, abstract, or letter

Cupples, Douglas W. Rev. of The Lost Colony of the Confederacy. By Eugene C. Harter. 30 Nov. 1998 <http://www.h-net.msu.edu/reviews/index.cgi>.

Article in a reference database, accessed on Internet

"Fermi, Enrico." Britannica Online. Vers. 98.1.1. Nov. 1998. Encyclopaedia Britannica. 30 Nov. 1998 <http://www.eb.com:180>.

Online posting on a discussion list

Franklin, Phyllis. "Climbing Mt. Everest." Online posting. 10 June 1977. E-GRAD. 15 Sept. 1998 <http://www.reg.unci.edu/UCI/HUMANITIES/ENGLISH/egrad.html>.

Personal e-mail message

Bell, Gordon R. "More Descendants of Benjamin Hooke." E-mail to the author. 28 Nov. 1998.

MLA Style

ELECTRONIC SOURCES NOT ON THE INTERNET Some materials, such as computer software and CD-ROMs, are accessed electronically but in themselves are not electronic. In addition to the information you would include for an electronic source on the Internet, you may need to provide a description of the medium (CD-ROM, diskette, etc.); the name of the database or vendor; and the date of electronic publication.

Computer program

Adobe Acrobat. Computer software. Ver. 5.0.5. CD-ROM. San Jose, CA: Adobe, 2001.

Material from a database accessed electronically

Identify the medium of the database you used: CD-ROM, diskette, videodisc, magnetic tape, and so on.

When you cite only part of a database, identify the title of that part within quotation marks.

Guerrini, Anita. "The Ethics of Animal Experimentation in Seventeenth-Century England." Historical Abstracts on Disc, 1982-1995. Spring 1995 update. CD-ROM. Retrieval Software, 1992. 15 Aug. 1995.

Underline or quote the title of the entry as MLA format would require in any other context.

Gainsborough, Thomas. The Morning Walk. Microsoft Art Gallery: The Collection of the National Gallery, London. CD-ROM. Redmond, WA: Microsoft, 1994.

When the material requires or includes more than one electronic medium, name all of them.

Perseus 1.0: Interactive Sources and Studies on Ancient Greece. CD-ROM, videodisc. New Haven: Yale UP, 1992.

Other Sources

For a wide range of other sources, provide some equivalent of author, title, and facts of publication. Because such sources usually have many persons identifiable as author in the broadest sense of the word, you will have to select those you consider necessary for locating the source and those important for your purpose in citing it. Include any information about writers or performers before or after the title with these abbreviations: Prod. for *Producer* or *Produced by*, Writ. for *Writer* or *Written by*, Dir. for *Director* or *Directed by*, Perf. for *Performer* or *Performed by*, Narr. for *Narrator* or *Narrated by*, Adapt. for *Adapter* or *Adapted by*, and Cond. for *Conductor* or *Conducted by*. Entries for the same source in two papers with different emphases, one on writers and the other on directors, would be constructed differently and would most likely provide different information. In either case, however, the reader should be able to identify and locate the material.

Television or radio program

An entry for a television or radio program includes the following information, if available and appropriate in a particular instance: title of the episode, in quotation marks; title of the program, underlined; title of the series; name of the network; call letters and city of the local station; and date of broadcast.

Jonathan: The Boy Nobody Wanted. Perf. JoBeth Williams and Chris Burke. WNBC, New York. 19 Oct. 1992.

"Some Can Sing." The Language of Life. Writ. and narr. Bill Moyers. Perf. Robert Hass, Claribel Alegría, and Carolyn Forché. PBS. WNET, Newark, NJ. 9 July 1995.

"Hiroshima: Why the Bomb Was Dropped." Peter Jennings Reporting. Prod. David Gelber and Martin Smith. ABC. WLOV, Columbus, MS. 27 July 1995.

Sound recording

For a recording of music or voice, underline the title of the complete work and place any segment of it within quotation marks. After the title, identify the medium (unless it is CD), the producer or publisher, and the date. The entry may begin with any of the composers, authors, or performers you wish to emphasize, identifying their function if it is not obvious. You may include identifying numbers or letters at the end of the entry.

MLA Style

Handel, George Frideric. <u>Water Music/Wassermusik</u>. Cond. Neville Marriner. Academy of St. Martin-in-the Fields. London: EMI, 1989.

Do not underline a musical composition identified by form, key, or number even when it is the title of a recording.

Brahms, Johannes. Symphony no. 3 in F major, op. 90. Cond. Sir Georg Solti. Chicago Symphony Orchestra. Recorded in Medinah Temple, Chicago, May 1978. Musical Heritage Society, 1989. 11170X.

Enclose a selection within quotation marks. If the name of the song writer is given, include it.

The Beatles. "The Long and Winding Road." By John Lennon and Paul McCartney. <u>Let It Be</u>. LP. Apple, n.d.

Dave Brubeck Quartet. "Far More Blue." <u>Time Further Out</u>. Audiocassette. New York: CBS, n.d.

Treat a spoken recording like a sound recording.

Thomas, Dylan. "Fern Hill." <u>Dylan Thomas Reading</u>. Vol. 1. LP. Caedmon, n.d.

<u>Family Counseling</u>. Narr. K. Hunter. Audiocassette. Washington, D.C.: American Psychological Association, 1989.

Performance A performance, such as a concert or play, usually begins with the title of the work. If you wish to emphasize any of the persons involved, place that person's name in the author position.

Molnar, Frederic. <u>The Play's the Thing</u>. Adapt. P. G. Wodehouse. Dir. Gloria Muzio. Roundabout Theatre Company. New York. 15 July 1995.

Close, Glenn, perf. <u>Sunset Boulevard</u>. By Andrew Lloyd Webber. Minskoff Theatre, New York. 1 Apr. 1995.

Beatty, Talley, chor. <u>Come and Get the Beauty of It Hot</u>. Perf. Marilyn Banks. Prod. Glory Van Scott. Symphony Space Theater, New York. 12 Sept. 1995.

Schwarz, Gerard, cond. Piano concerto in F major, K. 459. By Wolfgang Amadeus Mozart. Perf. Cecile Licad. Mostly Mozart Festival Orchestra. Avery Fisher Hall, New York. 28 July 1994.

Film or videotape The basic form for a film entry begins with the title, underlined, and includes the director, the distributor, and the year. You may also include the names of writers or performers, as relevant.

Country Life. Writ. and dir. Michael Blakemore. Perf. Sam Neill, Greta Scacchi, John Hargreaves, and Kerry Fox. Miramax, 1995.

Costner, Kevin, perf. Waterworld. Writ. Peter Rader and David Twohy. Prod. Charles Gordon and John Davis. Universal, 1995.

When a videocassette has a date different from that of the film, include both dates, as illustrated below.

Gilliam, Terry, dir. The Fisher King. Writ. Richard LaGravenese. Perf. Robin Williams and Jeff Bridges. 1991. Videocassette. Tristar, 1993.

Musical composition

An entry for a musical composition begins with the name of the composer, followed by the title of the piece. When the work is identified only by type or key, that identification is not underlined. When the composition goes by another title, that title is underlined.

Beethoven, Ludwig von. Sonata no. 19 in G minor, op. 49, no. 1.

Bach, Johann Sebastian. Brandenburg Concertos.

Musical scores

If you refer to the score in published form, cite it as a book, underlining and capitalizing principal words, even those for number and form, and providing the city of publication, publisher, and date.

Works of art

When referring to the actual work of art, provide the place where it can be found in addition to the artist and the title, underlined.

Gainsborough, Thomas. The Morning Walk. National Gallery, London.

When you use a reproduction of the work, provide the information in the entry above followed by publication information for your source. If you wish to provide the original date of the work, place it after the title, followed by a period.

Vallayer-Coster, Anne. The White Soup Bowl. 1771. Private Collection, Paris. Women Artists, 1550-1950. By Ann Sutherland Harris and Linda Nochlin. New York: Knopf, 1977. Plate 52.

Published letter

To cite a published letter, give the name of the writer, the name of the recipient, and the date, followed by the facts of publication for the source.

Crane, Stephen. Letter to Lily Brandon Munro. March 1894? Bradley, Sculley et al., eds. The Red Badge of Courage. 2nd ed. Norton Critical Edition. New York: Norton, 1976. 129.

Unpublished letter

Identify letter(s) you received as `Letter(s) to the author` and give the date(s). If the credentials of the letter writer require mention, place that information in the body of your text.

Mazzeo, Joseph A. Letters to the author. 8 Aug. to 31 Dec. 1996.

If the unpublished letters reside in an archive, provide the name of the collection and full information about the location.

Cockburn, Robert. Letter to Lord Melville. 17 May 1819. Manuscript Collection. Group 125. Rutgers U, New Brunswick, NJ.

Interview

Identify a published interview according to the format, whether book, television program, or radio broadcast.

Lipkowitz, Ina, and Andrea Loselle. "An Interview with Julia Kristeva." Critical Texts 3.3 (1986): 3-13.

Warner, Margaret. Interview with John Kenneth Galbraith. The News Hour with Jim Lehrer. PBS. WGBH, Boston. 5 Dec. 1995.

For an interview you conducted, identify the medium of communication, as for example, Personal interview for face-to-face communication, Telephone interview, E-mail interview. Place any identification of the person interviewed in the body of your text.

Jones, Tom. Personal interview. 26 May 1995.

Map or chart

World Climatology. Map. Times Atlas of the World. 1990 ed.

Cartoon

Schoenbaum, Bernard. Cartoon. New Yorker 2 Nov. 1992: 82.

Watterson, Bill. "Calvin and Hobbes." Cartoon. Miami Herald 22 July 1995, intl. ed.: 9A.

Advertisement

For an advertisement, use the name of the company as the author and identify the publication in which it appeared.

Infiniti. Advertisement. CBS. 10 Sept. 1995.

Tiffany and Co. Advertisement. New York Times 27 July 1995, late city ed.: A3.

Lecture or speech

If the lecture has a title, place it in quotation marks, followed by the name of the conference, the place, and the date.

Jochens, Jenny. "Gender Equality in Law?: The Case of Medieval Iceland." Center for Medieval and Early Renaissance Studies, 26th Annual Conference. Binghamton, NY. 15 Oct. 1992.

For a classroom lecture or informal meeting, designate the nature of the remarks after the name of the speaker.

Rittner, Robert. "The Great Awakening." Lecture to History 101. State University of New York. Buffalo, NY. 25 Apr. 1995.

Randall, Emily. Speech at student council meeting. Ventura County Community Coll. Ventura, CA. 15 Sept. 1996.

Manuscript or typescript Identify a manuscript or typescript with the appropriate abbreviation, ms or ts, and identify the location for unpublished material or the means of publication.

Scarborough, Dorothy. The Wind, ms. Dorothy Scarborough Papers. Texas Collection, Baylor U, Waco.

Legal sources Cite legal sources according to the *Uniform System of Citation* (see Appendix A), but place them in the reference list, rather than in footnotes (as they appear in legal documents and periodicals).

MLA Style

MLA-Style Shortened Forms of Publishers' Names and Imprints

In MLA style, publishers' names are shortened. When the name of the publisher is that of a person (J. B. Lippincott), cite the last name only (Lippincott). When the name of the publisher includes more than one surname (Houghton Mifflin), cite only the first (Houghton). Abbreviate *University* as *U*, and *Press* as *P*. The following is a selected list of shortened names.

SHORT FORM	COMPLETE NAME
Abrams	Harry N. Abrams, Inc.
ALA	American Library Association
Allen	George Allen and Unwin Publishers, Inc.
Allyn	Allyn and Bacon, Inc.
Appleton	Appleton-Century-Crofts
Ballantine	Ballantine Books, Inc.
Bantam	Bantam Books, Inc.
Barnes	Barnes and Noble Books
Basic	Basic Books
Beacon	Beacon Press, Inc.
Benn	Ernest Benn, Ltd.
Bobbs	The Bobbs-Merrill Co., Inc.
Bowker	R. R. Bowker Co.
Cambridge UP	Cambridge University Press
Clarendon	Clarendon Press
Columbia UP	Columbia University Press
Cornell UP	Cornell University Press
Dell	Dell Publishing Co., Inc.
Dodd	Dodd, Mead, and Co.
Doubleday	Doubleday and Co., Inc.

SHORT FORM	COMPLETE NAME
Dover	Dover Publications, Inc.
Dutton	E. P. Dutton, Inc.
Farrar	Farrar, Straus and Giroux, Inc.
Free	The Free Press
Funk	Funk and Wagnalls, Inc.
Gale	Gale Research Co.
GPO	Government Printing Office
Harcourt	Harcourt Brace and Company
Harper	HarperCollins, Publishers, Inc.
Harvard Law Rev. Assn.	Harvard Law Review Association
Harvard UP	Harvard University Press
Heath	D. C. Heath and Co.
Holt	Holt, Rinehart and Winston, Inc.
Houghton	Houghton Mifflin Co.
Humanities	Humanities Press, Inc.
Indiana UP	Indiana University Press
Johns Hopkins UP	The Johns Hopkins University Press
Knopf	Alfred A. Knopf, Inc.
Lippincott	J. B. Lippincott Co.
Little	Little, Brown and Company, Inc.
Macmillan	Macmillan Publishing Co., Inc.
McGraw	McGraw-Hill, Inc.
MIT P	The MIT Press
MLA	The Modern Language Association of America
NAL	The New American Library, Inc.
NEA	The National Education Association
Norton	W. W. Norton and Co., Inc.
Oxford UP	Oxford University Press
Penguin	Penguin Books, Inc.
Pocket	Pocket Books
Popular	The Popular Press
Prentice	Prentice-Hall, Inc.
Princeton UP	Princeton University Press
Putnam's	G. P. Putnam's Sons
Rand	Rand McNally and Co.
Random	Random House, Inc.
St. Martin's	St. Martin's Press, Inc.
Scott	Scott, Foresman and Co.
Scribner's	Charles Scribner's Sons
Simon	Simon and Schuster, Inc.
UMI	University Microfilms International
U of Chicago P	University of Chicago Press
U of Toronto P	University of Toronto Press
UP of Florida	The University Presses of Florida
Viking	The Viking Press, Inc.
Yale UP	Yale University Press

MLA also shortens the names of publishers' imprints (names given to groups of books within a company's publications) to one word, unless more are needed for accurate identification. To distinguish Laurel Editions from

MLA Style

Laurel Leaf, both imprints of Dell, the second word should be included. In MLA style, the name of the imprint, followed by a hyphen without spacing on either side, precedes the name of the publisher.

Below is a partial list of well-known imprints.

(Words modifying the name of the imprint, such as *Books* and *Editions*, may be omitted unless they are required for accurate identification.)

Laurel Editions-Dell
Laurel Leaf-Dell
Anchor-Doubleday
Dial-Doubleday
Image-Doubleday
Quantum-Doubleday
Harbinger-Harcourt
Harvest-Harcourt
Colophon-Harper
Perennial-Harper
Torchbooks-Harper
Owl-Holt
Clarion-Houghton
Riverside-Houghton
Dragonfly-Knopf
Reynal-Morris
Mentor-NAL
Plume-NAL
Signet-NAL
Poseidon-Pocket
Touchstone-Simon

[1/2 inch]

Michaels 1

[1/2 inch]

Jane Michaels

Professor Robert Barnes

English W3915

19 May 2002

The Effects of Serialization

on Elizabeth Gaskell's North and South

Many nineteenth-century novelists, including Charles Dickens and Anthony Trollope, published their novels in serial form. Consequently, they wrote under pressure of deadlines, and often they had not written beyond the latest installment. This method of publication naturally influenced the form of the novels, as I will demonstrate with Elizabeth Gaskell's North and South.

Gaskell herself conjectured about the effects of serialization on that novel. In late January 1855 she wrote to Anna Jameson that

10 spaces →

> in this way of publishing it, I had to write pretty hard without waiting for the happy leisure hours. And then 20 numbers [of installments] was, I found, my allowance, instead of the scant 22. Just at the very last I was compelled to desperate compression and at last the story is huddled and hurried up. (Chapple 130)

Some critics regard this pressure as having all but destroyed the coherence of the novel. Martin Dodsworth judges that the opening chapters "fail to establish any overall tone for the book" (10). He regards these chapters as disjointed and misleading because "she begins by setting up conventions against which she will offend, and

[1 inch]

[1/2 inch] Michaels 12

Works Cited

Burstyn, Joan. Victorian Education and the Ideal of Womanhood. Totowa, NJ: Barnes and Noble, 1981.

Chapple, J. A. V. Elizabeth Gaskell: A Portrait in Letters. Manchester, Eng.: Manchester UP, 1980.

Craik, W. A. Elizabeth Gaskell and the Provincial Novel. London: Methuen, 1975.

Dodsworth, Martin. Introduction. North and South, by Elizabeth Gaskell.

Duthie, Enid L. The Themes of Elizabeth Gaskell. New York: Macmillan, 1980.

Gaskell, Elizabeth. North and South. Ed. Dorothy Collin. Introd. Martin Dodsworth. Harmondsworth, Eng.: Penguin, 1986.

Lansbury, Coral. Elizabeth Gaskell. Boston: Twayne, 1984.

Sharps, John Gregory. Mrs. Gaskell's Observation and Invention: A Study of Her Non-Biographic Works. Sussex, Eng.: Linden, 1970.

Vicinus, Martha, ed. Suffer and Be Still: Women in the Victorian Age. Bloomington: Indiana UP, 1972.

MLA format sample page

9 American Psychological Association Style

Parenthetical Reference Citations in Text 246
Reference Forms 251
Periodicals 252
Books and Chapters of Books 255
Technical and Research Reports 259
Proceedings of Meetings 260
Dissertations and Theses 261
Unpublished Materials and Works of Limited Circulation 261
Reviews and Published Interviews 262
Audiovisual Media 263
Electronic Sources 264
The List of References 269
Sample Pages 271

The American Psychological Association (APA) requires citation of documentation within the text rather than endnotes or footnotes. The author's last name, the date of publication, and any other information necessary for locating the material cited may be incorporated into the text itself or placed within parentheses, as necessary for the particular sentence. An alphabetical reference list at the end of the research paper provides complete information about each source cited in the text. The specifications for creating the entries for numerous types of sources appear in the section entitled "Reference Forms." Instructions for organizing the list of references can be found in "The List of References." For information about when to use documentation, see Chapter 3 and "General Information on Documentation," page 136.

For additional information about APA style, consult the APA Web site <http://www.apastyle.org>.

Parenthetical Reference Citations in Text

Whether you quote directly or indirectly, you must provide the source of your information within the text. Documentation should be entered in a way that makes the identity of the source entirely clear while avoiding duplication and unnecessary clutter. As you write, you will want to keep in mind the need for parenthetical documentation, and occasionally you may want to revise a sentence to accommodate or reduce parenthetical material. The sources used in the examples below appear in reference list format on pages 250–251.

Author named in your text

If you mention the author's name in your text, cite only the date of publication in parentheses, immediately after the author's name.

```
Gould (1989) attributes Darwin's success to his gift for
making the appropriate metaphor.
```

Subsequent citation in same paragraph

When another sentence in the same paragraph refers to the same author, the parenthetical material, if it remains the same, need not be repeated. In any subsequent paragraph, however, you would need to provide the parenthetical information again. Use the last name only in both first and subsequent citations, except when two authors have the same last name (see page 248 below).

Author not named in your text

When you do not mention the author's name in your own text, that name, followed by a comma and the date of publication, appears in parentheses at the end of your sentence or, if you have referred to more than one source, at the end of the relevant clause.

```
As metaphors for the workings of nature, Darwin used the
tangled bank, the tree of life, and the face of nature
(Gould, 1989).
```

Citation of parts of sources

To indicate a precise location within the source, whether or not you quote from it directly, add the page or chapter number preceded by the appropriate abbreviation: `p.` for page, `pp.` for pages, `chap.` for chapter, `pt.` for part. In citing electronic sources in which portions of the document are numbered or designated in some other way, use an abbreviation for the marker used in the document, such as `sec.` for section and `par.` for paragraph.

```
(Gould, 1989, p. 14), (Gould, 1987, chap. 2), Tiihonen,
2000, sec. 3)
```

Author and date cited in text

If you use both the name of the author and the date in the text, a parenthetical reference is not needed.

```
In a 1989 article, Gould explores some of Darwin's most
effective metaphors.
```

APA Style

Direct quotation with name of author

When your sentence contains a quotation and includes the name of the author, place the publication date and page number in parentheses. Abbreviate the word *page* or *pages* (p. or pp.). The publication date follows the name of the author; the page number follows the end of the quotation.

```
Gould (1989) explains that Darwin used the metaphor
of the tree of life "to express the other form of
interconnectedness--genealogical rather than ecological--
and to illustrate both success and failure in the history
of life" (p. 14).
```

Direct quotation without name of author

When you use a quotation but do not identify the author in the sentence, the name of the author, date of publication, and page number appear in parentheses at the end of the sentence, followed by the period for the sentence.

```
Darwin used the metaphor of the tree of life "to express the
other form of interconnectedness--genealogical rather than
ecological" (Gould, 1989, p. 14).
```

Work by two authors

When you refer to a work by two authors, cite both names each time the reference appears. Within the parentheses use an ampersand (&), but within your text spell out the word *and.*

```
Sexual-selection theory has been used to explore patterns of
insect mating (Alcock & Thornhill, 1983). . . . Alcock and
Thornhill (1983) also demonstrate . . .
```

Three, four, five, or six authors

For a work by more than two authors but fewer than seven, cite all names in the first reference. In subsequent references, cite only the name of the first author and use et al.

```
Scientists have isolated a gene connected to circadian
rhythms in plants (Millar, Straume, Chory, Chua, & Kay,
1995, p. 1163). . . . They identified the mutations that
activated light-dependent pathways (Millar et al., 1995,
p. 1165). . . .
```

Seven or more authors

For a work by seven or more authors, give only the last name of the first author followed by et al. in both first and subsequent references.

```
Scientists have constructed a deletion map of the human Y
chromosome (Vollrath et al., 1992). . . . Their studies
resolved a region of the chromosome into ordered intervals
(Vollrath et al., 1992) . . .
```

Distinguishing entries with multiple authors

When two entries with multiple authors shorten to exactly the same form, cite as many names as you need to distinguish the two parenthetical references. If in addition to the article above with Vollrath as first author followed by Foote, you had another in which the name Smith followed Vollrath, the two shortened references would appear this way:

```
(Vollrath, Foote et al., 1992) . . . (Vollrath, Smith
et al., 1992).
```

If these two articles were published in different years, the second name would not be necessary to distinguish them:

```
(Vollrath et al., 1992) . . . (Vollrath et al., 1993).
```

Authors with the same last name

When you cite works by two or more authors with the same last name, use initials to identify the authors in the text even if the dates of publication differ.

```
R. Dawkins (1986) and M. S. Dawkins (1980) have contributed
to an understanding of consciousness in animals.
```

Work cited in another work

When the source of a direct or indirect quotation is a secondary source, refer to the source you actually used within parentheses and in the reference list.

```
Darwin's metaphors (as cited in Gould, 1989) . . .
```

If you use a direct quotation from the secondary source, the parenthetical reference reads `(as quoted by Gould, 1989).`

Work identified by title

When a work is noted in the reference list by title alone, a shortened version of the title is used to identify the work parenthetically in the text. Within the text, whether in parentheses or not, titles are presented differently from the way they are in the reference list. All words are capitalized, except words of four letters or more; the title of a book, report, brochure, or periodical is underlined; and the title of an article or chapter appears within quotation marks.

```
The National Endowment for the Humanities supports
"theoretical and critical studies of the arts" but not
```

APA Style

work in the creative or performing arts (*Guidelines*, 1994, p. 1).

Changes in the Medical College Admissions Test to begin in 1991 are expected to encourage more students to pursue general studies in the humanities, natural sciences, and social sciences ("New Exam," 1989).

Corporate author

When you cite a work by a group author, use the name of the corporation or organization as the author.

Retired officers retain access to all of the university's educational and recreational facilities (Columbia University, 1995, p. 54).

You may use well-known abbreviations of the name of a corporate author in subsequent parenthetical references or in the text itself. For example, you might use NSF for National Science Foundation, NIMH for National Institutes of Mental Health, and ERIC for Educational Resources Information Center. In this case, your first reference to the group or organization should include the abbreviation you intend to use.

The *Guidelines* (National Endowment for the Humanities [NEH], 1994) specify . . . The NEH gives block grants to states. . . . It funded a study of . . . (*Guidelines*, 1994)

Work explicitly identified as anonymous

If the title page actually gives the author's name as "Anonymous," use that word for the author and omit the title: (Anonymous, 1925). You will find few such instances, particularly among recent works.

Classical work

For a classical work, or any work so old that it was not published in the modern sense, cite the date of the translation you used: (Aristotle, trans. 1985). If the date of authorship is relevant, include it in your text. For identifying specific parts of a classical work, use conventional line, book, or section numbers, as appropriate for each particular case. The entry for the *Nicomachean Ethics* would read: (Aristotle, trans. 1985, 1123a34).

Bible or other sacred writing

Refer to passages in the Bible with citations of book, chapter, and verse and place the translation you used within parentheses, but not in the reference list: Jeremiah 48.18 (New Revised Standard Version). APA uses a period rather than a colon between chapter and verse: 2 Cor. 15.2.

Reference to more than one work

Parenthetical references may mention more than one work. Multiple citations should be arranged as follows:

List two or more works by the same author in order of date of publication: (Gould, 1987, 1989).

Differentiate works by the same author with the same publication date by adding an identifying letter to each date: (Bloom, 1987a, 1987b). The letters also appear in the reference list, where the works are alphabetized by title.

List works by different authors in alphabetical order by last name and use semicolons to separate the references: (Alcock & Thornhill; Gould 1989).

The following list provides bibliographical information for the works used in the above illustrations of APA reference citations. Reference lists should be double-spaced in manuscripts.

References

Alcock, J., & Thornhill, R. (1983). *The evolution of insect mating systems.* Cambridge: Harvard University Press.

Anonymous. (1925). *The wind.* New York: Harper.

Aristotle. (1985). *Nicomachean ethics* (T. Irwin, Trans.). Indianapolis: Hackett Publishing.

Bloom, H. (Ed.). (1987a). *Eugene O'Neill.* New York: Chelsea.

Bloom, H. (Ed.). (1987b). *John Dryden.* New York: Chelsea.

Columbia University. (1995). *Faculty handbook.* New York: Author.

Dawkins, M. S. (1980). *Animal suffering: The science of animal welfare.* London: Chapman & Hall.

Dawkins, R. (1986). *The blind watchmaker.* New York: Norton.

Gould, S. J. (1987). *Time's arrow, time's cycle: Myth and metaphor in the discovery of geological time.* Cambridge: Harvard University Press.

Gould, S. J. (1989). The wheel of fortune and the wedge of progress. *Natural History, 89*(3), 14, 16, 18, 20-21.

Guidelines. (1994). Washington, DC: National Endowment for the Arts.

APA Style

Guidelines and application form for directors, 1996 summer seminars for school teachers. (1994). Washington, DC: National Endowment for the Humanities.

The Holy Bible. (1989). (New Revised Standard Edition). Oxford: Oxford University Press.

Millar, A. J., Straume, M., Chory, J., Chua, N.-H., & Kay, S. A. (1995, 24 February). The regulation of circadian period by phototransduction pathways in *Arabidopsis. Science, 267,* 1163-1165.

New exam for doctor of future. (1989, March 15). *The New York Times,* p. B10.

Tiihonen, P. (2000). Second-level future studies. *IAIR International Journal of Futures Studies, 4.* Retrieved October 11, 2001, from http://www.systems.org/HTML/fsj-v04/Tiihonen1.htm

Vollrath, D., Foote, S., Hilton, A., Brown, L. G., Beer-Romano, P., Bogan, J. S., et al. (1992, 2 October). The human Y chromosome: A 43-interval map based on naturally occurring deletions. *Science, 258,* 52-60.

Reference Forms

This section provides reference forms for a wide range of sources from books and articles to electronic media. Because types of sources are proliferating rapidly, you may need to use some that are not mentioned here. In this case, you should look at the closest alternative and construct your own entry based on the basic principles of APA format. Also, you may have to refer to more than one of the examples given below. To create an entry for an article appearing in a book with three editors, for example, you would use the form for an article and the form for an unedited book, following the rules for works with two or more authors.

Periodicals

Basic entry

The basic entry for an article in a periodical begins with the last name(s), followed by the initials (not the entire first names), of all authors. The year of publication follows in parentheses; for magazine and newspaper articles, give the month and day (if any) or the season (capitalized). Next come the title of the article, not enclosed in quotation marks; the title of the periodical, including the article *the* italicized through the end punctuation mark, if any; the volume number, underlined or italicized through the end punctuation mark, if any; and inclusive page numbers. A period follows the author, the date, the title of the article, and the end of the entry. The name of the periodical, the volume number, and the page numbers are separated by commas. Only the first work of the article title, the first word of the subtitle, and proper names within both are capitalized. All words except articles and prepositions are capitalized in the title of the periodical, and the title is underlined or italicized. The abbreviation `p.` or `pp.` is used in references to daily newspapers but not to journals or magazines. Both numbers in inclusive pages include all digits.

Article by one author

Smith, J. (1995). The title of the article. *The Title of Journal, 1,* 101-105.

Simon, G. (1990). The significance of silence. *Paragraph, 13,* 202-216.

Article by two authors

For an article by two authors, invert the names of both authors, using a comma to separate surnames and initials. Place an ampersand (&) before the name of the second author.

McLaren, P., & Estrada, K. (1993). A dialogue on multiculturalism and democratic culture. *Educational Researcher, 22,* 27-33.

Article by three to six authors

List the names of all authors up to six, separating surnames and initials with a comma and placing an ampersand (&) before the name of the final author.

Dornbusch, S. M., Carlsmith, J. M., Bushwall, S. J., Ritter, P. L., Leiderman, H., & Hastorf, A. H. (1985). Single parents, extended households, and the control of adolescents. *Child Development, 56,* 326-341.

Seven or more authors

For an article with seven or more authors, list the first six names and use `et al.` to refer to the rest, no matter how many.

Vollrath, D., Foote, S., Hilton, A., Brown, L.G., Beer-Romano, P., Bogan, J.S., et al. (1992, 2 October). The human Y chromosome: A 43-interval map based on naturally occurring deletions. *Science, 258,* 52-60.

Names with suffixes

For names followed by a suffix such as Jr. or III, place the suffix after the initials for the first name, preceded and followed by a comma.

Harper, C. L., Jr., Nyquist, L. E., Bansal, B., Wiesmann, H., & Shih, C.-Y. (1995, January 13). Rapid accretion and early differention of Mars. *Science, 267,* 213-216.

When the name appears in regular rather than inverted order, no punctuation separates the name and the suffix: C. L. Harper Jr., Charles S. Levings III.

Journal paginated by issue

If each issue of a journal begins with page 1, give the issue number in parentheses after the volume number. The issue number is not italicized.

Brunsdale, M. M. (1991). Stages on her road: Sigrid Undset's spiritual journey. *Religion and Literature, 23*(3), 83-96.

Magazine article

The entry for an article in a magazine or newsletter with a volume number includes the month and day (if any), as well as the year, the volume, and the pages.

Osborn, M. (1994, March 11). Status and prospects of women in science in Europe. *Science, 263,* 1389-1391.

Most magazines have volume numbers, although in popular publications they are often not featured prominently. If you ascertain that the magazine has no volume number, follow the format for a newspaper article. If no author is given, begin the entry with the title of the article.

Newspaper article

Entries for articles in newspapers are constructed according to the principles for magazines, except that the volume number is omitted and the abbreviation p. or pp. is used to indicate page(s).

Morain, D. (1993, June 7). Poor counties hit hardest by budget cuts. *The Los Angeles Times,* p. A1.

Newspaper article, unsigned

An entry for a newspaper (or magazine) article without a byline or signature begins with the headline or title in the author position without italics, or quotation marks.

New exam for doctor of future. (1989, March 15). *The New York Times,* p. B10.

Newspaper article, discontinuous pages

When a newspaper article appears on discontinuous pages, give all page numbers and separate the numbers with commas.

Broad, W. J. (1989, March 14). Flight of shuttle begins flawlessly. *The New York Times,* pp. A1, C7.

Newspaper article in designated section

When you cite a newspaper article with a special designation, indicate its nature in brackets following the title.

Williams, R. L. (1992, May 13). National university is an outmoded idea [Letter to the editor]. *The Chronicle of Higher Education,* p. B4.

Special issue of a journal

In an entry for a special issue of a journal, identify the editors (if any) of the issue and the title of the issue. If the issue does not specify its editors, the title of the issue occupies the author position.

Political and social issues in composition [Special issue]. (1992). *College Composition and Communication, 43*(2).

Monographs

In an entry for a monograph, identify the nature of the material within brackets if the series or journal title does not, and give the volume number of the issue. Place additional identifying numerals, such as issue and serial (or whole) numbers, in parentheses after the volume number without an intervening space.

Hinde, R. A. (1990). The interdependence of the behavioral sciences [Monograph]. *Philosophical Transactions of the Royal Society, 329,* 217-277.

Kreutzer, M. A., Leonard, C., & Flavell, J. H. (1975). An interview study of children's knowledge about memory. *Monographs of the Society for Research in Child Development, 40*(Whole No. 1).

Abstract or synopsis

If you wish to cite the abstract of a published article rather than the article itself, provide a complete entry for the published article and cite the source of the abstract, if it is different, in parentheses. Place the designation Abstract within brackets after the title and before the period.

Dorin, J. R., Inglis, J. D., & Porteous, D. J. (1989). Selection for precise chromosomal targeting of a dominant marker by homologous recombination. [Abstract]. *Science, 243,* 1357-1360. (From *Science Abstracts,* 1989, *75,* Abstract No. 1153)

Article in press When an article either is being considered or has been accepted for publication, the phrase in press takes the position of the date, and the name of the journal follows, but no volume or page numbers are given.

Smith, S. (in press). An experiment in bilingual education. *Journal of Bilingual Education.*

Two such articles by the same author should be identified with lowercase letters preceded by a hyphen: (in press-a, in press-b).

▪ Books and Chapters of Books

Basic form The entry for a book begins with the last name of the author, followed by a comma and the initials of the author's first names, followed by periods. The date of publication appears in parentheses, followed by a period. Only the first word of the book title, the first word of the subtitle, and proper names within both are capitalized. The entire title and the end period are italicized. Facts of publication include the city of publication and, if the city might be unfamiliar to readers or confused with another location, the name of the state. Use U.S. Postal Service abbreviations for states (see Appendix B). The name of the location is followed by a colon and the name of the publisher. The entry ends with a period. The names of university presses are spelled out.

Nagel, P. C. (1992). *The Lees of Virginia: Seven generations of an American family.* New York: Oxford University Press.

Two or more authors For a book by more than one author, invert and list the names of all the authors. Use commas to separate surnames and initials. Place an ampersand (&) before the name of the last author.

Forsyth, A., & Thornhill, R. (1983). *The evolution of insect mating.* Cambridge: Harvard University Press.

Brochure Treat a brochure like a book, but designate it as a brochure within brackets.

APA Style

Edition other than the first

Identify an edition other than the first within parentheses following the title without any intervening punctuation. The number of the edition should be in serial form (2nd, 3rd, 4th, etc.) or, if it is a word, abbreviated (Rev. ed.).

Dreyfus, H. (1989). *What computers can't do* (2nd ed.). New York: Harper & Row.

Reprinted work

The entry for a reprinted work indicates the original date of publication within parentheses.

Darwin, C. (1964). *On the origin of the species: A facsimile of the first edition* (Introd. Ernst Mayer). Cambridge: Harvard University Press. (Original work published 1859)

The parenthetical reference in the text includes both dates: (Darwin, 1859/1964).

Treat a paperbound book issued in a year other than that of the hardcover edition as a reprinted work.

Jamieson, N. L. (1995). *Understanding Vietnam.* Berkeley: University of California Press. (First published in hardcover 1993)

The parenthetical reference in the text includes both dates: (Jamieson 1993/1995).

Edited volume

Indicate that a book is an edited volume by placing the abbreviation for editor (Ed.) or editors (Eds.) within parentheses in the author position.

Stanton, D. C. (Ed.). (1987). *The female autograph: Theory and practice of autobiography from the tenth to the twentieth century.* Chicago: University of Chicago Press.

Chapter or article in edited book

In a reference to a chapter or article in an edited book, place the name of the author of the chapter in the author position. The second part of the entry identifies the book in which the article appears. The name(s) of the editor(s) is (are) not inverted when not at the beginning of the entry. The page numbers for the individual chapter or article appear in parentheses after the title of the book.

Burghardt, G. M. (1984). On the origins of play. In P. K. Smith (Ed.), *Play in animals and humans* (pp. 5-42). Oxford: Basil Blackwell.

APA Style

For two or more editors, use the abbreviation `Eds.`

Dubin, F., Eskey, D., & Grabe, W. (Eds.). (1986). *Teaching second language reading for academic purposes.* Reading, MA: Addison-Wesley.

When the author of the article and the editor of the book are the same, but the book includes articles by other authors, list the name in both author and editor positions.

Olney, J. (1980). Autobiography and the cultural moment: A thematic, historical, and bibliographical introduction. In J. Olney (Ed.), *Autobiography: Essays theoretical and critical* (pp. 3-27). Princeton: Princeton University Press.

When all the chapters in a book are by the same author and you wish to cite one of them by title, place the word `In` before the book title. The example below indicates that Finke is the author of both the chapter and the book.

Finke, L. (1992). The rhetoric of desire in the courtly lyric. In *Feminist Theory, Women's Writing* (pp. 29-74). Ithaca: Cornell University Press.

Reprinted article When an article in a collection was published previously, list the version you actually used, but give the original citation in parentheses.

Howarth, H. L. (1980). Some principles of autobiography. In J. Olney (Ed.), *Autobiography: Essays theoretical and critical* (pp. 84-114). Princeton: Princeton University Press. (Reprinted from *New Literary History,* 1974, 5, 363-381.)

The parenthetical citation in the text includes both publication dates: `(Howarth, 1974/1980).`

Works without designated author Enter and alphabetize a book or brochure without an author or editor by title alone.

Guidelines and application form for directors, 1996 summer seminars for school teachers. [Brochure] (1994). Washington, DC: National Endowment for the Humanities.

APA Style

Author as publisher

When you consider the publisher as the author, replace the name of the publisher with Author.

Teachers Insurance and Annuity Association, College Retirement Equities Fund. [Pamphlet]. (1995). *The participant.* New York: Author.

Multivolume works

For a multivolume work published over several years, place in parentheses the year of publication of the first volume and that of the last volume, separated by a hyphen.

Ripley, C. P. (Ed.). (1985-1992). *The black abolitionist papers* (Vols. 1-5). Chapel Hill: University of North Carolina Press.

When referring to the entire multivolume work within the text, cite it as (Ripley, 1985-1992).

To refer to a single volume in a multivolume series, include only the relevant date, and place the volume number after the title without any intervening punctuation.

Ripley, C. P. (Ed.). (1987). *The black abolitionist papers* (Vol. 2). Chapel Hill: University of North Carolina Press.

When each volume has an individual title, provide both the multivolume and the volume titles, underlined continuously.

Freehling, W. W. (1992). *Secessionists at bay, 1776-1854: Vol 1. The road to disunion.* New York: Oxford University Press.

Translated work

Indicate the name of a translator within parentheses after the title by the initials of the first name(s) and the full last name. If you have used only the English translation, you do not need to include the original title. If you wish to do so, place it within brackets.

Derrida, J. (1976). *Of grammatology* (G. Spivak, Trans.). Baltimore: Johns Hopkins University Press. (Original work published 1967)

The parenthetical reference in the text should indicate the original date of publication as well as the date of the translation: (Derrida, 1967/1976).

Book in a foreign language

When you cite from a book in a foreign language, supply an English translation of the original title within brackets. If the work has not been translated, use your own translation or the English title by which the work is known. The bracketed title is not underlined or italicized.

Kristeva, J. (1983). *L'Histoires d'amour* [Tales of love]. Paris: Denoël.

Work in a series

The entry for an individually titled work in a series provides both the volume and the series titles.

Eiser, J. R. (Ed.). (1990). *Attitudinal judgment.* Springer Series in Social Psychology, no. 11. New York: Springer-Verlag, 1990.

■ Technical and Research Reports

Basic entry

Entries for technical and research reports should follow the basic format for a book entry. The identifying title, series, or number of the report, if any, should be placed in parentheses immediately after the title. The name of the agency publishing the report should not be abbreviated as an acronym, even if it is well known.

Gates, J. P. (1991). *Educational and training opportunities in sustainable agriculture* (U.S. Department of Agriculture). Beltsville, MD: National Agricultural Library.

Report from an information service

For a report that comes from an information service, such as the National Technical Information Service (NTIS) or Educational Resources Information Center (ERIC), identify the service and document number in parentheses at the end of the entry.

Groak, J. J. (1974). *Utilization of library resources by students in non-residential degree programs.* Washington, DC: U.S. Government Printing Office. (ERIC Document Reproduction Service No. ED121236)

Report from a university

When a university (as opposed to a university press) is the publisher, provide the name of the university, followed by the name of the specific unit or department.

Carter, G. E., Parker, J. R., & Bentley, S. (Eds.). (1984). *Minority literature and the urban experience.* LaCrosse: University of Wisconsin, Institute for Minority Studies.

Report from corporation or organization

American Museum of Natural History. (1995). *Annual Report, 1993-1994.* New York: Author.

▪ Proceedings of Meetings

When a presentation at a meeting appears in book form, the entry follows the format for an article in an edited book.

Eble, C. C. (1976). Etiquette books as linguistic authority. In P. A. Reich (Ed.), *The Second LACUS Forum, 1975* (pp. 468-475). Columbia, SC: Hornbeam.

Unpublished paper presented at meeting

For an unpublished paper presented at a conference or symposium, indicate the date of the presentation within parentheses after the name of the author and identify the conference as fully as necessary after the title. If the name of the city is well known, the name of the state may be omitted; otherwise, include both city and state.

Jochens, J. (1992, October). *Gender equality in law?: The case of medieval Iceland.* Paper presented at the 26th Annual Conference of the Center for Medieval and Early Renaissance Studies, Binghamton, NY.

Poster session

Gilbert, D. R. (1995, August). *Investigations into low temperature and low pressure deposition of diamond thin films.* Poster session presented at the Applied Diamond Conference 1995, National Institute of Standards and Technology, Gaithersburg, MD.

Dissertations and Theses

Microfilm of dissertation

When you use the microfilm of a dissertation as the source, give the microfilm number, as well as the volume and page numbers in *Dissertation Abstracts International.*

Baker, C. A. (1985). Multiple alliance commitments: The role of the United States in the Falklands war. *Dissertation Abstracts International, 45,* 4445B. (UMI No. 85-77, 123)

Typescript of dissertation

When you use the typescript copy of a dissertation, give the university and year, as well as the volume and page numbers in *Dissertation Abstracts International.* If the dates are different, provide the date of the dissertation after the name of the university.

Moskop, W. W. (1995). The prudent politician: An extension of Aristotle's ethical theory (Doctoral dissertation, George Washington University, 1984). *Dissertation Abstracts International, 45,* 4445B.

When the years are different, list them chronologically, separated by a slanted line, in the parenthetical reference: (Moskop, 1984/1985).

Unpublished dissertation or thesis

Treat a dissertation or thesis that does not appear in *Dissertation Abstracts International* as an unpublished work. Italicize the title and identify the university, the city, and, if necessary for identification, the state.

Peters, B. (1995). *The biographer as autobiographer: The case of Virginia Woolf.* Unpublished master's thesis, Pace University, Riverdale, NY.

Unpublished Materials and Works of Limited Circulation

Completed material not submitted for publication

When unpublished material is in completed form, italicize the title and indicate the unpublished status at the end of the entry.

Johnson, S. J. (1992). *The teaching of twelfth-grade advanced placement mathematics.* Unpublished manuscript, University of California, San Diego.

Manuscript submitted or accepted for publication

When an unpublished manuscript has been submitted or accepted for publication, designate it as `in press`.

Little, C. A. (1992). *Forms of childhood autism.* In press.

Draft material

When you refer to unpublished material in unfinished form, such as a rough draft or unorganized tabular data, put the name of the topic in brackets in the title position without underlining or italics. Indicate the status of the material at the end of the entry. Use the date you consulted the material.

Jensen, H. C. (1992). [Settlement patterns for Norwegian immigrants, 1890-1920]. Unpublished raw data.

Publication of limited circulation

When a work, although published, probably will not be available in most libraries, give the address at which a copy might be located or obtained.

Inouye, L. (1993, April). GECA--The organic agriculture training school, El Salvador. *Oxfam American project report,* pp. 1-4. [Brochure]. (Available from Oxfam America, 26 West Street, Boston, MA 02111-1206)

▪ Reviews and Published Interviews

Book review

Provide the title of the book under review within brackets following the title.

Moore, W. (1992, October 11). Great physicist, great guy [Review of the book *Genius: The life and science of Richard Feynman*]. *The New York Times Book Review,* p. 3.

If the review does not have a title, use the material within brackets as the title, retaining the brackets.

Kienitz, G. M. (1992). [Review of the book *Tennyson and the doom of Romanticism*]. *Religion and Literature, 24*(1), 87-90.

Film or video program review

Provide the title of the film or video program under review within brackets following the title. If the review does not have a title, use the material within brackets as the title, retaining the brackets, as shown above for a book.

APA Style

Canby, V. (1992, May 22). Cruise and Kidman in old-fashioned epic [Review of the motion picture *Far and away*]. *The New York Times*, p. C10.

Published interview

Follow the basic format appropriate for the book or periodical in which the interview is published. The name of the interviewer occupies the place of the author, and the person interviewed is identified by both first and last names within brackets.

Jahanbegloo, R. (1992, May 28). Philosophy and life [Interview with Isaiah Berlin]. *The New York Review of Books*, pp. 46-54.

Unpublished interviews, conducted through media such as telephone or e-mail, are cited parenthetically within the text as personal communications but are not listed as references.

▪ Audiovisual Media

In entries for audiovisual media, place the name of the principal organizer or creater in the author position, and in parentheses identify the person's function. The nature of the medium should be indicated in brackets immediately after the title. Enter the place and date of publication as for a book. If a work has limited circulation, provide an address from which it can be obtained.

Film

Eastwood, C. (Director). (1992). *Unforgiven* [Motion picture]. Hollywood: Warner Brothers.

Batty, P. (Producer). (1987). *The Divided Union* [Video]. Tinley Park, IL: Fusion Video.

Television broadcast

Entries for television series place the name of the producer in the author position. For an individual episode of a series or a single program, place the name of the writer or reporter in the author position and place the name of the producer in the position of the editor.

Television series

Moyers, B. (Writer and producer). (1995). *The language of life.* [Television series]. Newark, NJ: WNET.

Single episode from series

Jennings, P. (1995, July 27). Hiroshima: Why the bomb was dropped. [Television series episode]. In *Peter*

Jennings reporting (D. Gelber and M. Smith, producers). New York: ABC.

Individual program

Lacy, M. D. (1995, September 4). *Richard Wright: Black boy* (G.P. Land and J. Judin, Executive Producers, Independent Television Service and Mississippi Educational Television). New York: WNET.

Recording

Entries for recordings begin with the writer of the composition, followed by the original date.

Handel, G. F. (1771). Suite no. 1 in F major [Cond. N. Marriner, Academy of St. Martin-in-the-Fields]. On *Water music/Wassermusik* [CD]. Hayes, Middlesex, England: EMI. (1989)

Williams, M. (1971). Katydid's ditty [Recorded by Mannheim Steamroller]. On *Classical gas* [CD]. Omaha: American Gramaphone Records. (1987)

Cassette

When you have a number for a cassette or other material, include it with the description enclosed by parentheses.

Hunter, K. (Speaker). (1989). *Family counseling* (Audiocassette Recording No. 1175). Washington, DC: American Psychological Association.

Westen, D. (Author and speaker). (1995). *Is anyone really normal? Perspectives on abnormal psychology* (Videocassette No. 658). Springfield, VA: The Teaching Company.

▪ Electronic Sources

The citation for an electronic source should provide information sufficient to permit your reader to locate the material that is identical to the source you used. Because electronic sources can be easily altered or erased, meeting this criterion requires more information than is needed for print sources. Before submitting an article to an APA journal, you need to check all the URLs (electronic addresses) in your references for currency and to eliminate any citations that are no longer available. In the case of academic or work-related research papers, you might want to include printouts of some of your electronic sources in an appendix.

Electronic sources can be divided into two types: those available through the Internet and those not on the Internet.

SOURCES ON THE INTERNET Entries for materials from the Internet should include the same facts of publication necessary for print sources: last name of the author followed by the initial(s) of given names; the date of publication within parentheses; the title of the section you used; the title of the database, project, or site, italicized. In addition, citations for electronic sources include the date you accessed the site and the URL. You may break a URL only after a slash. Do not insert a hyphen into a URL and do not follow it with a period. You may also include, as appropriate, information such as the date of the latest version of the site; the number of pages, paragraphs, or sections; and the e-mail address of the Webmaster maintaining the site. To locate some of this information, you may have to explore the entire site carefully. Also, some of the copyright information may be on the Home page from which the site branches: to find this page, remove the final segments of the address until you reach the Home page or click the appropriate link on the site. If you cannot find some of the required information, cite anything you have that will be useful to readers.

Internet articles identical to a print source

Corbett, K. J. (2001, Winter). The big picture: Theatrical moviegoing, digital television, and beyond the substitution effect. [Electronic version]. *Cinema Journal, 40,* 17-32.

When the electronic and print versions are identical, only the bibliographic information for the print source is required.

Article in an Internet-only periodical

Youngblood, G.M. (1999, Summer). Web hunting: Design of a simple intelligent web search agent. *ACM Crossroads, 5.* Retrieved October 15, 2001, from http://www.acm.org/crossroads/xrds5-4/webhunting.html

Provide the URL that links directly to the article. An Internet-only periodical does not usually have page numbers.

Newspaper article, electronic version

Chang, K. (2001, October 19). Precursor to tiniest chip is developed. *The New York Times.* Retrieved October 19, 2001, from http://www.nytimes.org/pages/science/html

Document created by a private organization, no date

The Literacy Volunteer Connection (n.d.). *Tips for volunteer tutors*. Retrieved October 17, 2001, from http://literacyvolunteer.homestead.com/TipsForTutors.html

When an individual is not identified as the author, use the name of the organization in place of the author.

Document, no author identified, no date

Advice for job hunters. (n.d.). Retrieved October 1, 2001, from http://www.howard.dowding.ukgateway.net/

When neither an individual nor an organization is identified as taking responsibility for creation of the site, place the title of the document at the beginning of the entry. Use the abbreviations n.d. (no date) for undated documents.

Chapter or section in a document, no page numbers

Stone, G. (2000, March). Lead length and voice in U.S. newspapers (conclusions and readability). *Web journal of mass communication research, 3*. Retrieved October 10, 2001, from http://www.scripps.ohiou.edu/wjmcr/vol03/3-2a.htm

Cite the entire document when pages or sections are not marked.

Report on government agency Web site, no date

United States Senate. (n.d.) *Senate oral history program*. Retrieved October 19, 2001, from http://www.senate.gov/learning/learn_history_oralhist.html

Private organization report on organization Web site

Oxfam International.(n.d.). *Towards global equity: Strategic plan summary 2001-2004*. Retrieved October 20, 2001, from http://www.oxfam.org/strategic_plan/equity.htm

Organization document, from Web site of a different organization

American Council of Learned Societies. (2000, November). *Report on History E-book Project*. Retrieved October 25, 2001, from Columbia University, Center for Comparative Literature and Society Web site: http://www.columbia.edu/cu/research/

APA Style

For a document accessed from the Web site of an organization other than the one that produced the document, identify and cite the URL of the provider you used.

U.S. government report online

Department of Energy. (2001, March 13). *Protection of human subjects.* Retrieved October 26, 2001, from http://www.access.gpo.gov/nara/cfr/waisidx_01/10cfrv4_01.html#706

Paper presented at a virtual conference

Mackieh, A., & Cilingir, C. (1996). *Effects of performance shaping factors on human error.* Paper presented at the CybErg 96 virtual conference. Retrieved October 26, 2001, from http://www.curtin.edu.au/conference/cyberg/centre/paper/mackiehpaper.html#

Because a virtual conference takes place online, no place can be specified.

Message posted to a newsgroup

Stonehouse, R. (2001, October 25). Did the Trojan War occur? Message posted to newsgroups://soc.history.ancient.humanities.classics

When you have other relevant sources, avoid referring to newsgroups because the messages usually do not remain online very long, and the origin of the message is not verifiable. Provide the precise date of the posting; the subject heading, not italicized; and the address of the newsgroup.

Message posted to online forum or discussion group

Adams, E. (2001, October 4). Question to Martha Nussbaum. Posted to http://chronicle.com/colloquylive/s002/1/10/nussbaum/chat

ELECTRONIC SOURCES NOT ON THE INTERNET Some materials, such as computer software and CD-ROMs, are accessed electronically but in themselves are not electronic. In addition to the information you would include for an electronic source on the Internet, you may need to provide a description of the medium (CD-ROM, diskette, etc.); the name of the database or vendor; and the date of electronic publication.

Journal article retrieved from an electronic database

Robinson, D. T., & Smith-Lovin, L. (2001, September). Getting a laugh: Gender, status, and humor in task discussions. *Social Forces, 80,* 125-158. Retrieved October 19, 2001 from http://muse.jhu.edu/journals/social_forces/v080/

Encyclopedia or dictionary entry

Sobel, Robert D., ed. (1900). *Smith, Charles Emory.* Biographical directory of the United States executive branch. Retrieved October 25 from http://lexis-nexis.com/hisuniv/

Abstract obtained from a database

Brown, L., & Halweil, B. (2001, May). Virtual water. *Canada and the world backgrounder, 66.* Abstract retrieved October 25, 2001, from Readers Guide Abstracts: http://firstsearch.oclc.org

Electronic version of U.S. government report available from GPO access database

U.S. Senate (2001, October 22). Joint Committees of the Congress. *Senate Calendar of Business, 107th Congress.* Retrieved October 29, 2001, from Senate Calendar Online via GPO Access: http://www.access.gpo.gov/congress/browse-sc.html

Data file, available from NTIS Web site

North Atlantic Treaty Organization. (1990, May). *NATO Thesaurus Project* [Data file]. Available from National Technical Information Service Web site: http://neptune.fedworld.gov/

Computer software

In an entry for computer software, include the name of the author or producer; the year of development or publication; the title, not italicized; immediately after the title, a description of the material in brackets; the facts of publication; and any additional information necessary for locating and running the program.

Adobe Systems (Producer). (2001). Adobe Acrobat (Version 5.0.5) [Computer software]. San Jose, CA.

Knowledge Revolution (Producer). (1992). Interactive physics II [Computer software]. San Francisco.

APA Style

```
AAPEX (Producer). (1995). Quotation reference collection
     [Computer software]. Reno. Available: AAPEX Software,
     955 South Virginia, Suite 116, Reno, NV 89502.
```

The List of References

In APA style, the list of sources is entitled "References." This list should be confined to those works actually cited within the article, report, or dissertation, and it must include all of the cited works. If you wish to provide a list of additional readings or the full range of works you consulted, you may do so in a bibliographical appendix (not acceptable for an article to be submitted to an APA journal). For a sample reference list, see pages 250–251 and 275.

Order of entries

Entries appear in alphabetical order according to the last name of the author or, if there is no author, the first word in the title, excluding articles. For the principles of alphabetization in a reference list or bibliography, see pages 139–140.

Two or more works by same author

Two or more works by the same author appear in chronological order by date of publication, beginning with the earliest.

```
Jones, J. J. (1995).

Jones, J. J. (1996).
```

Two or more works by the same author and with the same publication date appear in alphabetical order by title and are identified by serial lowercase letters after the date. Repeat the name of the author in each entry.

```
Jones, J. J. (1995a). Breakdown in communication . . .

Jones, J. J. (1995b). Businesses organize . . .
```

One-author entries precede two-author entries beginning with the same author, even if the publication date is later; two-author entries precede three-author entries, and so on.

```
Jones, J. J. (1995).

Jones, J. J., & Smith, S. S. (1987).
```

Sources with the same first author are alphabetized by the surname of the second author. If the first two names are the same, alphabetize by the third author, and so on.

```
Jones, J. J., Smith, S. S., & Adams, A. A. (1994).

Jones, J. J., Smith, S. S. & Bentley, B. B. (1988).
```

An author entry precedes an entry for the same person as an editor, which precedes an entry for the same person as a coauthor or coeditor.

`Jones, J. J. (1995).`

`Jones, J. J. (Ed.) (1995).`

`Jones, J. J., & Smith, S. S. (1995).`

`Jones, J. J., & Smith, S. S. (Eds.) (1995).`

Different authors with same surname

Authors with the same surname should be alphabetized by the initial of the first name.

`Jones, J. J. (1995).`

`Jones, M. J. (1995).`

Anonymous work

For a work explicitly identified as anonymous, use the word `Anonymous` as the author entry and alphabetize accordingly.

`Anonymous. (1996).` *`Primary Colors.`* `New York: Random House.`

Legal citation

Place citations for legal documents in the reference list (not at the bottom of the page as in legal documents and periodicals). Enter them without italics, and alphabetize them by the first significant word in the entry.

`Jones v. Smith, Volume, Source, Page (Court Date).`

`Smith v. Jones, " " " " .`

Within the body of your paper, give the names of the contenders, underlined or italicized, and the date of the decision within parentheses. For the format and content of legal references, see Appendix A.

APA Style

[1 inch]

running head
Counterfactual Thinking

[4 line spaces]

Counterfactual Thinking title

[double spaced]

Neal J. Roese student's name

Northwestern University affiliation

Title page, APA

[1 inch]

Abstract

[4 line spaces]

Counterfactuals are mental representations of alternatives to the past and produce consequences that are both beneficial and aversive to the individual. These apparently contradictory effects are integrated in a functionalist model of counterfactual thinking. The author reviews research in support of the assertions that (a) counterfactual thinking is activated automatically in response to negative affect, (b) the content of counterfactuals targets particularly likely causes of misfortune, (c) counterfactuals produce negative affective consequences through a contrast-effect mechanism and positive inferential consequences through a cause-inference mechanism, and (d) the net effect of counterfactual thinking is beneficial.

Abstract page, APA

[1 inch]

Counterfactual Thinking

Look in my face: my name is Might-have been;

I am also called No-more, Too-late, Farewell.

-Dante Gabriel Rossetti

Popular wisdom typically equates thoughts of what might have been with negative emotional consequences. As the quotation above suggests, those who dwell on possibilities that never were, that is, on *counterfactual* versions of the past, are doomed to regret, despair, and an excruciating sense of loss. This theme echoes through numerous literary narratives: If only Madame Bovary had married someone other than the dull Henry Bovary . . .; if only Cyrano had mustered sufficient courage to pursue directly his love Roxanne . . . .[1] John Greenleaf Whittier (1898) wrote what is perhaps the most famous assertion of this theme: "For all sad words of tongue or pen, the saddest are these: 'It might have been!'" (p. 153).

Although philosophers have long pondered the enigmatic character of counterfactuals (e.g., Goodman, 1947), social psychologists have only more recently examined their significance for feeling and thinking (e.g., Roese & Olson, 1955d). Research has indeed confirmed that negative emotions may result from counterfactual thinking. Other research, however, has shown that separate beneficial effects may also emerge from counterfactual thinking. Specifically, thoughts of what might have been may suggest paths to what may yet be. From this latter vantage point, short-term negative affect may be offset by inferential

APA Style

First page of text, APA

[1 inch]

benefits that may aid the individual on a longer term basis. That counterfactual thinking is generally beneficial, or functional, for the individual forms the conceptual basis for the present theoretical overview of the counterfactual literature. This review is intended to be both comprehensive, in that the majority of studies conducted by social psychologists are considered, and theory driven, in that diverse threads of counterfactual research are woven into an integrated functionalist tapestry.

Five main sections comprise this article. First, I define counterfactuals. Second, I articulate the theoretical framework of counterfactual functionality. Third, I examine determinants of counterfactual thinking in light of the functional approach. Fourth, I review consequences of counterfactual thinking, and finally I consider implications that integrate both beneficial and harmful consequences under the rubric of functionality.

Several assertions are subordinated under the central idea that counterfactual thinking has a net benefit for the individual. To begin with, counterfactual thinking is activated by negative affect. In functional terms, counterfactual thoughts thus come to mind in response to those experiences where corrective thinking would be most beneficial. Second, the content of counterfactuals often focuses on extreme or unusual antecedent events, which are particularly likely sources of the misfortune in question. Third, counterfactuals produce negative affective consequences through a contrast-effect mechanism, but these effects are offset by positive inferential consequences

Second page of text, APA

References

Alloy, L. B. & Tabachnik, N. (1984). Assessment of covariation by humans and animals: The joint influence of prior expectations and current situational information. *Psychological Review, 91,* 112-149.

Bandura, A. (Ed.). (1995). *Self-efficacy in changing societies.* New York: Cambridge University Press.

Bargh, J. A. (1996). Automaticity in social psychology. In E. T. Higgins & A. W. Kruglanski (Eds). *Social psychology: Handbook of basic principles* (pp. 169-183.) New York: Guilford.

Bohner, G., Bless, H., Schwarz, N., & Strack, F. (1998). What triggers causal attributions? The impact of valence and subjective probability. *European Journal of Social Psychology, 18,* 335-345.

Boninger, D. S., Gleicher, F., & Strathman, A. (1994). Counterfactual thinking. From what might have been to what may be. *Journal of Personality and Social Psychology, 67,* 297-307.

Bouts, P., Spears, R., & van de Pligt, J. (1992). Counterfactual processing and the correspondence between events and outcomes: Normality versus value. *European Journal of Social Psychology, 22,* 387-396.

Branscombe, N. R., Crosby, P., & Weir, J. A. (1993). Social inferences concerning male and female homeowners who use a gun to shoot an intruder. *Aggressive Behavior, 19,* 113-124.

Reference page, APA

[1 inch]

Counterfactual Thinking 34

Footnotes

[1]See Flaubert (1857/1950) and Rostand (1898/1971), respectively.

(The list of footnotes, correlated to superscripts in the text, continues. In APA journal format footnotes would appear at the bottom of the appropriate page.)

Footnotes page, APA

References

Alloy, L. B., & Tabachnik, N. (1984). Assessment of covariation by humans and animals: The joint influence of prior expectations and current situational information. *Psychological Review, 91,* 112–149.

Bandura, A. (Ed.). (1995). *Self-efficacy in changing societies.* New York: Cambridge University Press.

Bargh, J. A. (1996). Automaticity in social psychology. In E. T. Higgins & A. W. Kruglanski (Eds.), *Social psychology: Handbook of basic principles* (pp. 169–183). New York: Guilford.

Bohner, G., Bless, H., Schwarz, N., & Strack, F. (1988). What triggers causal attributions? The impact of valence and subjective probability. *European Journal of Social Psychology, 18,* 335–345.

Boninger, D. S., Gleicher, F., & Strathman, A. (1994). Counterfactual thinking: From what might have been to what may be. *Journal of Personality and Social Psychology, 67,* 297–307.

Bouts, P., Spears, R., & van der Pligt, J. (1992). Counterfactual processing and the correspondence between events and outcomes: Normality versus value. *European Journal of Social Psychology, 22,* 387–396.

Branscombe, N. R., Crosby, P., & Weir, J. A. (1993). Social inferences concerning male and female homeowners who use a gun to shoot an intruder. *Aggressive Behavior, 19,* 113–124.

Branscombe, N. R., & Weir, J. A. (1992). Resistance as stereotype–inconsistency: Consequences for judgments of rape victims. *Journal of Social and Clinical Psychology, 11,* 80–102.

Brendl, C. M., & Higgins, E. T. (1996). Principles of judging valence: What makes events positive or negative? In M. P. Zanna (Ed.), *Advances in experimental social psychology* (Vol. 28, pp. 95–160). San Diego, CA: Academic Press.

Breslauer, G. (1996). Counterfactual reasoning in Western studies of Soviet politics and foreign relations. In P. E. Tetlock & A. Belkin (Eds.), *Counterfactual thought experiments in world politics: Logical, methodological, and psychological perspectives* (pp. 71–94). Princeton, NJ: Princeton University Press.

Buck, M. L., & Miller, D. T. (1994). Reactions to incongruous negative life events. *Social Justice Research, 7,* 29–46.

Carver, C. S., Blaney, P. H., & Scheier, M. F. (1979). Reassertion and giving up: The interactive role of self-directed attention and outcome expectancy. *Journal of Personality and Social Psychology, 37,* 1859–1870.

Collins, R. L. (1996). For better or worse: The impact of upward social comparison on self-evaluations. *Psychological Bulletin, 119,* 51–69.

Crocker, J. (1981). Judgment of covariation by social perceivers. *Psychological Bulletin, 90,* 272–292.

Davis, C. G., & Lehman, D. R. (1995). Counterfactual thinking and coping with traumatic life events. In N. J. Roese & J. M. Olson (Eds.), *What might have been: The social psychology of counterfactual thinking* (pp. 353–374). Mahwah, NJ: Erlbaum.

Davis, C. G., Lehman, D. R., Silver, R. C., Wortman, C. B., & Ellard, J. H. (1996). Self-blame following a traumatic event: The role of perceived avoidability. *Personality and Social Psychology Bulletin, 22,* 557–567.

Davis, C. G., Lehman, D. R., Wortman, C. B., Silver, R. C., & Thompson, S. C. (1995). The undoing of traumatic life events. *Personality and Social Psychology Bulletin, 21,* 109–124.

Dunning, D., & Madey, S. F. (1995). Comparison processes in counterfactual thought. In N. J. Roese & J. M. Olson (Eds.), *What might have been: The social psychology of counterfactual thinking* (pp. 103–131). Mahwah, NJ: Erlbaum.

Dunning, D., & Parpal, M. (1989). Mental addition and subtraction in counterfactual reasoning: On assessing the impact of actions and life events. *Journal of Personality and Social Psychology, 57,* 5–15.

Einhorn, H. J. & Hogarth, R. M. (1986). Judging probable cause. *Psychological Bulletin, 99,* 3–19.

Fearon, J. D. (1991). Counterfactuals and hypothesis testing in political science. *World Politics, 43,* 169–195.

Fillenbaum, S. (1974). Information amplified: Memory for counterfactual conditions. *Journal of Experimental Psychology, 102,* 44–49.

Fischhoff, B. (1975). Hindsight ≠ foresight: The effect of outcome knowledge on judgment under uncertainty. *Journal of Experimental Psychology: Human Perception and Performance, 1,* 288–299.

Fischhoff, B. (1976). The effect of temporal setting on likelihood estimates. *Organizational Behavior and Human Performance, 15,* 180–194.

Flaubert, G. (1950). *Madame Bovary* (A. Russell, Trans.). London: Penguin. (Original work published 1857)

Funder, D. C. (1987) Errors and mistakes: Evaluating the accuracy of social judgment. *Psychological Bulletin, 101,* 75–90.

Gavanski, I., & Wells, G. L. (1989). Counterfactual processing of normal and exceptional events. *Journal of Experimental Social Psychology, 25,* 314–325.

Gilbert, D. T. (in press). Ordinary personology. In D. T. Gilbert, S. T. Fiske, & G. Lindzey (Eds.), *Handbook of social psychology* (Vol. 4). New York: McGraw-Hill.

Gilbert, D. T., & Malone, P. S. (1995). The correspondence bias. *Psychological Bulletin, 117,* 21–38.

Gilovich, T., & Medvec, V. H., (1994). The temporal pattern to the experience of regret. *Journal of Personality and Social Psychology, 67,* 357–365.

Gilovich, T., & Medvec V. H. (1995a). The experience of regret: What, when, and why. *Psychological Review, 102,* 379–395.

Gilovich, T., & Medvec, V. H. (1995b). Some counterfactual determinants of satisfaction and regret. In N. J. Roese & J. M. Olson (Eds.), *What might have been: The social psychology of counterfactual thinking* (pp. 259–282). Mahwah, NJ: Erlbaum.

Girotto, V., Legrenzi, P., & Rizzo, A. (1991). Event controllability in counterfactual thinking. *Acta Psychologica, 78,* 111–133.

Gleicher, F., Boninger, D., Strathman, A., Armor, D., Hetts, J., & Ahn, M. (1995). With an eye toward the future: The impact of counterfactual thinking on affect, attitudes, and behavior. In N. J. Roese & J. M. Olson (Eds.), *What might have been: The social psychology of counterfactual thinking* (pp. 283–304). Mahwah, NJ: Erlbaum.

Gleicher, F., Kost, K. A., Baker, S. M., Strathman, A. J., Richman, S. A., & Sherman, S. J. (1990). The role of counterfactual thinking in judgments of affect. *Personality and Social Psychology Bulletin, 16,* 284–295.

References page as printed in APA journal

10 *Columbia Guide to Online Style*

Humanities style 279
Scientific style 279

When you have numerous electronic sources of widely various types, you may want to consult *The Columbia Guide to Online Style,* by Janice R. Walker and Todd Taylor (New York: Columbia University Press, 1998). For an introduction to the book and changes or updates see <http://www.columbia.edu/cu/cup/cgos/>.

This guide provides citations in a generic humanities style, which differs from either *Chicago Manual* or Modern Language Association style, and a generic scientific style, which differs from American Psychological Association style. Nevertheless, the book may be helpful because it contains extensive coverage of the problems involved in citing online sources and gives examples of a wider range of electronic sources than any of these style sheets.

When using *CGOS* you should use footnotes, endnotes, or parenthetical references for the style sheet you are using. If, for example, you are using MLA or APA format and consult *CGOS* about a citation, provide the information within parentheses in the text just as you would for a print source. Similarly, when using endnotes in the *Chicago Manual* style, your endnotes should take the form you use for other sources.

This introduction to *CGOS* provides examples of bibliographical formats in the humanities style and the scientific style. All entries use the hanging indention (the first line on the left margin and subsequent lines indented five spaces). If a publisher prefers to receive your manuscript without the commands for indention, you may start all lines at the left margin and leave a line of space between entries. Titles are italicized rather than underlined. To emphasize the differences between the styles, the same sources appear in both humanities and scientific style.

▪ Humanities style

Complete work Audi, Robert. *Moral Knowledge and Ethical Character.* New York: Oxford University Press, 1997. Electronic Text Service, Columbia University. https://www1.columbia.edu/sec/dlc/oup/audi/ (1 Nov. 2001).

Portion of a complete work Marcone, Joan. "Chalk in the Electronic Classroom." *Online Pedagogy.* 2000. http://www.teaching.com/onlinepedagogy/smartclassrooms/screens/ (2 Nov. 2000).

Article with print equivalent Campbell, James. "Alfred Nobel and His Prizes." *Boston Review* 26:5 (2001). http://bostonreview.mit.edu/BR26.5/Campbell.htm (29 Oct. 2001).

Newspaper article Schiff, David. "Leonard Bernstein: The Man Who Mainstreamed Mahler." *New York Times.* 4 Nov. 2001. http://www.nytimes.org/2001/11/04/arts/music/04SCHI.html (6 Nov. 2001).

Home page Smith, Michael W. http://www.gse.rutgers.edu/people/mws.htm (15 Oct. 2001).

Computer program *Adobe Acrobat Vers. 5.0.5.* San Jose, CA: Adobe, 2001.
(Notice that *CGOS* abbreviates version to vers.)

▪ Scientific Style

Complete work Audi, R. (1997). *Moral knowledge and ethical character.* New York: Oxford University Press. Electronic Text Service, Columbia University. https://www1.columbia.edu/sec/dlc/oup/audi/ (1 Nov. 2001).

Portion of a complete work

Marcone, J. (2000). Chalk in the electronic classroom. *Online pedagogy*. http://www.teaching.com/onlinepedagogy/smartclassrooms/screens/ (2 Nov. 2000).

Article with print equivalent

Campbell, J. (2001). Alfred Nobel and his prizes. *Boston review*, 26(5). http://bostonreview.mit.edu/BR26.5/Campbell.htm (29 Oct. 2001).

Newspaper article

Schiff, D. (2001, Nov. 4). Leonard Bernstein: The man who mainstreamed Mahler. *New York Times*. http://www.nytimes.org/2001/11/04/arts/music/04SCHI.html (6 Nov. 2001).

Home page

Smith, M.W. (2001, Feb. 19). http://www.gse.rutgers.edu/people/mws.htm (15 Oct. 2001).

Computer program

Adobe Acrobat Vers. 5.0.5. (2001). San Jose, CA: Adobe.

Appendix A

Legal Citation

Most legal writing, particularly briefs and other documents filed with courts, employs only notes. Citations are made either parenthetically in the text or in footnotes. There is only one format for legal references, whether they are placed within the text or at the bottom of the page. If you wish to include legal documents in a bibliography, the entries should take the same form as the notes.

The Harvard Law Review Association booklet *A Uniform System of Citation,* 17th ed. 2000 (known as *The Bluebook*), is the standard guide in matters of format and interpretation of entries. For meanings of abbreviations not contained there, consult *Black's Law Dictionary.*

In the United States, primary sources are judicial, statutory, and quasi-statutory material.

■ Judicial Material

The most common category of judicial material includes the reported decisions of court cases and the documents related to these decisions, such as briefs submitted by the parties or the transcript of a trial. The order of the elements in the citation of a reported decision is as follows: (1) names of the parties (only the first party on each side); (2) volume number; (3) name of the report or service in which the decision appears; (4) page on which the decision begins, or paragraph number of the decision, followed by the page on which the cited material appears; (5) in parentheses, the court of decision (if not apparent from the name of the report) followed by the year of decision; and (6) the subsequent history of the case.

U.S. Supreme Court

[41] Traux v. Corrigan, 257 U.S. 312, 327 (1921).

The decision in the *Traux* case, cited in note 41, is contained in volume 257 of the official reports of decisions of the United States Supreme Court (*United States Reports*). It begins on page 312; the cited material appears at page 327. The decision was handed down in 1921; the court of decision is apparent from the name of the report.

State court, parallel citations

[42] 3 N.Y. 2d 155, 143 N.E.2d 906, 164 N.Y.S.2d 714 (1957).

Note 42 gives the citation to *Sabo v. Delman*. The name of the case appears in the text, where it is italicized; only the citation is given in the note. The fact that the abbreviation of the official report—*N.Y.* for *New York Reports*—is also the abbreviation of the name of the state indicates that the decision was handed down by the state's highest court (in this case, New York's Court of Appeals). The designation 2d indicates that the decision is found in the second series of *New York Reports*. A parallel citation is also given to two unofficial reports, the *North Eastern Reporter, Second Series*, which gathers cases from several states into a single volume, and the *New York Supplement, Second Series*, which reports New York cases from several different levels.

Many decisions are reported only in unofficial reporters, particularly loose-leaf services, which attempt to compile the decisions relevent to a particular subject matter.

Decisions in unofficial reporters

[43] Omega-Alpha, Inc. v. Touche Ross & Co., [1976-1977 Transfer Binder] Fed. Sec. L. Rep. (CCH) 95,663, at 90,268 (S.D.N.Y. 1976).

The decision cited in note 43 is reported at Paragraph 95,663 of the *Federal Securities Law Reporter*, compiled by the Commerce Clearing House, Inc. Although the decision first appeared in the "Current" binder of that service (updated weekly), it has now been transferred to the permanent binder of decisions handed down in 1976 and 1977. The particular material cited within the case is found at page 90,268 of the volume.

When the citation is to an unreported decision, the docket number of the case, the court in which it is pending, and the actual date of the decision are given.

Unreported decision

[44] Lannen v. Simpson, No. 79-1527-J (162nd Jud. Dist. Ct. Tex., Feb. 3, 1980).

Materials submitted to a court or generated during court proceedings are cited by reference to a reported decision, if one exists, or to the case name, docket number, and court, if one does not.

Brief, U.S. District Court

[45] Brief for Plaintiff at 10, Jones v. Smith, 139 F. Supp. 730 (W.D. La. 1956).

The reference in note 45 is to material appearing at page 10 of Jones's brief submitted to the United States District Court for the Western District of Louisiana in connection with a case with a decision reported in volume 139 of the *Federal Supplement*.

■ Statutory Material

The second kind of primary source material includes constitutions, statutes, bills and resolutions, and international agreements. Some of the elements found in judicial material are obviously not a part of statutory citations. The order of those elements that are relevant is the same, at least by analogy. The following examples indicate how this kind of citation can be read by someone who is familiar with legal abbreviations.

U.S. Constitution

[46] U.S. Const. amend. XXI, § 2.

[47] U.S. Const. art. III, §§ 1-2.

Notes 46 and 47 refer to the United States Constitution, section 2 of the twenty-first amendment and sections 1 and 2 of article III, respectively.

State constitution, with date

[48] N.Y. Const. art. II, § 6 (1894, amended).

In note 48, citation of section 6, article II of the New York Constitution includes a date because the portion referred to has since been substantially amended or is no longer in force.

Statute, official and common names

[49] Labor Management Relations (Taft-Hartley) Act § 301 (a), 29 U.S.C. § 185 (a) (1986).

In note 49, the citation is to a federal enactment by both its official and common names, section 301, subsection (a); the law is codified in title 29 of the *United States Code*, section 185, subsection (a), 1986 edition. The citation should also be to the latest edition of the code.

Bill not enacted into law

[50] S. 1975, 89th Cong., 1st sess., 111 Cong. Rec. 10502 (1965).

Note 50 refers to Senate Bill 1975, introduced in the first session of the Eighty-ninth Congress and cited in volume 111 of the *Congressional Record*, beginning on page 10502; the bill had not been enacted into law at the time of citation, 1965.

Senate resolution

[51] S. Res. 218, 83d Cong., 2d sess., 100 Cong. Rec. 2972 (1954).

Note 51 refers to Senate Resolution number 218, adopted at the second session of the Eighty-third Congress, 1954, and recorded in volume 100 of the *Congressional Record*, beginning on page 2972.

International agreement

[52] Agreement on Rural Health Services, Sept. 30, 1976, United States-Egypt, 28 U.S.T. 8877, T.I.A.S. No. 8775.

The agreement cited in note 52 was signed on 30 September 1976 and can be found in volume 28 of *U.S. Treaties and Other International Agreements*, the official source of such treaties, beginning on page 8877. Parallel citation is made to the Department of State publication *Treaties and Other International Acts Series*, number 8775; the latter is an unofficial source.

▪ Quasi-statutory Material

Rules, regulations, and the like that are promulgated by nonlegislative organs of government are classified as quasi-statutory material. By analogy, citations to them are read in the same way as are citations to judicial and statutory sources.

Presidential Executive Order

53 Exec. Order No. 10540, 19 Fed. Reg. 3983 (1954).

Note 53 refers to Presidential Executive Order numer 10540, which is to be found in volume 19 of the *Federal Register* (an official report), 1954, beginning on page 3983.

Internal Revenue ruling

54 Rev. Rul. 131, 1953-2 Cum. Bull. 112.

Note 54 refers to Revenue Ruling 131, which appears in part 2 of the 1953 volume of the *Cumulative Bulletin*, beginning on page 112. This is an Internal Revenue ruling of the Treasury Department.

Federal regulation

55 SEC Reg. A, 17 C.F.R. §§ 230.251-230.264 (1980).

In note 55, the citation of Securities and Exchange Commission Regulation A to the Code of Federal Regulations shows that the regulation is currently in force. It is found in title 17, sections 230.251 through 230.264 in the 1980 edition.

Appendix B

Abbreviations of State Names

Usually, the name of the city is all that is needed to identify the place of publication in a note or a bibliographical reference. If one city might be confused with another (such as Lexington, Kentucky, and Lexington, Massachusetts) or if the location of a city is not well known, include the name of the state or territory, using abbreviations. Use these abbreviations only in bibliographical references or in tables; do not use them in the text.

STATE NAME	TRADITIONAL ABBREVIATION (*CHICAGO MANUAL*)	U.S. POSTAL SERVICE ABBREVIATION (MLA AND APA)
Alabama	Ala.	AL
Alaska	Alaska	AK
American Samoa	Amer. Samoa	AS
Arizona	Ariz.	AZ
Arkansas	Ark.	AR
California	Calif.	CA
Canal Zone	C.Z.	CZ
Colorado	Colo.	CO
Connecticut	Conn.	CT
Delaware	Del.	DE
District of Columbia	D.C.	DC
Florida	Fla.	FL
Georgia	Ga.	GA
Guam	Guam	GU
Hawaii	Hawaii	HI
Idaho	Idaho	ID
Illinois	Ill.	IL
Indiana	Ind.	IN
Iowa	Iowa	IA
Kansas	Kans.	KS
Kentucky	Ky.	KY
Louisiana	La.	LA
Maine	Maine	ME
Maryland	Md.	MD
Massachusetts	Mass.	MA
Michigan	Mich.	MI
Minnesota	Minn.	MN
Mississippi	Miss.	MS

STATE NAME	**TRADITIONAL ABBREVIATION (*CHICAGO MANUAL*)**	**U.S. POSTAL SERVICE ABBREVIATION (MLA AND APA)**
Missouri	Mo.	MO
Montana	Mont.	MT
Nebraska	Nebr.	NE
Nevada	Nev.	NV
New Hampshire	N.H.	NH
New Jersey	N.J.	NJ
New Mexico	N.Mex.	NM
New York	N.Y.	NY
North Carolina	N.C.	NC
North Dakota	N.Dak.	ND
Ohio	Ohio	OH
Oklahoma	Okla.	OK
Oregon	Oreg.	OR
Pennsylvania	Pa.	PA
Puerto Rico	P.R.	PR
Rhode Island	R.I.	RI
South Carolina	S.C.	SC
South Dakota	S.Dak.	SD
Tennessee	Tenn.	TN
Texas	Tex.	TX
Utah	Utah	UT
Vermont	Vt.	VT
Virginia	Va.	VA
Virgin Islands	V.I.	VI
Washington	Wash.	WA
West Virginia	W. Va.	WV
Wisconsin	Wis.	WI
Wyoming	Wyo.	WY

Glossary

This glossary lists terms and abbreviations that occur frequently in notes, parenthetical literary references, and bibliographical entries. Many of these terms, particularly those in Latin, are no longer recommended for current use, but because they are part of the tradition of scholarly research and writing, they appear frequently in literature.

When you are deciding whether to use one of these terms or abbreviations, your first guide should be the requirements of the style you are following. Your second consideration should be brevity and clarity. If an abbreviation will save space and contribute to understanding, go ahead and use it; if it will merely obfuscate, write out the word or expression.

Foreign words and phrases not yet Anglicized should be italicized (underlined in typing). Conclusions concerning which foreign words have become Anglicized vary among disciplines, institutions, and journals, but the trend is toward Anglicizing abbreviations and terms. Italicized words in parentheses are the Latin originals.

For words and expressions not included here, consult a standard dictionary.

ABBREVIATION OR TERM	MEANING
abbr.	abbreviation, abbreviated
abr.	abridged, abridgment
adapt.	adapter, adapted by
anon.	anonymous
app.	appendix
art.	article
ASCII	American Standard Code for Information Interchange
b.	born, brother
BBS	Bulletin Board Server, a meeting place in cyberspace where participants can exchange messages
bibliog.	bibliography, bibliographer, bibliographical
biog.	biography, biographer, biographical
bk., bks.	book(s)
bookmark	an electronic marker that stores a link to a favorite or frequently used URL

Boolean search	an electronic search using terms such as *and*, *or*, and *not* to limit or expand the keyword
bulletin board	computers and software that permit users to send (post) and view messages to all connected computers
c., cc.	chapters (in legal citations only)
ca., c. (*circa*)	about (with dates)
CD-ROM	compact disk read-only memory
cf. (*confer*)	compare (not see)
chap., chaps.	chapter(s)
chor.	choreographer, choreographed by
col., cols.	column(s)
colloq.	colloquial, colloquialism
comp.	compiled by, compiler
Cong.	Congress
cont.	continued
copr., cop., or ©	copyright
d.	died, daughter
database	a set of structured data that is digitized, or accessible electronically
digital, digitized	electronically accessible
dir.	director, directed by
diss.	dissertation
div., divs.	division(s)
download	to copy a file from a Web site or other electronic medium onto your computer
ed.	edited by, editor, edition
eds.	editors or editions
e.g. (*exempli gratia*)	for example
e-journal	journal published in electronic form
E-mail, e-mail, email	electronic mail
enl.	enlarged
esp.	especially
et al. (*et alii*)	and other(s)
etc. (*et cetera*)	and so forth
et passim	and here and there
ex., exs., exx.	example(s)
f., ff.	and the following page(s), line(s), etc.
FAQs	Frequently Asked Questions. A feature of some Web sites listing answers to questions frequently asked by users or anticipated by the creators of the site
fig., figs.	figure(s)
fl. (*floruit*)	flourished
fn.	footnote (also see n.)
fol., fols.	folio(s)
ftp	file transfer protocol; see protocol
f.v. (*folio verso*)	on the back of the page
fwd.	foreword, foreword by

gen.	general, genitive
govt.	government
hit(s)	the site(s) identified by a keyword search; visit(s) to a Web site
http	hypertext transport protocol; see protocol
hyperlink, hotlink	a highlighted URL or icon that, when clicked, automatically accesses another Web site
hypertext	a collection of electronic documents organized by their relation to each other through hyperlinks (rather than organized sequentially)
icon	a logo or symbol that, when clicked, links to another site
ibid. (*ibidem*)	in the same place
id. (*idem*)	the same
i.e. (*id est*)	that is
illus.	illustrated by, illustrations(s), illustrator(s)
inf. (*infra*)	below
introd.	introduction by
ISP	Internet Service Provider; a service, either commercial (e.g., America Online, Hotmail) or institutional (e.g., a college or company), that provides access to the Internet
keyword	the word or phrase entered to attempt to search or access information on the Internet
l., ll.	line(s)
LISTSERV™	a commercial electronic mailing list
lit.	literally
lkd.	linked from; used for connection between sites on the Internet
loc. cit. (*loco citato*)	in the place cited
menu	equivalent of a table of contents for a Web site
misc.	miscellaneous
MS, MSS or ms., mss.	manuscript(s)
n., nn. or n, nn	note(s), endnote(s), footnote(s)
NB, N.B. (*nota bene*)	take careful notice, mark well
n.d.	no date (of publication)
no., nos.	number(s)
n.p.	no place (of publication), no publisher
n. pag.	unpaginated, no page
n.s., ns	New Series
N.S., NS	New Style
obs.	obsolete
online or on-line	connected to the Internet
op. cit. (*opere citato*)	in the work cited
orch.	orchestrator, orchestrated by

OS, OSS, os., oss.	Old Series, Old Style
p., pp.	page(s)
par., pars.	paragraph(s)
passim	throughout
perf.	performer, performed by
pl., pls.	plate(s), plural
prod.	producer, produced by
protocol	the first element in many electronic addresses; defines the method a browser or other software must use to access data, e.g., hypertext transfer protocol (http), file transfer protocol (ftp), telnet, gopher
pseud.	pseudonym
pt., pts.	part(s)
pub., publ.	published by, publisher
q.v. (*quod vide*)	which see
rev.	revised by, revision; review; reviewed by
rpt., repr.	reprint, reprinted
sc.	scene
sec., secs.	section(s)
ser.	series
sic (*sic*)	thus
sup. (*supra*)	above, earlier in the text
supp. (MLA) or suppl. (APA)	supplement
s.v. (*sub verbo* or *voce*)	under the word or heading
syn.	synonym, synonymous
tech. rep.	technical report (APA)
trans., tr.	translated by, translation, translator, translators
TS, TSS, ts., tss.	typescript(s)
univ.	university
URL	Uniform Resource Locator; an electronic address used to access a Web site
ut sup. (*ut supra*)	as above
v. (*vide*)	see
v.	versus (in legal citations only)
v., vv., vs., vss.	verse(s)
var.	variant
vers., ver.	version
viz or viz. (*videlicet*)	namely
vol., vols.	volume(s)
vs. (*versus*)	against
Web site	an electronic location created to provide information about a particular topic
writ.	writer, written by
WWW, Web	World Wide Web, the documents residing on all Internet servers that use http protocol

Index

NOTE: Forms specific to a particular style sheet appear next to their abbreviations in boldface; entries in regular type apply to all styles. If you do not find an entry for the style sheet you are using, follow the cross references to a related entry. Sample pages appear in italics.

Abbreviations, 287–290
in body of paper, 87–88
ibid., 146–147
for missing information, 157
in notes/appendixes, 88
numbers with, 95–96
state names, 285–286
APA: in reference forms, 251–269
Ch.: in endnotes, 146–147; journal titles, 159; of months, 158
MLA: of publisher names, 221, 239–240
Abstracts
dissertation/thesis, 40, 202, 203
format for, 130
APA, 254–255, 272; electronic database, 268
Ch., 202, 203; online, 212, 213
MLA: online, 234
Acknowledgments, 44, 132
Active voice, 84
A.D., 96
Addresses. *See* Lectures; Numbers; Speeches/addresses
Advertisements
APA: newspaper article, 253–254
Ch., 190, 191
MLA, 238
Alignment: of epigraphs, 126; of numbers, 124; in outlines, 98; of quoted poetry, 64
Alphabetization, 139–140
American Psychological Association (APA) style, 17, 239, 245–277; abstracts, 40; audiovisual media, 263–264; avoiding bias in, 86; books, 255–259; capitalization, 93; dissertations/theses, 261; electronic sources, 264–269; headings in, 48; periodicals, 252–255; proceedings, 260; quotation indentation in, 64; reference forms, 251–269; References list, 250–251, 269–270; reviews/interviews, 262–263; sample format pages, *271–277;* technical/research reports, 259–260; in text citations, 246–251; unpublished/limited circulation materials, 261–262
Amplifying ideas, 137–138
Analysis, organization by, 21–22
Annotated bibliographies, 28, 130;
Ch.: sample, *36–37*
Anonymous works
APA, 249, 270
Ch., 152
MLA, 224; magazine articles, 230
Anthologies
APA: edited volume, 256–257
Ch.: edited work or compilation, 153–154, 180–183
MLA, 224–225
Appendixes: dissertation/thesis, 48; format for, 133; tables in, 100
Approval sheets, 40
Articles. *See* Edited works; Journals; Magazines; Newspapers
Art works. *See* also Nonprint sources: **Ch.,** 172, 206, 207; **MLA,** 237
Atlases. *See also* Reference works: **Ch.,** 163, 196, 197
Audiocassettes. *See* Sound recordings
Audiovisual media. *See* Nonprint sources
Authors
qualifications and perspective of, 14
APA: corporate/group, 249, 257–258; and date cited in text, 246; multiple, 247–248, 255; named/not named in text, 246; names with suffixes, 253; as publisher, 258; with same last name, 248
Ch.: corporate/group, 153, 180; editor/compiler as, 153; groups/corporations as, 153, 180; of introductions/forwords, 154; missing, 178; multiple, 144, 178; multiple works by the same, 144; with same last name, 144–145; subsequent references to, 143–146
MLA: corporate/group, 216, 224; multiple, 215; multiple works by the same, 217; named in text, 215; not named in text, 215; with same last name, 216

Back matter, 133. *See also* Appendixes; Bibliographical notes; Endnotes; Glossaries; Indexes; Lists of works cited
Ballets. *See also* Musical compositions; Performances: titles of, 91
Bar graphs, 107–108, 112–113
B.C., 96
Berkman, Robert, 13
Bias, avoiding in language, 85–87
Bibliographical notes, 138
Bibliographic databases, 7
Bibliographies
alphabetization in, 139–140
annotated, 28, 36–37, 130
capitalization in, 93
Ch., 150–175; books, 151–157, 179, 181, 183, 185; dissertations, 169, 203; electronic sources, 173–175, 209, 211, 213; entry arrangement, 150; facts of publication, 155–157; journal articles, 158–159, 187; magazine articles, 160; microform materials, 209; missing information in, 157, 178; multiple works by one author, 150–151; multivolume works and series, 157–158, 185, 187; newspaper articles, 160–161, 189, 191; nonprint sources, 169–172, 203, 205, 207, 209; periodicals, 158–162; public documents, 164–167, 197, 199, 201; references to multiple works, 150–151; reference works, 163–164, 195, 197; reviews, 161–162, 191, 193; sacred works, 162–163;

sample, 35–38, 179–213; spacing in, 129; titles in, 155; unpublished sources, 167–168, 201, 203; works of literature, 162–163, 193, 195
dissertation/thesis, 49
final copy format for, 129
format for, 28, 129
types of, 140
working, 5
Bills not enacted into law, 283
Blue Book, The. See Uniform System of Citation, A
Bookmarks, electronic, 13
Book Review Digest, 14
Book Review Index, 14
Books. *See also* Edited works; Multivolume works
chapter titles, 91
division titles, 92
indexes to parts of, 10
APA, 255–259; basic form, 255; chapter/article in, 256–257; edited, 256–257; editions, 256; foreign language, 259; group authors, 257–258; multiple authors, 255; multivolume works, 258; reprinted, 256, 257; reviews, 262; in series, 259; translated, 258–259
Ch.: anonymous, 152; authors with same last name, 152; multiple authors, 151–152; online, 173, 210, 211; pseudonyms, 152; reviews of, 161
MLA: edited/compiled/translated, 224; foreign language, 227; with missing information, 228; by multiple authors, 223–224; online, 232–233; reference to entire, 215; reviews, 230; in series, 226; by single author, 223
Boolean logic, 11–12
Brackets: additions to quotations with, 78; capitalization and, 73; for corrections/clarifications/comments, 126
Brochures
APA, 255
Ch.: paperbound editions, 156, 184–185
MLA: pamphlet, 227
Browsers, 13

Capitalization, 93–94; of captions, 43; of direct quotations, 71–73
Captions: capitalization of, 43; figure, 109, 128; graphs, 107; table, 101–102, 128
Cartoons: **Ch.,** 190, 191; **MLA,** 238
Cause-and-effect organization, 21
CD-ROM databases, 11
Centered material, 123
Chapter numbers, 129
Checklist of United States Public Documents, 164
Chicago Guide to Preparing Electronic Manuscripts for Authors and Publishers, 121
Chicago Manual of Style, The, 17, 28, 141–213; bibliographies, 150–175, 179, 181, 183, 185; endnotes/footnotes, 142–150, 178, 180, 182, 184; quotation indentation in, 62, 63; sample paper in, *29–38*
Chronological organization, 21
Classical works. *See also* Books: **APA,** 249; **Ch.,** 149, 163, 194, 195
Clearance forms, 44
Coherence, 85
Columbia Guide to Online Style, The (Walker, Taylor), 17, 278–280
Comparison and contrast, 21
Compilations
APA: edited volume, 256–257
Ch., 154, 180
MLA, 224
Compilers. *See also* Editors: **Ch.,** 151, 153, 180; **MLA,** 216.
Computer programs: **APA,** 268–269; **CGOS,** 279, 280; **Ch.,** 174–175, 208, 209; **MLA,** 234
Conference proceedings
APA, 260; virtual, 267
Ch., 182, 183, 186, 187
MLA, 227
Congressional hearings, 196, 197, 198, 199
Congressional Record, 166; **Ch.,** 196, 197; **MLA,** 227–228
Consistency: in outlines, 24–25
Constitution of the United States, 166, 283. *See also* Government publications; Public documents; **Ch.,** 198, 199
Constitutions, state, 283
Convention proceedings, 200, 201
Copies, of final drafts, 121
Copyright, fair use and, 62
Copyright pages, dissertation/thesis, 42–43, 54; format for, 130–131
Corporate authors
APA, 249, 257–258; reports from, 260
Ch., 153, 180–181
MLA, 216, 224
Court cases, 281–282
Cross-references, 137

Databases: **APA,** 267–269; **Ch.,** 175, 210, 211; **MLA,** 234; research on, 11–12
Data files: **APA,** 268–269
Dates, 95–96
APA: citations in text, 246
Ch.: abbreviations for, 158; of publication, 155–157
MLA: of publication, 222–223
Decimal outlines, 22–23
Dewey Decimal system, 6
Diction, 81
Dictionaries. *See also* Reference works: **APA:** electronic, 268; **Ch.,** 163, 196, 197
Direct quotations, 61–79; additions to, 78–79; **APA:** with/without author name, 247; brackets with, 126; capitalization of, 71–73; epigraphs, 66, 126; extended, 63–67; indentation of, 62, 63–64; indicating emphasis in, 90; indicating omissions from, 75–78; introducing, 68–71; **MLA:** setting off prose, 125; note taking with, 18, 19; poetry, 62, 64–65; prose, 62, 63–64; punctuating, 71–78; short, 62
Discussion lists, online: **APA,** 267; **Ch.,** 174, 212, 213; **MLA,** 234
Dissertation Abstracts International (DAI), 40
Dissertations/theses, 39–57
back matter, 133
body of, 44–48
chapter organization in, 44–47
chapter titles/headings in, 47–48
copyright page, 42–43, 54
end matter, 48–49
front matter, 39–44
sample, 51–57
titles for, 40–42
titles of, 92
APA, 261
Ch., 169, 202, 203
MLA: published, 228; unpublished, 228–229
Documentation, 28, 136–140; of indirect quotations, 59–61; list of sources, 138–140; note-bibliography, 136; parenthetical-reference, 136; during research, 17
Drama
quotations of, 65–66
titles of, 91

Ch.: act, scene, line, 192, 193; performance, 204, 205; reviews, 161, 190, 191
MLA, 217–218; online, 233

Economy, writing with, 82
Edited works. *See also* Editors, Compilers: **APA,** 256–257; **Ch.,** 192, 193; **MLA,** 220, 224, 226
Editing, 27, 98
Editions
newspaper, 161
titles, 92
APA, 256
Ch., 154–155, 182, 183; paperbound, 156–157, 184, 185
MLA: reprinted work, 226
Editorials. *See also* Newspapers
APA, 253–254
Ch., 161, 188, 189
MLA, 230; online, 234
Editors. *See also* Authors, Compilers
APA, 256–257
Ch., 151, 153; of multivolume works, 157; references to, 145, 180; series, 158
MLA, 216; multiple works by the same, 221
Electronic indexes, 11–12; documenting, 17; evaluating information on, 15–16
Electronic sources
APA, 264–269
Ch., 173–175; availability of, 175; computer programs, 174, 208, 209; databases, 175, 210, 211; Internet, 173–174, 210–213; sample entries, *208–213*
MLA, 218, 232–235; articles, 233; books, 232–233; computer programs, 234; databases, 234–235; discussion lists, 234; drama, 233; e-mail, 234; Internet, 232–234; online documents, 233; online newspapers, 233; poetry, 233; professional/personal sites, 234; reference databases, 234; reviews/editorials/abstracts/letters, 234; scholarly projects, 233; undated documents, 234
Electronic submissions, 121
Ellipses, 126; indicating omissions with, 75–78
E-mail: **Ch.,** 206, 207; **MLA,** 234
Encyclopedias. *See also* Reference works
article titles, 91
APA: electronic, 268
Ch., 163–164; signed entries, 196, 197; unsigned entries, 194, 195
End matter: dissertation/thesis, 48–49
Endnotes
dissertation/thesis, 49
location of, 127
numbering, 127
purposes of, 136–138
quotations in, 126
spacing of, 127
superscripts for, 125, 126
Ch.: designation of in text, 142–150; first references, 143; Latin abbreviations in, 146–147; multiple, 146; numbering, 142; parenthetical, in text, 149–150; sample, *34;* subsequent references, 143–146; title only references, 147–149
Enumeration, 97–98. *See also* Numbers
Epigraphs, 66–67, 126
Equations, 123
Equipment, for final drafts, 120–121
Executive documents: **Ch.,** 166–167, 198, 199
Executive Orders, 284
Exploratory writing, 25

Facts of publication
APA, 255–256; state name abbreviations, 285–286
Ch., 155–157; government publications, 165–166; missing information, 157, 184, 185
MLA: missing, 228
Fair use, 62
Federal regulations, 284
Figures, 99, 104–110; captions, 109, 128; footnotes for, 128; graphs, 105–109; illustrations, 108; lists of, 132; notes for, 110; numbering, 109; placement of, 128; sample, *116–119;* text and, 109
Figures, lists of, 43
Films. *See also* Nonprint sources
reviews of, 161
titles of, 91
APA, 263; reviews, 262–263
Ch., 169–170, 202, 203; reviews, 190, 191
MLA, 236–237; reviews, 231
Filmstrips. *See also* Films; Nonprint sources: **Ch.,** 202, 203
Final drafts, 120
Find It Fast: How to Uncover Expert Information on Any Subject (Berkman), 13
Finished copies, 120–133; equipment/supplies for, 120–121; printing, 121–133
First drafts, 25. *See also* Writing
Fonts, 120–121
Footnotes. *See also* Endnotes: **APA,** 276; continued, 127; dissertation/thesis, 49; for figures, 110; location of, 127; numbering, 127; quotations in, 126; spacing of, 127; superscripts for, 125, 126; table, 103–104
Foreign language works
APA, 259
Ch.: translated works, 154, 182–183
MLA, 227
Foreign words, 287; capitalization of, 94; italics in, 90
Forewords: **Ch.:** authors of, 154; **MLA,** 225
Format: outline, 22–23; research paper, 27–28
Formulas, 123
Fractions, 95
Front matter, 39–44; format for, 130–132

Gender bias, 85–87
Glossaries: dissertation/thesis, 49; format for, 133
Google, 13
Government publications
Ch. (*See* Public documents [**Ch.**])
indexes to, 10
APA: electronic, 268; online, 266–267
MLA, 227–228
Graphs, 105–109; bar, 107–108, 112–113; captions, 107; line, 105–106; pie charts, 106–107; presenting numerical data in, 108; sample, 112–114
Group authors: **APA,** 257–258; **Ch.,** 153, 180; **MLA,** 226
Guidelines for Bias-Free Writing (Schwartz), 87
Guidelines for Nonsexist Language in APA Journals..., 86
Guide to Reference Books Covering Materials from 1985–1990 (Balay, Sheehy), 10
Guide to Reference Books (Sheehy), 10

Handbook for Academic Authors (Luey), 121
Headings: capitalization of, 94; within chapters, 127–128;

dissertation/thesis, 47–48; in outlines, 24–25; table column, 128–129; in tables, 102–103
Humanities, indexes in, 9
Humanities style, 278–279
Hyphenation, 88–89, 123
Hypotheses: topics stated as, 5

Ibid., 146–147
Illustrations, 108–109. *See also* Figures; Tables
Imprints, publishers', 156; **Ch.,** 182, 183; **MLA,** 226
Indentation: printing final papers and, 123; of quotations, 62, 63–64, 125
Indexes: dissertation/thesis, 49; electronic, 11–12; format for, 133; information collection with, 9–10
Indirect citations: **APA,** 248; **Ch.,** 145–146, 178, 180; **MLA,** 217
Indirect quotations, 59–61
Information: collecting, 5–19; evaluating, 14–16; identifying sources of, 137; recording, 17; sources of, 6–13; understanding, 17–19
Information notes, 137–138
Information service reports, 259
Interest, in topic choice, 3
Internal Revenue rulings, 284
International agreements, 283
Internet sources
  documentation of, 17
  evaluating information on, 15–16
  figures from, 108
  research on, 12–13
  APA, 264–267; articles, 265; chapter/section in documents, 266; discussion lists, 267; newsgroups, 267; newspapers, 265; reports, 266–267; virtual conference papers, 267
  CGOS, 279, 280
  Ch.: books online, 173, 210, 211; discussion lists, 174, 212, 213; journals/magazines, 174, 210, 211; newspapers, 174, 212, 213; poetry online, 173, 210, 211; reference works, 174, 210, 211; reviews, 174, 212, 213; sample entries, 210–213; scholarly projects, 174, 212, 213
  MLA, 218, 232–234
Interviews: **APA,** 263; **Ch.,** 172; **MLA,** 238
Intransitive verbs, 84
Introductions: **Ch.:** authors of, 154, 162, 182, 183; to direct quotations, 68–71; **MLA,** 225
Italics: indicating with underlining, 89; titles in, 91; uses of, 90

Journals
  article titles, 91
  indexes to, 10
  titles of, 91
  APA: articles with multiple author, 252–253; articles with one author, 252; basic entry, 252; electronic database, 267–268; online, 265; paginated by issue, 253; in press articles, 255; special issues, 254
  CGOS, 279, 280
  Ch.: continuously paged, 158; issue vs. volume numbers, 159, 186, 187; online, 174, 210, 211; quotations in titles, 159; reprinted articles, 180, 181, 182, 183; reviews in, 190, 191; sample entries, 186, 187; separately paged, 158–159, 186, 187; series numbers, 159, 186, 187; title abbreviations, 159
  MLA, 229; abstracts, 231; online, 233; previously published articles, 225
Justification, text, 122–123

Language, Gender, and Professional Writing: Theoretical Approaches and Guidelines for Nonsexist Usage (Frank, Treichler), 86
Language, unbiased, 85–87
Laws. *See* Legal citations
Leaders, 125
Lectures: **APA,** 260; **Ch.,** 172, 208, 209; **MLA,** 238–239; titles of, 91
Legal citations, 281–284; **APA,** 270; case titles, 91; judicial material, 281–282; **MLA,** 239; quasi-statutory material, 283–284; statutory material, 282–283
Letters
  APA, 262; quotations from, 64
  Ch., 206, 207; to the editor, 190, 191; online, 212, 213
  MLA, 237–238; to the editor, 230; online, 234
Library catalogs, 6–8
Library of Congress system, 6
Line graphs, 105–106
Lists: enumeration in, 97–98
Lists of works cited. *See* Works cited lists

Literature, works of. *See also* Drama; Plays; Sacred writings
  Ch.: classical works, 149; edited, 192, 193; introduction writers, 162; plays, 192, 193; references to, 147–149; sample entries, 192–195; translators, 162
  MLA, 217–218; verb tense and discussion of, 82–83
Literature reviews, 45; verb tense and, 83

Magazines
  APA, 253
  Ch., 160, 188, 189; online, 174
  MLA, 230; online, 233
Magnetic tapes. *See also* Nonprint sources: **Ch.,** 208, 209
Manageability of topics, 4
Manuscripts. *See also* Unpublished sources: **APA,** 261–262; **Ch.,** 168, 200, 201; **MLA,** 239
Maps/charts. *See also* Reference works: **MLA,** 238
Margins, 122–123
Mechanics, writing, 87–98; abbreviations, 87–88; capitalization, 93–94; editing/proofreading, 98; enumeration, 97–98; hyphenation, 88–89; italics, 89–90; numbers, 94–96; spelling, 87; titles of works, 90–93
Microform materials
  APA, 261
  Ch, 208, 209; dissertations, 169, 202, 203
  MLA, 231
MLA Handbook, The, 17
Modern Language Association **(MLA)** style, 17, 214–244; avoiding bias in, 86; books, 223–229; citation content, 214–218; citation placement/punctuation, 219–220; electronic sources, 232–235; nonprint sources, 235–239; periodicals, 229–231; publisher names/imprints, 221–222, 239–241; quotation indentation in, 63–64; sample format, 243–244; works cited list, 220–223
Monographs. *See also* Books; Pamphlets: **APA,** 254
Monthly Catalog of U.S. Government Publications, 164
Movies. *See* Films
Multivolume works
  APA, 258

Ch., 157–158, 184, 185; first and subsequent references to, 145
MLA, 216–217, 225–226
Musical compositions: **Ch.,** 171, 204, 205; **MLA,** 237; titles of, 91
Musical performances. *See also* Performances
Ch., 170, 204, 205; reviews, 162, 192, 193
Musical scores: **Ch.,** 171; **MLA,** 237

Newsgroup postings: **APA,** 267
Newspapers
article titles, 91
indexes to, 10
titles of, 91
APA, 253–254; online, 265
CGOS, 279, 280
Ch., 160–161; advertisements, 190, 191; cartoons, 190, 191; city/state names in, 160–161, 188, 189; editions, 161, 188, 189; letters to editor, 190, 191; online, 174, 212, 213; sample entries, 188–191; section numbers, 160; special article types in, 161
MLA, 229–230; online, 233
Nonprint sources
APA, 263–269
Ch., 169–172; films, 169–170; musical compositions/scores, 171; performances, 170; personal contacts, 172; sound recordings, 171–172; speeches/addresses, 172; television/radio programs, 170; works of art, 172
MLA, 235–239; advertisements, 238; art works, 237; cartoons, 238; films/videotapes, 236–237; interviews, 238; lectures/speeches, 238–239; legal sources, 239; letters, 237–238; manuscripts/typescripts, 239; maps/charts, 238; musical compositions/scores, 237; performances, 236; sound recordings, 235–236; television/radio programs, 235
Notes. *See* Endnotes; Footnotes
Note taking, 17–19; direct quotations in, 67
Number-letter outlines, 22–23
Numbers, 94–96; alignment of, 124; dividing, 123; fractions, 95

Objectivity, 14
Omissions: ellipses for, 126; indicating in quotations, 75–78
Online library catalogs, 6–7, 8
Online materials. *See* Internet sources; Web sites
Operas. *See also* Musical compositions: titles of, 91
Ordinal numbers, 96
Organization: dissertation/thesis, 44–47; of notes, 18
Originality: in topic choice, 4
Outline pages, 27; **Ch.,** 31
Outlines, 20–25; alignment in, 98; formats for, 22–23; logical consistency in, 24–25; organizing, 20–22; parallelism in, 23–24; thesis statement in, 20; types of, 22
Out of print works, 156

Page numbers: **APA,** 96, 122; front matter, 39, 122; **MLA,** 96, 122; with tables and figures, 128
Paintings: titles of, 91
Pamphlets. *See also* Books: **MLA,** 227; titles of, 91
Paper, for final drafts, 121
Parallelism: in outlines, 23–24; writing style and, 84–85
Paraphrases, 19; indirect quotations, 59–61
Parenthetical documentation
of poetry, 65
purposes of, 136–138
APA, 245–277; anonymous works, 249; author named in text, 246; author not named in text, 246; authors with the same last name, 248; classical/sacred works, 249; corporate authors, 249; direct quotations, 247; multiple authors, 247–248; parts of sources, 246; reference to multiple works, 249–250; in text citations, 246–251; works cited in other works, 248; works identified by title, 248–249
Ch., 149–150
MLA, 214–244; abstracts, 231; advertisements, 238; anonymous works, 224; art works, 237; author named in text, 215; author not named in text, 215; authors with same last name, 216; books, 223–229; books by single author, 223; books in a series, 226; conference proceedings, 227; content of, 214–218; corporate authors, 216, 224; edited works, 226; editorials, 230; editors/compilers, 216, 224; electronic/Internet sources, 218, 232–235; entire book referenced, 215; films/videotapes, 236–237; foreign language works, 227; front matter emphasized, 225; government publications, 227–228; interviews, 238; journal articles, 229; lectures/speeches, 238–239; legal sources, 239; letters, 237–238; letters to editor, 230; literary works, 217–218; magazine articles, 230; manuscripts/typescripts, 239; maps/charts, 238; material cited in another source, 217; microform collections, 231; missing information, 228; multiple authors, 215, 223–224; multiple citations, 217; multiple publishers, 227; multiple works by same author, 217; multivolume works, 216–217, 225–226; musical compositions/scores, 237; newspaper articles, 229–230; pamphlets, 227; performances, 236; periodicals, 229–231; placement/punctuation of, 219–220; previously published articles in collections, 225; published dissertations, 228–229; publisher's imprints, 226, 240–241; publisher's names, 239–240; reference books, 225; reprinted works, 226; reprinted works with new titles, 225; reviews, 230–231; sample pages, 243–244; serialized articles, 231; sound recordings, 235–236; television/radio programs, 235; titles within titles, 228, 231; translated works, 226; unpublished dissertations, 228; works by title only, 216; works cited list, 220–223; works in anthologies, 224–225
Part-title pages, 129
Passive voice, 84
Performances
Ch., 170, 204, 205; reviews, 192, 193
MLA, 236; reviews, 230
Periodicals. *See also* Journals; Magazines; Newspapers: **APA,** 252–255; **Ch.,** 158–162; **MLA,** 229–231

Personal contacts: **Ch.,** 172, 206, 207
Personal pronouns, voice and, 81–82
Personal sites: **MLA,** 234
Philosophy, verb tense and discussion of, 83
Photocopies: **Ch.,** 168, 202, 203; note taking via, 18
Pie charts, 107
Plagiarism, 59, 60–61
Plates. *See Figures*
Plays, titles of, 91. *See also* Drama
Poetry
  brief quotations of, 62
  excerpts of, 125
  extended quotations of, 64–65
  indicating omissions in quotes of, 78
  parenthetical documentation of, 65
  partial lines in, 65
  titles of, 91
  Ch.: long, 174, 195; online, 173, 210, 211; short, 174, 195
  MLA, 217–218; online, 233
Poster sessions: **APA,** 260
Prefaces, 132; dissertation/thesis, 44
Preliminaries. *See* Front matter
Primary sources, 15
Printing: numbering pages and, 122; spacing and, 122–125
Printing papers, 121–133
Proceedings. *See* Conference proceedings
Professional sites: **MLA,** 234
Proofreading, 28, 98
Pseudonyms. *See also* Anonymous works: **Ch.,** 152, 178
Public documents (**Ch.**), 164–167. *See also* Government publications; acts of Congress, 198, 199; author entry for, 164–165; cabinet reports, 198, 199; city/state, 167, 198, 199, 200, 201; congressional, 166; congressional hearings, 196, 197, 198, 199; *Congressional Record,* 166, 196, 197; Constitution, U.S., 166, 198, 199; convention proceedings, 200, 201; executive documents, 166–167, 198, 199; facts of publication of, 165–166; sample entries, 196–201; title entry for, 165; treaties, 198, 199; unpublished, 167; untitled, unpublished, 200, 201
Publishers
  APA: author as, 258
  Ch.: imprints, 156, 182, 183; shortened names of, 155
  MLA: government publications, 227–228; imprints, 226, 241; multiple, 227; shortened names of, 221, 239–240; in works cited lists, 221
Punctuation: bibliography/lists of works, 129; of numbers, 94–95; spacing around, 124; in titles, 91; **MLA,** 219–220

Quasi-statutory material, 283–284
Quotation marks: direct quotations and, 73–74; indirect quotations and, 61; titles in, 91–92
Quotations, 58–79; additions to, 78–79; copyright and, 43; direct, 61–78; indentation of, 125; indicating omissions from, 75–79; indirect, 59–61; plagiarism and, 59; run-in, 74, 125; superscripts with, 125; **Ch.:** parenthetical references with, 149–150

Radio programs. *See also* Sound recordings, Audiovisual media: **Ch.,** 170, 204, 205; **MLA,** 235
Reference materials. *See* Back matter; Reference works
References list (**APA**), 250–251, 269–270; authors with same surname, 270; multiple authors, 270; multiple works by one author, 269–270; order entry, 269; sample of, 275, 277
Reference works. *See also* Books; Edited works
  research with, 9–12
  APA: books and chapters of books, 256–257
  Ch., 163–164, 194–197; online, 174, 210, 211
  MLA, 225
Reprints: **APA,** 256, 257; **Ch.,** 180, 181, 182, 183; **MLA,** 225, 226
Republished works: **Ch.,** 184, 185
Research papers. *See also* Bibliographies; Organization; Writing: sample, 29–38; style for, 80–87; writing, 2–38
Research reports: **APA,** 259–260
Resources: availability of and topic choice, 4
Reviews
  evaluating information with, 14
  indexes to, 10
  APA, 262–263
  Ch., 160–161; online, 174, 212, 213; sample entries, 190–193
  MLA, 230–231; online, 234
Revision, 26
Roman numerals, 96

Sacred writings
  titles of, 92
  APA, 249
  Ch., 162–163, 194, 195; references to, 148–149
Safire, William, 80
Scholarly projects: **APA,** 268; **Ch.:** online, 174, 212, 213; **MLA,** 233
Sciences, indexes in, 9
Scientific style, 279–280
Sculptures: titles of, 91
Search engines, 13. *See also* Internet sources; Web sites
Secondary sources, 15
Senate resolutions, 283
Sentence outlines, 22, 24
Sentence structure, 83–84
Serialized articles: **MLA,** 231
Series
  APA, 259
  Ch., 158, 186, 187
  MLA, 226; journals with multiple, 229
Sheehy, Eugene P., 10
Short stories: titles, 91
Slides. *See* Nonprint sources
Social sciences, indexes in, 9–10
Songs: titles, 91
Sound recordings. *See also* Nonprint sources: titles of, 91; **APA,** 264; **Ch.,** 171, 204, 205, 206, 207; **MLA,** 235–236
Sources, lists of, 138–140. *See also* Bibliographies; Endnotes
Spacing: around headings within chapters, 127–128; around punctuation, 124; bibliographies, 129; centering material, 123; of footnotes/endnotes, 127; of quoted poetry, 65; of quoted prose, 125
Spatial pattern organization, 21
Speeches/addresses, 208, 209; **APA,** 248–249; **Ch.,** 172, 206, 207; **MLA,** 238–239
Spell checkers, 121
Spelling, 87
Spoken recordings, 206, 207. *See also* Sound recordings
State name abbreviations, 285–286
Statistics: graphs and, 105–109; tables and, 99–100
Statutory material citations, 282–283

Style, 80–87. *See also* Coherence; Diction; Parallelism; coherence, 85; diction, 81; economy, 82; parallelism, 84–85; sentence structure, 83–84; tone, 81; unbiased language and, 85–87; verb tense and, 82–83; voice, 81–82
Summaries: indirect quotations, 59–61; in note taking, 19
Superscripts, 125, 126; **Ch.,** 142
Supreme Court cases, 281
Symbols, handwritten, 121
Synopsis: **APA,** 254–255

Tables, 99–104; capitalization in, 94; captions, 101–102, 128; columns/rows in, 102–103; computer generated, 100, 104; footnotes for, 103–104, 128; headings, 102–103; large, 104; leaders with, 125; lists of, 43, 56, 132; numbering, 102; placement of, 128; relationship of with text, 100–101; rules in, 103; sample, 115; spacing in, 128–129; **APA,** 102, 103
Tables of contents: dissertation/thesis, 43, 55; format for, 131–132; leaders with, 125
Tapes. *See also* Sound recordings; Videocassettes: **Ch.,** 171–172
Technical reports. *See also* Government publications; Public documents: **APA,** 259–260
Telephone conversations, 206, 207
Television programs
  reviews of, 161
  APA, 263–264
  Ch., 170, 204, 205; reviews, 192, 193
  MLA, 235
Theory, verb tense and discussion of, 83
Theses. *See* Dissertations/theses
Thesis statements, 5; topic choice and, 2; writing, 20
Title pages, 27; **APA,** 271; **Ch.,** 30; dissertation/thesis, 40–42, 52–53; format for, 130
Titles of works, 90–93
  chapter, 129
  dissertation chapter, 47–48
  selecting, 40–42
  two-part, 41–42
  books, 91
  capitalization of, 93
  italicized, 91
  quotation marks with, 91–92
  within titles, 92–93
  APA: within titles, 92; works identified by, 248–249
  Ch.: shortening, 143–144, 147–148; supplied for unpublished works, 168; within titles, 93, 155
  MLA: within titles, 228, 231
Tone, 81
Toner cartridges, 121
Topic outlines, 22, 24
Topics: choosing, 2–5; defining, 3–4; working statements of, 4–5
Transitional expressions, 85
Translations
  APA, 258–259
  Ch., 154–155; emphasis on author, 182, 183; emphasis on translator, 182, 183
  MLA, 224, 226
Translators
  Ch., 151, 155, 162; emphasis on, 182, 183
  MLA, 226–227
Treaties. *See also* Government publications; Public documents: Ch., 198, 199
Typescripts. *See also* Unpublished sources: **APA,** 261; **Ch.,** 168, 200, 201; **MLA,** 239
Type size, 120–121

Uniform System of Citation, A, 239, 281–284
University reports, 260
Unpublished sources
  APA, 260, 261–262
  Ch., 167–168; manuscripts, 168, 200, 201; photocopies, 168, 202, 203; sample entries, 200–203
  MLA, 237–238
Unsigned works. *See* Anonymous works
URLs (Uniform Resource Locators), 13, 15

Validity, establishing, 137
Vehicles: names of, 91
Verb tense, 82–83. *See also* Parallelism
Videocassettes. *See also* Nonprint sources
  APA: reviews, 262–263
  Ch., 171–172, 206, 207
  MLA, 236–237; reviews, 231
Voice, 81–82

Web sites. *See also* Internet: evaluating, 15–16; CGOS: home pages, 279, 280
Without Bias: A Guidebook for Nondiscriminatory Communication, 87
Word division, 123
Word processors: editing on, 27; final drafts and, 121; first drafts on, 25; revising with, 26; tables/charts with, 99
Words as words, 90
Working bibliographies, 5
Working topic statements, 4–5
Works cited lists, 138
  dissertation/thesis, 49
  MLA, 220–223; articles in edited volumes, 220; entire edited volumes, 220; multiple works by same editor/compiler, 221; publisher names in, 221
Writing, 2–38; editing, 27; the finished copy, 120–133; format in, 27–28; information collection for, 5–19; mechanics of, 87–98; outlines, 20–25; revising, 26; theses/dissertations, 39–57; topic choice in, 2–5

Yahoo!, 13
Years, 95–96